Praise for *Voodoo Days at La Casa Fabulosa...*

"David Dominé's vivid writing style will leave you captivated. *Voodoo Days at La Casa Fabulosa* is a wonderfully well-written page turner."

~ Rose Pressey, *USA Today* bestselling author

"An unconventional memoir, indeed. A phenomenal memoir and a new all-time favorite. This book kept me up laughing until the wee hours of the morning—and leaving the lights on in the meantime."

~ Kelly Creagh, author of the *Nevermore* trilogy

"David's style of writing is engaging and very entertaining. I couldn't put the book down. *Voodoo Days at La Casa Fabulosa* is a warm tribute to Old Louisville and all the quirkiness that makes it such an amazing place to live!"

~ David Williams, reviewer for the *Courier-Journal*

"Encountering mysterious events while renovating a haunted house inspired David Dominé's hilarious *Voodoo Days at La Casa Fabulosa*. Ghostly episodes, chock full of house design and sumptuous dinner parties, and woven with neighborhood tales of witches, black magic, and strange characters, will start an avalanche of curious enthusiasts to the streets of Old Louisville. "

~ Mary Popham, author of *Back Home in Landing Run*

D1283633

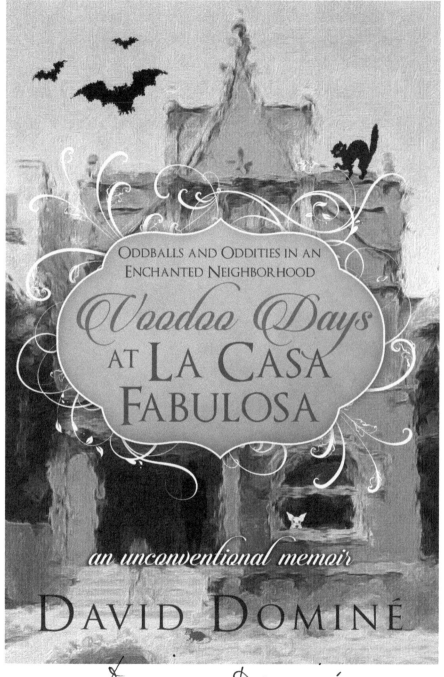

ODDBALLS AND ODDITIES IN AN
ENCHANTED NEIGHBORHOOD

Voodoo Days
AT LA CASA
FABULOSA

an unconventional memoir

DAVID DOMINÉ

If you feel the urge, don't be afraid to go on a wild goose chase.
What do you think wild geese are for anyway?
– Will Rogers

I love to visit the other side now and then but on my social passport Bohemia
is indelibly stamped, without regret on my part.
– Tennessee Williams

If there's no coincidence, there's no story.
– Chinese Proverb

The stories and events in this book are based on actual happenings that occurred while I lived in a Victorian house in the Kentucky historic preservation district known as Old Louisville. The time span is from roughly November 1999 through May 2001. Aside from a small amount of artistic license when I rearrange and condense experiences in the chronology of events for dramatic effect, I have tried to recreate the incidents as faithfully as possible in what I hope to be an entertaining and informative work of creative nonfiction.

All of the characters are real, although some of the names have been changed.

CONTENTS

For my god-daughter, Olivia Rose

Prologue

A dead leaf loosened itself from a branch overhead and tumbled down. Borne aloft now and then in the light breeze that swayed the limbs of the large maple tree, it danced through the air and fluttered across the façade of the old house. More than a month's worth of chill fall days and periodic winds had shorn the tree of most of its foliage and only a handful of leaves clung to the spindly fingers of gnarled wood. Overhead they interlocked and wove together to form a canopy that clacked in the wind. Beyond the patches of orange and yellow, the cloudless sky had that crystal tint of azure so typical of late autumn afternoons. As I stood on the sidewalk in front of the tall house, I craned my neck to see the steeply pitched gable hovering over the ornate façade. Another soft gust raced across the yard and the solitary leaf came to land at my feet as a bat fluttered overhead in the still-bright sky.

After studying it for a moment, my eyes returned to the front of the structure. Although an unseemly coat of battleship gray covered the brick face, exposed patches of red and oxidized brown peeked through here and there where the elements had done their work. Time had also eroded many of the intricate details that embellished the flamboyant façade, but after only a momentary glance, it became apparent that I stood before an impressive piece of architecture.

Up under the gable, three small windows formed a horizontal band, framed on either side by ornamental pedestals with intertwined bases. At the second-story level, two additional pedestals appeared to anchor the windows to the façade. On the ground level next to the front entrance, a large window—its rounded top nestled in a scalloped terra cotta arch adorned with laurel wreath and garland—afforded a glimpse of the front parlor, where an elegant mahogany mantel reflected a sheen of golden light. Standing there, I could imagine the past lives of the old house. As the cold fall air entered and left my lungs, I inhaled visions of previous generations flashing before my eyes.

My eyes squinted as I scrutinized the scene before me. It needed some work, but the building at 1228 South Third Street was possessed of an unkempt charm that tugged at my heartstrings. I loved old houses, and I had always dreamed of living in a Victorian one at that. As it turned out, this one had everything I had wanted: three floors, a staircase at the front of the house, a staircase at the back of the house, hardwood flooring, and lots of fireplaces. There was no carriage house and the yard was rather small, but I could live with that.

Whether I could live with the outdated wallpaper and smallish kitchen was another thing. I was an aspiring food writer who had just started work on his first cookbook, and I would be spending many hours on recipe development and testing. I wanted a spacious kitchen with up-to-date appliances—and the kitchen in this house, unfortunately, did not fit the bill. I had just been inside for another look around the house, and this kitchen was tiny—something not altogether surprising for a Victorian house.

Although the kitchen had its issues, it did have its charms. And according to Margaret, the woman who was looking to sell the house, the kitchen even came with its own ghost. "Her name's Lucy, and she's a poltergeist," she had said. "If she doesn't like what you're doing to the place, she'll let you know. She'll break things. Knock pictures off the wall. You'll hear her walking around in the middle of the night. You'll smell her cooking things in here when nobody is around. Stuff like that." When I tried to laugh off these warnings, Margaret had fixed me with a somber gaze and said: "I'm serious. There's a ghost in this house."

Despite my love of spooky stories, however, I didn't really believe in ghosts, so I wasn't too worried about spectral inhabitants in the residence. Much more daunting was the maintenance that such a property would require. The interior needed painting and decorating and then there was the outside. The front yard was patchy and riddled with weeds. The roof needed repairs, and the chimneys had to be rebuilt. The tuckpointing would cost a fortune, and someone would have to pull off the ivy and fix a spot of water-damage on the inside before replastering a wall. And something needed to be done about the paint job as well. Not to mention, the utilities would be expensive and the bathrooms needed to be updated.

In addition, the block the house sat on was not one of the more desirable blocks in the neighborhood. Across the street stood the Hillebrand House, a 1960s high-rise apartment building that towered over mostly 19th-century dwellings. Interspersed among the single-family homes were old houses that served as apartment houses and office space. The residence immediately to the south had been converted into a business, a "barber college" to be exact, and it didn't appear that the new tenants were keeping it in very good shape. And several houses down the block, to the north, was Oak Street, a once-thriving commercial corridor that had fallen on hard times. Although several shops and restaurants—one of them, the Rudyard Kipling, was an icon in the city—still lined the street, most people in the area knew Oak Street as a place frequented by panhandlers and other unsavory characters. Semis and other large vehicles were always trying to cut through to the Interstate, and it could be loud at all hours of the day.

The bat returned and darted by, this time with two friends, as one by one, I ticked off the reasons why it would be an unwise decision to buy the house.

Within a month, we signed the contract and moved in.

The Tuesday Night Dinner Club

The box made a muffled thud as it landed at my feet. I straightened up and looked around the room, working a cramp out of my forearm. After three days of non-stop moving, everything had been transported from the old apartment to the new house on South Third Street, barely a half mile from downtown Louisville. Ramon and our friend Skippy had done most of the hard lifting since I couldn't take off from teaching, and it had been up to me to get things situated in the new place. Now, a couple of days later, the boxes and big pieces were in the right rooms, and all it needed was some rearranging to make the place feel like home.

Up on the third floor, I looked through the three small windows at the front of the house down to the street below. The house sat on a small plot of land along a stretch of antique homes known as Millionaires Row, about a third of the way between Louisville's city center and the famous racetrack at Churchill Downs. Although our friends called it a mansion, to me it was a big house and nothing more. Yes, it did have six bedrooms but that wasn't large enough to be a mansion in my book. There was no ballroom for one, and real mansions had ballrooms. Besides, the new house wasn't grand enough either. Although there were loads of elegant details such as the parquet floors, ornate fireplace mantels, and intricate millwork, the house itself had a certain Victorian practicality that toned it down.

I picked up a lace curtain and threaded it onto the rod above one of the windows. Once all three curtains were hung, I adjusted them and pushed one aside to look outside again, where winter weather had arrived. From the gray skies above, random snowflakes tumbled through the air and showered down on an old man peddling his pinwheel-bedecked bicycle along the sidewalk. As the bike passed, his grizzled face looked up, and he yanked off the Confederate hat atop his head and waved it at me before wheeling out of sight, his long white beard fluttering in the cold wind.

This was life in Old Louisville. Locals touted it as "America's largest Victorian neighborhood" but I sometimes wondered if "America's craziest neighborhood" might not be more apt. In my six previous years of living in the area, I had already met untold numbers of colorful characters so I could only imagine what it would be like for the next six years now that I was living in the middle of it all. I smiled to myself and started unpacking books and placing them in the shelves that lined the walls of the spacious room that would serve as my office.

Once the cartons had given up all of their contents, I walked into the adjacent room, the only other large space on the top floor, and took a look around. With the adjoining kitchenette and bathroom, and access to the small rooftop deck at the back of the house, it would make an ideal guest suite. All it needed was some furniture. With over a dozen rooms to decorate, it had become evident that we'd be busy hitting the antique stores and thrift shops in search of the right furniture for the old house. But, that would have to wait until the new year. Christmas was right around the corner, and we had to make it through Thanksgiving first.

From somewhere up in the attic, there came a loud rumbling, a shuffling noise, and I turned my eyes to the ceiling and waited. But I didn't hear the sound again. Birds or squirrels, I guessed. Fighting back a shudder against the cold, I went to the drafty door that led out onto the rooftop and pulled it open. Outside an icy wind had begun to roar and pockets of snow were collecting along the creases of the slate and shingle roofs. From my vantage point atop the deck at the back of the house, I peered down into several yards and across the rooftops of carriage houses along the brick alley that divided the block in half.

Without a sound, a black Mercedes crept down the alleyway and swerved around an abandoned shopping cart near an overflowing dumpster. When the car passed, a gray shadow emerged from behind the dumpster and, head lowered against the chill wind, slowly made its way down to Oak Street. After a number of steps, the figure stopped, turned, and looked up at me, oblivious as the blustery weather blew her dark coat open and billowed out her skirts. On her head rested a tightly wound turban with a gleaming brooch pinned over the forehead. An exotic-looking necklace with what appeared to be ivory tusks dangled at her breast, which heaved with exertion. Although I couldn't tell for sure, the woman's eyes appeared to have a defiant look and she mustered a severe gaze before pulling the coat tightly around her and disappearing down the alley.

Slightly unnerved, I retreated to the warmth of the house, the wind slamming the door shut behind me. I took the stairs down to the second floor and walked the length of the narrow hallway that ran from the large room at the front of the house to the smaller one at the back. The front room had a sleeping alcove against the southern wall, in addition to an intricately carved mahogany fireplace in the middle of the wall to the north. To the east, two big windows with interior shutters afforded a view of Third Street. Next to a closet by the alcove, a door led into a smaller room that I surmised had originally been a nursery, and that, in turn, connected to another bedroom through a pocket door. Back in the hallway, another door bisected the corridor, running past a second staircase that led down to a coatroom and a bathroom on the ground floor before ending in a smallish room at the rear.

I poked my head through the door to this room and looked around. While all the other rooms on the middle floor seemed to have irregular shapes and extra doors and angles, this one was a simple square with a small closet. A solitary window looked out over the modest back yard, and another in the southern wall provided a glimpse of the rear of the large mansion next door. This room had a fireplace like most of the other rooms in the house, but unlike the seven others, the mantel in this room was a small, simple piece carved from oak. Under my feet was a layer of thick beige carpet that I hoped to remove in the spring, when the time came to restore the hardwood floor underneath.

The wind picked up, causing the windowpanes to rattle violently in their casings. Almost inaudible, a faint groan seemed to rise from the floorboards as the house braced itself against the gathering storm. Outside, darkness had fallen and blowing snow swirled and fluttered in the dim cone of illumination under the streetlight. When I turned on the sconce over the mantelshelf, there was a bright flash and a loud popping noise as the bulb blew out. When I hit the switch on the wall it appeared that the bulb in the ceiling fixture had burnt out as well. Great.

There's something interesting about this room, I thought to myself as my eyes scanned the interior. It was noticeably smaller and plainer than the other rooms on the second floor and seemed a bit isolated. I pulled the door to and descended the back stairs to the bottom floor.

Under the staircase in the coatroom, a small door led down a narrow flight of steps to the basement. Two larger doors led to the front and back of the house, and I walked through one into a small room that had originally served as the butler's pantry. To one side was the kitchen; to the other was the dining room. I pushed through the swinging door and walked into the dining room, my footsteps echoing as I made my way across the parquet floor.

Past the walnut fireplace surround, and through the double pocket doors into the foyer, I came to stand in the cozy entryway with the oaken stairwell leading upstairs. Two stained glass windows with elegant designs in yellow, amber, and rose caught the light from the neighbor's porch lamp and scattered random patterns on the shiny floor. I gazed through a pair of transomed French doors into the front parlor, where a large brass chandelier cast a golden glow across the mirror embedded in the mahogany fireplace surround. Despite the cracks in the wall, the room appeared elegant and inviting. I scanned the room and smiled, reminded of how glad I was to have bought the house. Despite all the work ahead, I looked forward to making it a home.

At my feet, there was a gentle snoring. From the looks of it, our little schnauzers, Rocky and Bess, had already made themselves at home and they snoozed contentedly on their furry pallets on the floor. Bess grumbled in her sleep and rolled over on her side.

Suddenly, a loud electric buzz reverberated throughout the house, and I jumped. It was the doorbell, one of those old annoying kinds, and I still hadn't gotten used to it. Barking, Rocky and Bess bolted from their beds and skittered to a stop at the front entry. I ran and turned the knob to see who was there. It was Tuesday night—time for the once-a-week get-together with our friends—and someone had apparently arrived. It was our friend Wendy, showing up early as usual, and I let her in. Out on the sidewalk, a tall man with a long coat and a knit cap ambled by, a violin case swinging at his side. Waving a bottle of Maker's Mark in my face, Wendy breezed past me and headed for the kitchen.

"My hair appointment didn't take that long, so I decided to come right over." She found herself a glass tumbler, filled it with ice and sloshed in some bourbon. I followed her lead and helped myself.

Wendy turned and surveyed the kitchen. "The place is really shaping up." Despite the disorder in the rest of the house, I had managed to get the kitchen put together as soon as we moved in and the space already looked comfortable and lived in. The faux-hardwood linoleum floors would have to go, and the walls needed a new coat of paint, but it was still bigger and nicer than my last kitchen. When you're a food writer, you need a good kitchen, and I was dreaming of the day I could afford to update the one at the new house.

I popped open the oven door and checked on the chickens roasting inside, and a delicious wave of smells filled the room. On top of the stove, a pot of potatoes simmered away, waiting to be mashed with garlic, cream, and butter. A batch of crusty wheatberry rolls cooled on a rack on the counter. With a tossed green salad and the gingerbread I had baked for dessert, it would all make a nice winter supper.

"So, any ghosts yet?" Wendy took a sip of bourbon and looked at me.

"Ghosts? Not that I know of. A couple of weirdoes, but that's typical for Old Louisville." I stopped and let my eyes roam around the room. Despite the denial, I was recalling the pictures and prints that had mysteriously fallen from the walls in the kitchen and adjacent butler's pantry during the previous week. I had no inkling that anything other than a poor job of hanging them might have been the culprit, but even after the frames had been hung the third and fourth times—with bigger nails and in different locations—most of them refused to stay put. I paused and scratched my head. "Actually, some odd things have been happening with the pictures I've been hanging," I said. "But it's probably nothing. I'm sure they weren't hung right in the first place."

"Well, did you ask the ghost if it was okay to start hanging things on the wall?" She stood with her hands on her hips and stared.

"Huh?" I lit the candles on the table by the large window and put out a dish of salted cashews.

"You know," she said, "a house this old has got to have a ghost or two. My

6

grandmother knew about spooks and she always said when you move into a new place you need to ask the spirits there if it's okay." Her ice cubes clinked together as she took another sip of bourbon. "If you don't," she said, "they'll cause trouble for you."

"Well, truth be told," I said somewhat sarcastically, "I hadn't gotten around to that yet." From a nearby desk, I picked up an old lithograph that originally hung over the stove. It depicted a huge pig standing in an English barnyard, and I had found it at antique store shortly after moving in. It had fallen for the third and final time, so I decided it would look better sitting on the old oak desk. Examining it in my hand, I wondered if I shouldn't try to hang it one last time.

"All you have to do is let them know what your plans are," Wendy said, the tone of her voice reminding me about the warnings from Margaret, the previous owner. Although I hadn't taken it seriously when she had insisted that the house came with a ghost, I had found some comfort in Margaret's reassurances that Lucy, for the most part, was supposed to be a benevolent spirit.

But that was neither here nor there, because even if I loved a good ghost story, I considered myself a skeptic and didn't believe in phantoms. I might be a firm believer in the unexplained, but chain-rattling ghosts were something else.

Just then, something crashed and a breaking noise reverberated at the back of the house. Walking quickly to the butler's pantry, we found another framed picture lying in the middle of the floor. I went over to the section of wall where it had hung and studied a nail still sticking out of the plaster. Behind me, Wendy clucked her tongue. "See? I told you so." She walked around the broken glass and stood next to me, reaching up to test the nail. "How do you explain that?"

I rolled my eyes and ignored the question, retreating to the kitchen for a dustpan and broom. Back in the butler's pantry, I knelt down to collect the bits of broken glass scattered around the floor as Wendy picked up the mangled frame and put it out on the back deck. "I told you so," she said under her breath.

The annoying buzzer rang again as I deposited the last of the debris in the trash, and I went to open the front door and let in several friends. Outside, the wind churned up the thin layer of snow that had collected on the ground, where it had taken on a strange iridescent quality in the gray light. Outside, a streetlamp shone dull yellow as a figure, bundled against the wind, noisily pushed an old shopping cart along the bumpy sidewalk.

"Who's that with the cart?" It was our friend Tim, otherwise known as Skippy, and he rushed up the steps. "Another homeless person?" He hurried inside while I propped the door open.

"Could be," I answered, "but who knows? Some people around here without cars don't want to carry their groceries home so they take the whole cart." As people greeted and exchanged hugs and kisses, I closed the door and watched the shopping cart slowly retreat into the darkness.

7

Gathering up jackets and scarves, I went to hang them in the coatroom while the others helped themselves to drinks and then went to admire the undecorated Christmas tree that stood in the front parlor. It was a 12-foot spruce and it looked perfect in its spot in front of the large window. A cheery fire blazing in the hearth, the sounds of laughter and friendly banter soon drowned out the strains of holiday music coming from the radio. It was December 6, St. Nick's Day, the perfect date for a tree-trimming party, and people quickly got to work stringing the lights and hanging ornaments.

In the kitchen, I was putting together a tray of smoked trout and cream cheese on toast points when another crash, a kind of dull thud, echoed through the bottom floor. It was an eerie—and familiar—sound and it seemed to resonate from the walls and the ceiling. I froze and waited, the noise fading into utter silence.

Although it was unlikely, I wondered if the Christmas tree had toppled over and knocked down a piece of furniture, so I clenched my teeth and hurried to the front of the house to survey the damage. I pushed my way through the swinging door of the butler's pantry. "Did the tree fall over again?" I said. "It kept falling over yesterday, but I thought I finally got it to stay in place." The group of friends gathered in the parlor, however, had run into the foyer and met me with the same expectant look of dread in the dining room, their heads craning around me to see what had caused the noise. They were looking into the butler's pantry and beyond.

"Didn't that come from the kitchen?" asked Laura.

"No, I thought it came from the parlor," I said.

Beth widened her eyes, shrugged her shoulders and giggled nervously. Cautiously, we clumped together and wandered from room to room in search of the source of the noise. From the sound of it, we decided that a large chandelier could have fallen somewhere, but it soon became clear that all the chandeliers were still in place. A thorough search of the ground floor yielded absolutely nothing, and we moved to the second and third floors with the same results. We pulled down the steps to the attic and searched it to no avail and then made our way back down through the house and ended up in the dreary basement. Nothing there seemed to explain the huge crash either. A quick inspection around the outside of the house in the frigid winter air resulted in the same puzzled looks and lack of explanation.

Back in the front parlor, the tree stood stock still, anchored in place by an invisible bit of wire that stretched between the crown molding and the top of the trunk. I had decided on the wire tether in case the tree should decide to topple again, and I was glad to see the wiring had done its job.

Wendy placed her hands on her hips and glared at me as she had done before. "See? You have to okay it with the ghost first!" But before I could shrug off the unexplained sound with another scoff, she ran to the kitchen, picked up the hammer lying on the counter and returned to the parlor. Punctuating her words as she spoke, the hammer had been raised over her head and waved to and fro.

"What are you doing with that hammer?" asked Skippy. "You look like an insane woman! Better watch out or you'll end up like one of those crazy people over on Oak Street." He pulled a chair up to the fire and started leafing through a copy of *Old Louisville: The Victorian Era* by local historians Sam Thomas and William Morgan.

Ignoring the comments, Wendy raised her eyes and began addressing an unseen guest. "We want to hang some nice pictures here," she said. "You'll like them, so please don't knock them down anymore. We don't want to bother you and we understand it's your house. Thank you!"

I flinched at the last comment, and Wendy started gathering nails to make better use of the hammer. Within five minutes she had managed to re-hang all but one of the pictures and we sat down to eat. The pig lithograph would stay on the desk in the foyer, I decided, but it needed to be reframed first.

The next Tuesday, the same group of friends gathered for our weekly dinner, a tradition kept alive since our days of working together at the Seelbach Hotel. A week later, the pig still sat proudly atop the old oak desk in the entry hall, and in the kitchen and dining room all the pictures had managed to stay put where Wendy decided to hang them. Back in the kitchen, she assumed her usual stance and slowly turned around to admire her handiwork, a smug grin painted on her face. "I told you so." She emptied her glass of wine in one gulp and opened another bottle. I ignored her and started to get dinner ready.

Even though Ramon and I had been in the house for only a short period of time, it already had a cozy, homey feel to it. I had started work on a cookbook with Kentucky-inspired recipes and stories, and everyone was eager to do me the favor of sampling my handiwork. After baked brie and pears in the parlor, we sat down to the table in the dining room for a dinner of Bibb lettuce salad and pork tenderloin with roasted potatoes and red cabbage. For dessert there was warm apple crisp and whipped cream, and when the bourbon was passed around, talk turned to the resident ghost. During the previous week the strange noises and dull thuds had continued throughout the house, and word had gotten around to my friends. When they all brought up the odd occurrences, I told them it had to have something to do with the house settling or something else perfectly explainable. Not of all them were convinced, however.

"So, what did the previous owner tell you about the spook in the attic?" Skippy poured generous amounts of Woodford Reserve into large snifters before passing them around. He worked at the distillery where it was made, so we were always assured of a steady supply of that particular bourbon. Moving to the fire in the front parlor, I repeated Margaret's warnings that Lucy didn't like to see things changed too much and that she would let us know if that was the case. "I guess it must be a poltergeist, then," he said. "Aren't they the ones that like throwing stuff around and breaking things?"

"Maybe we should get out the Ouija board and see if we can contact her," Laura said, looking around the room for approval. Bess had crawled up into her lap and was enjoying the attention.

"Ay, no! No way." Ramon stood hastily and bolted for the kitchen. "No way. I don't like those things. They're bad news!" He disappeared and left behind a trailing epithet of curses in Spanish. In the kitchen, water could be heard running in the sink as he started cleaning up the dishes.

"Yeah, if we make contact, maybe she could tell us why she's been knocking over the Christmas tree this past week," said Wendy. She grabbed a decanter from the sideboard and filled her glass with bourbon. Then she passed it around to the others.

"That Christmas tree?" asked Skippy, pointing to the fully decorated tree that stood in the window. Twinkling white lights danced in the reflection on the glass. "The one we decorated last week?"

From the looks of it, you couldn't tell that anything bad had happened to it. To the contrary, I had evened out the decorations and added dozens of cinnamon stars and gingerbread men baked during the previous week. They had been dusted in powdered sugar and hung with gold ribbons. It all added an old-fashioned touch to the tree.

"Yes." I was hesitant to answer because I didn't want them to jump to any conclusions. "It's fallen three times since you guys were here, and it broke all the best ornaments. I've had to run to the store twice for new ones." I had also had to bake several new batches of cookies.

"But, I thought you anchored it to the wall." Skippy poured himself another drink.

"I did, but the wire kept coming undone somehow." I went over to the tree and checked behind it. The wire from the tree was still connected to the nail.

"Don't worry about it falling anymore," assured Wendy. "I asked Lucy to leave it alone when you were all in the kitchen, and it'll be fine now."

"I hope so," I said, "because I can't afford any more ornaments."

Something in the kitchen caused us all to jump, the sudden sound of glass crashing on the floor and shattering to pieces. We stared at each other and waited.

"Ramon? Was that you . . . or the ghost?" Our friend Beth, who had showed up in time for dessert, stood and placed a snifter on the mahogany mantel.

Several seconds later, Ramon appeared at the parlor doors with a meek smile on his face. "Oops." He held a shard of glass out for inspection. "I dropped another one of your Waterford champagne flutes, David. Sorry." He turned and walked back to the kitchen.

Laura, our friend from across the river in Indiana, chuckled as she grabbed a tray of bourbon balls and passed them around. "I guess we all know what you'll be getting for Christmas." She put the dish down and moved her chair closer to the hearth. The wind roaring outside, she appeared to have no plans to leave the fireside any time soon.

Another loud noise echoed from somewhere outside the room, vibrations seeming to rumble through the floorboards. The little white lights danced on the tree and I could see ornaments shaking on the branches. "Ramon?" I walked to the door and looked into the foyer. "Was that you?"

"If that was a champagne flute hitting the ground, that was one *huge* piece of stemware," said Skippy, getting to his feet.

Steps could be heard in the dining room and Ramon walked through the opened pocket doors into the foyer. "What was that?" he asked, drying his hands on a checkered dishtowel.

"You mean that wasn't you?" I said. "It sounded like it came from the kitchen or the dining room."

"No. I thought it came from the foyer or the parlor. But I suppose it could have been in the dining room." He went to the table, pulled out a chair and looked underneath.

"It sounded like something fell. Something big." Beth went to the back stairs and looked up. "I don't see anything back here."

One by one, we wandered off to different parts of the house in search of the noise. I grabbed a coat and went outside to see if I could find anything. Five minutes later we had all gathered in the foyer, no one having discovered the source of the disturbance.

"Well, since I'm up and about, I guess I better start heading home," said Laura. I went and got her coat from a hook on the wall. When the others saw me doling out coats, they decided it was time to leave as well. As they left, they all wished us good luck trying to find out where the odd noises were coming from.

I closed the door after the last of the guests headed out into the wintry night. I tidied up a bit and made the rounds of the rooms to turn off the lights before hurrying upstairs and ducking under the covers. Only after I had snuggled in did I recall seeing that the pig print on the desk in the foyer had either fallen or been pushed over so that it lay face down. I debated getting out of bed and standing it up again, but another sudden loud noise downstairs startled me. It was like a large *boom*, maybe in the basement. I got out of bed and went down to investigate.

A sound was coming from the small bathroom under the front steps, and the closer I got to it, the more it sounded like a hissing noise. Pushing the door all the way open, I turned on the light and inside I could see the little black cat we had adopted back at the old place. She stood on all fours with her back arched and hissed at something unseen. Then she ran into the tiny closet next to the toilet and refused to emerge. This had become her new home as of late. Ever since moving into the new house, the previously mischievous troublemaker had turned into a literal scaredy cat. No amount of coaxing would make her leave the confines of the tiny bathroom, and she refused to come out to eat or drink unless someone brought the food and water to her. After several minutes of reassuring pats, I left her in the little closet and returned to the second floor.

On the landing, the chandelier outside the bedroom was slowly swaying back and forth. I stood and watched it for several moments, but it soon tapered off and stopped. Had it been caused by my motion coming up the stairs? I couldn't be sure, but I hoped that was the reason. Tiny pinpricks of gooseflesh began running down my shoulders and arms and, when I looked around, I realized that the house somehow still had a big, empty feel to it.

When the strong smell of coffee woke me the next morning, I had all but forgotten the odd events of the previous night.

"Are you sure you didn't make coffee this morning?" I turned to Ramon as we sat watching television late the next afternoon. "When I woke up and went down to the kitchen this morning, it smelled like someone had just brewed a pot. It was really strong, too."

"No," he answered. "I didn't have time so I got some at the drive through."

"Hmmm. I wonder where that smell is coming from," I mumbled. "It's not the first time I've smelled coffee when nobody was down there to make it."

"Is that what you wore to school today?" Ramon had given me the once-over and was shaking his head. "Those baggy pants and sweater make you look like a hobo."

Looking down at my attire, I frowned. "I like this outfit," I said. "It's comfy."

"Hobo."

I got up and walked to the window to look outside. Most of the last snowfall had already disappeared, and the street had a barren, deserted look about it. But in the gathering darkness, I saw a large, stray dog warily cross the street, its shaggy black fur reflecting a thin strip of yellow light from the nearest street lamp. It looked up at me and paused; then its head dropped and the creature bolted across the front yard and around the side of the house. I closed the shutters over the windows, went down to the kitchen, and put a kettle of water on to boil. After grabbing an oatmeal cookie, I brewed a pot of tea and carried it up to my office on the third floor.

Since moving into the house at 1228 South Third Street, I had become obsessed with uncovering its secrets and wanted to find out everything possible about its previous owners. I tapped on walls and panels, hoping to reveal a secret passageway or at least a hidden compartment, but discovered nothing. Then I embarked on a series of fruitless searches for significant dates scribbled in pencil across the rafter beams in the attic or stashes of family documents in the basement. When that failed, I tried a more practical approach and spent hours researching on line, ravenous for the least bit of information that could open a door to the past.

Like most addresses in Old Louisville, 1228 South Third Street had seen its share of history, so I was fairly certain there was information to be found. The only problem was how to track it down. Since my housemate Ramon worked as a title examiner downtown, it was relatively easy to dig up the deeds to the property and get a glimpse at the names of its previous owners, and after a week or so, I was able to piece together some basic information about the early days of the house.

As it turns out, the residence saw its first inhabitants around 1895, when it was built for the Widmer family. The original owner's name was Jacob C. Widmer, and his wife appeared to be Kate Webb Widmer. I was actually hoping to discover that the earliest residents had an aristocratic-sounding last name, a name that would lend the house a bit of class. Ophelia Merriwether, for example, was a regal-sounding name that would have looked fabulous on a brass plaque at the front of the house, but she wasn't one of the original occupants and hadn't lived in the house that long. *The Ophelia Merriwether House* had a certain ring to it. *The Jacob Widmer House*? Not so much.

Snooping through old city directories, I learned that Widmer had been the business manager of the National Tobacco Works, one of many warehouses in Louisville, a city that processed half of the world's Burley back in the day. At one time, the National Tobacco Works employed some five hundred workers and produced more than six million pounds a year. With the help of old Sanborn fire maps at the Filson Historical Society, I also learned that the house Jacob Widmer had bought sat at one time on a larger plot of land originally owned by a neighbor to the south, J.S. Bockee. His old place was the gray mansion immediately next door, a structure that was used as the ramshackle barber school and a noisy day care center during our tenancy of Widmer House.

Mr. Bockee had also worked in Louisville's thriving tobacco industry. Although he had already made a name and fortune for himself as an astute broker of Kentucky's most famous crop, Bockee realized money could also be made by the sale of land already in short supply at that time. He took his piece of land to the north, removed an older building there, and then equally divided the plot into two smaller parcels where he built larger homes with identical floor plans. Our house was one of them. The neighbors to the north had the other house, which was originally built for the Goren family.

Although I was never able to locate the original plans for the house, I found similar plans by Charles D. Meyer, one of Louisville's first and foremost architects of national acclaim, so it's possible that he designed the spacious town home to make the most of the small plot of land. From the original deed, I was amazed to discover that the original sales price had been $12,500.00. Working with the Louisville Landmarks Commission, I learned that the house had been built in the Châteauesque style, its unique façade perhaps more reminiscent of a home in a medieval village in northern Europe or of one of the many whimsical movie palaces built across this country in the late 1920s than in early Kentucky. I only needed to find out more about the actual people who used to live there.

Eventually I found a neighborhood web site and continued snooping. By the

1920s the Widmers had already sold the house, and ownership then passed through several hands, most of them single females. Several years before the Second World War, they turned our place into a rooming house, a not uncommon fate for many of the grand residences in Old Louisville. World War II ended, and for most prosperous cities around the nation the next several decades bore witness to a dark period in terms of urban development. Louisville, like all the rest, suffered a period marked by neglect of its grandest neighborhoods. Many gracious homes fell victim to the wrecking ball, and mansions in Old Louisville became flophouses and bordellos, passed to absentee landlords or sat abandoned.

A look through the *Caron's City Directories* of the mid 1900s showed that a large number of these stately residences served as boarding houses for single men and women employed in the Louisville workforce. Widmer House, as we halfheartedly decided to call it, provided rooms for employees of the nearby Louisville & Nashville Railroad and continued as a boarding house until the 1970s. Although much of the original character remained, the former residence of Jacob and Kate Widmer had seen better days when a small family bought it in the 1980s. Over the next fourteen years—and with no small amount of elbow grease—they patiently converted the former rooming house into a comfortable single-family residence. Now it was our turn to add a chapter to the history of Widmer House.

Another owner of the house was Sallie Sevier. *The Sallie Sevier House* would have had a nice French ring to it, I thought. Sallie M. Sevier was a resident of 1228 South Third Street from 1916 to 1933, and several old-timers confided that she had been quite a character in her day. I was never able to dig up any written substantiation for these claims, but according to stories shared with me in a local genealogy chat room, Sallie loved the cinema and was often found downtown at movie houses such as the Loew's Theater on South Fourth Street. It was at a showing of *The Sheik* in 1921 that she supposedly developed a crush on its star, Rudolph Valentino, and gained a subsequent appreciation of her house's exotic Persian influences as well. Soon thereafter she was reported to have given the elaborate façade a colorful makeover, restyling it in a romanticized notion of what a Moroccan-inspired palace in Spain might have looked like.

Given its mosque-like finials and dramatic roofline, it's hardly surprising that locals in fact referred to it at one time as the "Moorish Palace," a name that has stuck until this day. What I did find revealing was that Sallie reputedly hosted lavish parties in the 1920s that played on the *Lawrence-of-Arabia* theme, encouraging her guests to come dressed as sheiks and harem girls. Someone even told me that at one party the papers reported that she had pitched a huge striped tent and tethered an ornery camel in the front yard. So it looked like the newest tenants of the Widmer House would have big shoes to fill.

It was very dark outside. Downstairs, footsteps echoed as Ramon walked through the hallway and opened a door. I finished what I was doing on the third floor, grabbed the teapot and headed down to the kitchen to boil another kettle of water. As I waited for the steam to whistle, I walked over to the window and surveyed the backyard through the frosted glass. There was no sign of the black dog I had seen before, however a fat, bristly possum inched along the top of the fence, no doubt making its way to the garbage cans in the alley. Upstairs, Ramon made another pass in the corridor running the length of the house. When furniture in the little room above the kitchen started to scrape along the floor, I stopped and looked up at the ceiling. What was Ramon up to? Had he decided to rearrange the furniture in that room? It would be midnight in an hour and half, so why on earth had he decided to move things around when it was so late? I shook my head and waited for the water to boil. Overhead, several loud footsteps reverberated through the floorboards.

A minute or two later, the teapot startled me with its shrill whistle. But that was nothing like the fright I got when the knob on the back door rattled and began to turn. Somebody was trying to get in.

Something in the Basement

The door suddenly opened, filling the kitchen with a gust of icy air, and in walked Ramon out of the cold and bluster. Relieved, I watched as Rocky and Bess bounded in after him and began dancing around for their usual post-walk treat. After closing the door, he unhooked the dogs from their leads and fished out two biscuits from a basket on the counter. He hung the leashes from a nearby hook and went to the coat rack to hang up his jacket.

That's when I remembered the footsteps on the floor above. "What–?" I slowly looked up at the ceiling, thinking about the scraping noises in the little room overhead. Several hairs stood up on the back of my neck, triggering a rash of goose bumps that traveled down my spine.

"What were you saying?" Ramon returned from hanging his coat and poured hot water into the pot and added tea leaves. "Good. I could use a cup of tea. It's cold out there."

"Where were you?" I asked, my eyes darting back to the ceiling.

"I took the dogs out for a walk," he said matter-of-factly. "The usual route." He stirred the tea and put the cover back on the pot.

"How long were you gone?" I turned, crossed through the next room and started to go up the back stairs.

"Half an hour or so," he called out. "I took them through the park and around the fountain at St. James Court like we always do. Why? What's going on?"

At the top, I bent over the railing and shouted down to the kitchen. "Well, while you were gone, it sounded like someone was walking around up here and moving things in the little bedroom."

I walked down the hall and opened the door to the back room. I flicked on the light and poked my head inside, but nothing appeared out of place. Although I had just changed the bulb, there was a rapid flickering and then the light burned out. I went to the mantel and turned the light on there.

Ramon walked up behind me, a cup of tea in hand. "Are you sure it was steps?"

"That's what it sounded like." I opened the closet door and looked inside. Then I looked out the back window. Finally, I turned off the light and closed the door. "And I could have sworn someone was in that room, moving the furniture around. I could hear something scraping along the floor like someone was pushing or pulling it."

"Probably the house settling or something like that–you know what they say about old places." Ramon walked back to the TV in the big room at the front of the house and resumed the movie he had started. Rocky and Bess emerged at the top of the stairs and joined him on the sofa, where they eventually curled up and dozed.

"Hmm." I mumbled to myself, looking over my shoulder to the solitary door at the end of the hallway. "Let's hope so." I returned to the kitchen to retrieve my pot of tea and took it back to the third floor. Outside, the wind was howling and it whistled and whipped around the corners of the house.

Christmas came, and it seemed that the house would burst with a steady stream of family, friends, and out-of-town visitors that didn't abate until the holiday decorations came down on the sixth of January. My weekly dinner friends came over that night and we had a taking-down-the-tree party with more recipes I was testing for the new cookbook. The dreary weather that followed in the next two months provided ample opportunity for our group to gather in front of the fire in the parlor, and it seemed that Widmer House had effortlessly transformed itself into a familiar friend.

Nonetheless, I looked forward to the warm weather right around the corner, not only for the pleasant temperatures, but also for the chance to do some major work on the house. Three rooms still sat practically untouched, for the most part in need of furniture, wallpaper and drapes, and I couldn't wait to tear up the outdated shag carpeting that covered the entire second floor. From what I could tell, all the original hardwood flooring was still there, but it would be a major project to sand and refinish them. The crumbling façade would most likely have to wait a while, perhaps till the following year by which time I would have scoured antique shops for the right light fixtures and furnishings for the interior of the house.

I was standing in the foyer one afternoon in January, deciding where to put an old rosewood settee, when the doorbell rang. I went to answer it, noticing how blue the cloudless sky seemed that day. It was my friend Jill, another former coworker from my days waiting tables at the Oakroom down at the Seelbach Hotel. She was passing by and wanted to say hello, so I took her into the front parlor. A pot of freshly brewed tea sat on the sideboard, and I poured her a cup as we began to chat.

"Who was that weird guy out front?" she asked, taking a sip.

"What weird guy? We've got quite a few down here in Old Louisville." I passed her a plate with a piece of apple cake I had made earlier in the day.

"That old guy out front," she said. "He was just standing on the sidewalk staring at the place."

"I didn't notice any old guy in particular," I said, "but there are lots of them around here. Probably one of the men looking for work at the day laborer place around the corner."

"Maybe." She bit into a forkful of cake and smiled. "But it's odd, because he looks exactly like this old Cajun guy I used to see down here all the time when I studied at the University of Louisville."

"How did you know he was Cajun?" I sat back and pulled Rocky closer to me. Bess lay on the floor, curled up in front of the fireplace.

"I don't really know that he was Cajun," she said, "but he had that look, you know? Sort of dark and swarthy. And he had a different kind of accent."

"Really? So what made him so memorable, other than the fact that he was a displaced Cajun in Kentucky?" I drained the last of my tea from the cup and set it down on the saucer.

"Well, there was this one time in particular," she began. "The day before, my boyfriend and I had visited the library on York Street, where I'd found this huge ledger of old wives' tales and witchcraft and stuff like that. All stuff from Kentucky back in the 1800s."

"Okay, so where does the Cajun guy come in?" I leaned forward and poured myself another cup of tea. A fat squirrel scampered onto the window ledge outside and peered in at us. Rocky's ears perked up as he let out a low growl.

"Well, it's sort of weird. I read this creepy warning that you should not sweep at night because you might sweep up spirits," she said. "I didn't think much of it, but the next night, right before the sun went down, I decided to sweep the dead leaves from my front porch where we were living over on Second Street. I had totally forgotten the story I had read."

"And?" I pushed another piece of cake in her direction. The squirrel bounded off the window ledge and Rocky jumped down from my lap and ran to the window, where he stood on his hind legs and barked a warning.

"Well, I'd glance up after every few sweeps to see what was going on out in the street, and I looked up to see this old man gliding by with the setting sun shining at his back. But the thing is, it didn't look like he was walking at all. He seemed to be floating."

"So, what did he do?"

"He didn't really do anything," she said, "but he stopped when he saw me looking at him. And then in this eerie Cajun dialect he said very deliberately, 'It is bad to sweep in the night.'"

"'It is bad to sweep in the night'?"

"Yes, and I thought it was really strange because I had just read about it the day before. I tried to be friendly and told him I had only a few more leaves to sweep up. And you know what he said?"

Shaking my head, I cupped the tea between my hands.

"Well, the old guy stopped short, turned his head in my direction and repeated his warning in that thick accent of his. 'But it is *bad* to sweep in the night,' he said."

"Yes, I suppose that is sort of creepy."

"It was odd." She nodded and sat back against a cushion. "A gold tooth flashed from his grin, and I felt totally mesmerized by his glare. I thought about it for a minute and said, 'You're right. I'm done.' I turned to go inside. But when I looked back three seconds later to say good-bye, no one was there."

"So, he just disappeared?"

"I don't know, but curiosity made me walk to the sidewalk and look both ways. There was an empty lot next door and a man couldn't have shot out of sight so quickly. I looked to the other side and still I saw no one. It was really freaky."

"So, did you find out what happened to him?"

"No, but I would see him every now and then, and it always seemed like he'd be gone when I looked back. I always wondered if he wasn't a spirit that I swept up."

"Well, he seems to keep reappearing," I said. "If that's who it was standing out front just now."

"Yeah, maybe, but you know what?" She looked out the window to the sidewalk in front of the house. "As I was walking up to your front steps after I saw him, it dawned on me that he was the old Cajun guy, so I turned back to look at him—"

"Let me guess," I said. "When you looked back, there was nobody there?"

"Yes!" Her eyes widened as she said it. "It couldn't have been more than a second or two, so where did he go?"

"Yes, but some people tend to lurk in Old Louisville. I think it has something to do with us being so close to downtown. We get more than our share of crazies. I wish we could send some of them to the East End."

"Yeah, I know what you mean. They could use a colorful character or two out there," she said. "But it was still odd nonetheless. Make sure you keep an eye out for that guy."

"I will. Maybe there's some voodoo going on in Old Louisville that we don't know about and maybe he has something to do with that."

Jill took another bite of cake and laughed. "Watch out for little dolls with pins sticking out of them showing up on your front steps."

"If I find something like that," I said, "it will probably be Ramon who did it."

Later that evening, I was at home, alone, and thankful the day was almost over. I had taught in the morning, and most of the afternoon was spent cleaning and organizing. The day before, I had moved a small sofa and several chairs into the butler's panty, along with a TV, and it had been transformed into an inviting little nook. Under a blanket on the sofa, with the dogs on their cushions on the floor, I looked forward to a quiet evening watching the History Channel and the

Food Network.

As I flipped through the channels, it seemed that something rattled the small door leading down to the basement. Sitting up, I turned off the volume and listened intently, but nothing happened. After a minute's silence, I put the sound back on. Rocky and Bess hadn't given any indication that they had heard noise, so no big deal. I continued pressing buttons on the remote control and finally settled on a show about haunted houses.

After several minutes, I could hear some kind of noise. It sounded like maybe someone had grabbed the door handle from the other side and had tried to slowly pull the basement door open. I muted the TV and listened carefully, but nothing could be heard. Perhaps it was a draft causing the old door to rattle. Not overly concerned, I returned my attention to the television set and unmuted the volume. There was supposed to be a documentary about Bigfoot coming on next, and I love Bigfoot.

After another fifteen minutes or so, I had stopped thinking about the rattling of the basement door when a distinctly audible noise rattled it again, and an apparent whoosh of air caused one of the curtains behind the TV to lift a bit and flutter briefly before settling back down. I turned off the volume and started to push back the blanket so I could go and check the door, when the dogs suddenly stood up and shook themselves awake. After several good shakes, they scanned the room and then raised their heads to look at me. Both of them had cocked their heads to the side and gazed at me with mild perplexion.

"You need to go outside?" I said.

But instead of erupting in a whirlwind of happy jumps, they stood and stared at me with their heads inclined somewhat to the left. I started to get up from the couch and head for the back door when I realized they hadn't been staring at me, but rather at something behind me. I turned around to see what had captured their attention, but there was nothing there, save for a bare spot of wall where their eyes were focused. It was where the pictures had kept falling. Intrigued, I noticed that when I rose from the sofa and positioned myself next to the dogs, neither of them moved their eyes from the wall.

"You need to go for a walk?" I asked, a little louder. But nothing seemed to faze them. I suddenly felt a distinct change in the air, almost as if an electrical charge had atomized the atmosphere. "You're only freaking yourself out," I mumbled, not totally convinced this was true as I walked into the kitchen. I grabbed a sandwich from the refrigerator and returned to the little TV room to find Rocky and Bess in the same position, their eyes glued to the wall behind the sofa.

After several seconds, they both turned their heads to the left and appeared to follow something with their eyes. I saw nothing myself, but their eyes seemed to be following an invisible form as it made its way to the little door under the back stairs. Bess, curious as ever, trotted over to the door and leaned down to have a sniff at the threshold. Not satisfied with her olfactory explorations, she reached out a paw and started to scratch at the thin crack under the door. Somehow, I wasn't surprised when the door suddenly began to rattle in its frame; however, I was taken aback when Bess suddenly withdrew from the door and quickly scooted backward toward me, evidently startled by something. Then, she deliberately turned and looked up at me, a confused look on her face as the fur on her back and sides slowly lifted and stood on its ends. She gradually rolled her eyes up to see why the hair on top of her head was standing straight up, and then she quickly shook the hair back down and ran to me, standing so I could pick her up. Rocky looked on, a puzzled look on his face as well. This time when I asked them if they wanted to go outside, their floppy ears perked up and their wagging tails let me know they didn't want to be in that room any longer.

After letting them outside, I went to the door under the stairs and opened it. Only darkness greeted me until I turned on the light that illuminated the narrow wooden stairs leading into the cellar. I was tempted to go down and snoop around the brick and limestone rooms for a bit, but I decided to save it for another day. Apart from the washer and dryer, there wasn't much down there besides storage boxes and a few odds and ends left behind by the previous occupants. Even if I didn't believe in ghosts, I didn't relish the idea of being down there all by myself either. I was discovering that being alone in a big old house had its spooky moments now and then—especially at night.

Ghosts for Dinner

Although I was perfectly content with two dogs and a cat, Ramon decided he wanted another rescue schnauzer. On a cold day of drizzle and gray clouds in February, I walked into the front parlor and found a little silver schnauzer by the name of Fritz. He was obviously overcome by his new surroundings and looked timidly up at me, but once I knelt down and put a hand out for him to sniff, he bounded to me. After several minutes of pats and belly-rubs, he had won me over. From that point forward, there were few times when Fritz wasn't at my side in Widmer House.

To celebrate Fritz's arrival, and because February was cold and dreary, I decided it was time for a dinner party. It would serve as the official welcome to the new house, and I would make it a long, drawn-out affair with many courses in homage of the home's Victorian past. I would serve smoked salmon and toast points to start with, and then we'd move on to a cream of asparagus soup. Both would be served with champagne. After that, we'd open a bottle of chardonnay and move on to broiled trout with creamed spinach and then have sliced turkey with chestnut dressing. After taking a break in the parlor for a cup of punch romaine, we'd return to the table and enjoy beef tenderloin with bordeaulais sauce and roast potatoes, all washed down with a nice bottle of claret. To finish the extravaganza, there would be a cheese plate, orange soufflés, and cherry tart with sauternes. Back in the parlor, we'd linger over bourbon and chocolates in front of a blazing fire. Cold, dreary months did have their advantages.

In the dining room I stood and looked at the table, satisfied with my handiwork. The table had green skirting with a cream-colored Jacquard cloth draped over it, and eight high-backed chairs had been arranged around it. Each place setting had a gold charger with various gilt-rimmed plates of descending sizes stacked on top. On the smallest plate, I had placed printed linen napkins folded in the shape of the fleur-de-lis, an appropriate symbol for Louisville. With nice silverware and wineglasses, and two large silver candelabra in the center, the setting looked splendid. When I got up in the morning, all I'd have to worry about was the actual cooking.

The grandmother clock in the hall had struck midnight, and I trudged up to bed and jumped under the covers. Outside, the wind had picked up and could be heard whistling between the houses; inside Ramon snored away like a Bulgarian sailor. Despite the racket, I settled in, looking forward to a good night's sleep. Soon I began to drift off.

Not too long after that, right before complete sleep took hold of me, I sat bolt upright in bed, jarred awake by a loud crash from downstairs. It sounded like something, perhaps a chandelier, had crashed to the floor in the dining room. "Did you hear that?" I called out to the darkness, afraid to move, but listening as Ramon stirred.

"Yes," he answered, groggily. "Something fell. Go see what it was."

I grabbed the Louisville Slugger near the side of the bed and crept downstairs after flicking the lights on in the stairwell. In the foyer, all was quiet and nothing appeared out of order so I cautiously entered the dining room and hit the light switch. But nothing appeared out of place. I jumped a bit as the windows suddenly began to rattle, no doubt jostled by the wind outside, and I went into the next room. In the butler's pantry, I remembered the incident with the dogs and the rattling door, and I opened it and peered down into the darkness. All was quiet so I walked through the butler's pantry and into the kitchen, where I searched for the source of the noise. Eventually I returned back through the coatroom and through the foyer into the front parlor. With bright lights illuminating the room, it became apparent that nothing was amiss. I scratched my head, doused the lights and headed back upstairs. Could it have been the house settling or something like that?

Back under the covers, I snuggled in and enjoyed the warmth, thankful that I didn't have to be outside in the weather. After tossing and turning several times, I realized that I had missed my opportunity; I wasn't tired anymore, and it would probably take another hour or two for me to fall asleep.

Listening to the wind roar outside, I lay there and tried to come up with ways to induce slumber. I thought about the menu for tomorrow night's dinner; I went over decorating plans for the house in my head; I enumerated all the things that needed to be fixed and debated what should be fixed first. The bathroom on the second floor needed some major work, but there were crumbling chimneys on the roof that really needed attention before they collapsed and killed someone. The back part of the roof was looking pretty rough as well. Nearly an hour passed that way, but I wasn't any closer to sleep than before.

Suddenly, another loud crash emanated from the room immediately below, the dining room, and the floorboards seemed to shudder. It sounded as if a large piece of furniture—perhaps the armoire in the dining room—had been tipped over and fell to the ground. I could hear Ramon as he groaned a bit in his sleep and turned to one side. "Did you hear that?" I whispered, straining my ears for further noises.

"Yes," he answered, groggily. "Something fell. Go see what it was."

Louisville Slugger in hand, I stole out of the bedroom, past the dogs—they had also become alarmed at the noise and rose from their spots on the padded bench at the foot of the bed—and snuck quietly down the back stairs. Down in the coatroom, I listened in the dark for more activity. Other than the wind outside, all was still. On tiptoes, I crept into the butler's pantry and doubled back into the dining room, reaching my hand out for the light switch on the wall. Holding my breath, I slowly turned on the chandelier, my eyes adjusting as they wandered from the large armoire against the wall to the marble-topped buffet and then the walnut fireplace mantel.

Everything looked fine again. After scanning the room a second time, I walked across creaking floorboards into the foyer and turned on the lights. Nothing had tipped over there, either. In the parlor and the kitchen, it was the same. A cold draft hit my bare feet as they slid across the icy tiles and approached the back door; I opened it and looked outside. The stark light of a streetlamp in the alley illuminated the entire rear of the house, and nothing seemed out of place. I closed the door and went quickly to the front of the house, where I quietly pulled the front door open and found myself standing on the porch. Other than bare branches rattling in the wind, Third Street was desolate of any activity until the cold air whipped up an empty plastic grocery bag and sent it fluttering down the sidewalk. My feet chilled from the cold concrete, I went back inside and closed the door.

Still trying to find something to explain the strange sound, I ran up to the third floor and took a gander, but nothing appeared out of place. Then I trotted back down to the second floor and checked the two rooms at the front of the house before peering inside the bathroom on my way to the little room at the back of the structure. I opened the door and turned on the light. Everything was fine, except the freezing cold in the space caught me off guard. Since there were three exposed walls, it shouldn't have been surprising, but I wasn't expecting it. An old wooden tambour clock ticked away on the mantel, its round face showing it was almost half past one as I slowly studied the silvery numbers. Realizing I was finally starting to get tired again, I closed the door and returned to the bedroom.

Fritz had wriggled himself out from under the blankets and shadowed me, but Bess and Rocky were still standing on the settee at the foot of the bed. I picked them up and bundled them under the covers, convincing myself I was imagining things. It was time to go to sleep so I snuggled in and let myself relax, looking forward to dreams about the dinner party the next evening.

Although I didn't succumb to sleep entirely, I lay in a deeply relaxed state for another half hour or so, before a third loud crash reverberated through the downstairs. Again, I had the impression that it came from the dining room. The dogs stuck their sleepy heads out from under the covers and gave me confused looks. I asked Ramon if he had heard the noise again.

"Yes," he answered, groggily. "Something fell. Go see what it was."

Bat in hand, I stealthily made my way down to the dining room and flipped on the light. But instead of finding a piece of furniture tipped over, I saw the table perfectly laid out for my party the next evening. In the foyer, the grandmother clock provided me my only solace, a steady tick-tock that echoed quietly through the shining woodwork. Light from the chandelier reflected in the crystal champagne flutes and gleamed in the polished silver on the table as I scrutinized the dining room. All was fine.

More determined than before, I quickly went from room to room and turned on the lights, and then out the front and back doors where everything looked to be in place. Before double-checking the upper floors, I remembered the basement and opened the small door under the back stairs, my eyes trained on the darkness at the bottom of the steps. Slowly I followed the creaky stairs down to the washroom and pulled the string that illuminated a lone bare bulb in the ceiling. Then I listened. The wind still howled outside, but in the basement silence reigned, for the most part.

I checked the three adjacent cellar rooms and found nothing to arouse suspicion. It was a typical basement in an old Victorian house, utilitarian and inherently scary, and it exuded the sense of foreboding that is part and parcel of old underground rooms. The more I stood and examined the drab walls of stone and brick and the wispy cobwebs dangling from the bare rafters, the more my sense of unease increased: I was freaking myself out, so I ran up the stairs and closed the door. After checking the second and third floors another time, I found myself back under the covers, once more hoping to finally get some sleep.

Outside, two people—no doubt they were patrons leaving one of the neighborhood bars—began yelling in the back alley. From the face of the digital clock next to the bed I could see it was almost 2:30 and, after a quick calculation, I realized there was still a chance at getting five or six hours of sleep, so I concentrated on relaxing my feet and working up to my head. But every time I got up to my stomach I started thinking about the tart I had made for dessert the following evening. I debated sneaking downstairs to help myself to one of the extras I had made. In addition, a block of twelve-year-old cheddar I had brought back from a recent trip home to Wisconsin seemed to be calling my name. My stomach emitted a long, painful growl.

Fifteen minutes later my thoughts finally got off food and I was relieved to feel my eyelids drooping. I pulled the covers tight around me and began to drift off.

Crash! The crack of breaking glass made me jump out of bed. It sounded like a windowpane had broken, and I could hear large shards falling to the hardwood floors. All three of the dogs stirred and a growling Fritz made for the foot of the bed.

"Did you hear that?" Gripping the Louisville Slugger tightly, I rushed over to Ramon and flipped on the light.

"Yes," he answered, groggily. "Something—"

"Yeah, yeah, I know," I said. "'Something fell. Go see what it was.' *You* go see what it was." I poked him with the baseball bat.

"I'm too tired." He groaned and turned over. "Stop being such a hobo."

A second large crash echoed downstairs, again sounding like a broken window, and I could hear something like a large stone or brick bouncing across the parquet floors. After several seconds of silence, it happened a third time, the loud sound of breaking glass finally causing Ramon to right himself in the bed and listen. "Are those windows breaking?" he whispered.

"I think someone's trying to break in." My voice quavered, as I nervously picked up my cell phone and prepared to call 911.

From downstairs came another loud noise and the sound of broken glass falling to the floor. It sounded like stones were hitting the ground as well.

Ramon got up from the bed and snatched an aluminum bat leaning up against the wall on his side; two seconds later, we were inching our way down the front stairs. At the bottom of the steps, I quickly hit the switch and the foyer flooded with light. The face of the grandmother clock indicated that it was half past three as we cautiously entered the dining room, which was empty. Ramon went to the back of the house, and I searched the front, but everything seemed to be fine. After putting on some shoes and hurrying around the outside of the house, I checked the basement while Ramon scoured the top floors. Nothing. With all the lights on, we went from window to window on the ground floor, examining the panes for cracks or any signs of breakage. Then we checked all the remaining windows in the house and found not so much as a hairline fracture. What had made those sounds?

We turned off all the lights and cut through the foyer to ascend the steps to the second floor, but as we passed the grandmother clock, I realized that the tick-tocking had stopped. I looked at the face of the timepiece and was surprised to discover that it still read 3:30, even though the cell phone in my hand indicated it was 3:50. The weights hadn't even descended halfway down, so I was at a loss to explain why the mechanism had simply stopped. Anxious to get back to a warm bed, I quickly opened the door and reset the hands before pulling up the weights and setting the pendulum in motion. With the comforting tick-tock behind me, I made for the bedroom.

"Maybe it came from the neighbor's house or something," said Ramon, already tucked in under the covers.

"But it sounded like it came from the dining room," I answered. "Like all the other sounds before." I turned and looked into the darkness of the hallway, half expecting something to emerge from the shadowy recesses of the staircase. "If you ask me, something weird is going on in this house."

"Humph." With that Ramon promptly fell asleep and his loud snoring resumed.

Standing near the open bedroom door, I could still hear the clock ticking away in the foyer; a moment later, a series of four deep, melodious chimes marked the hour. Tiredness stung my eyes and my shoulders ached with tension, so I went to bed, pressed my eyes shut and willed myself to sleep. I'd be lucky to get three hours. The wind roaring outside, I cushioned my head against the pillows. Eventually, I dozed.

Boom! Sometime later, a loud thud sounded from downstairs. Groggy, I reached for the cell phone and saw that it was 5:10. Ramon stirred a bit but then I heard nothing. I debated getting up to check on the noise, but I soon decided against it. Why go downstairs if I was going to find nothing anyway? I closed my eyes and tried to recapture sleep.

Sometime later there was another dull thud. My eyes snapped wide open and a silent curse formed on my lips. I grabbed the cell phone and saw it was 6 o'clock on the dot. Ramon started mumbling something, and although I couldn't understand every word, the essence of it was: "Something fell. Go see what it was."

As adrenaline rushed through my veins, it became crystal clear that I was not meant to get any sleep this day. I stoically pushed back the covers and gave an unsatisfying stretch. Through the window next to the bed, the faintest sliver of rose and yellow appeared above the horizon, signaling the waning bit of darkness. The sun would be up soon, so I might as well get out of bed and start the day with a cup of strong black coffee. Leaving Rocky and Bess in their warm nest, Fritz dutifully followed as I trudged downstairs to grind some beans.

My hand on the rail as I descended the stairs at the front of the house, I could hear the neighborhood slowly coming to life. Outside, a car door slammed, and several vehicles sped by on Third Street. I opened the drapes over the window in the foyer to let in a bit of light, but it was still mostly dark outside. On the sidewalk, a neighbor was walking her dog. I turned on a small floor lamp and headed back to the kitchen, eager for the first cup of coffee.

But as I cut through the darkened dining room and pushed my way through the swinging door into the butler's pantry, my shin struck something hard and I grimaced in pain. I reached out for the light switch and turned it on, rubbing the part of my leg under my knee with the other hand. There in front of me, one of the dining room chairs blocked the doorway. Nonplussed, I stared, then grabbed it and turned to put it back in place at the table. That's when I froze, failing to comprehend the scene before me.

"Ramon!" I yelled. "Come down here right now."

Josephine

It took several more shouts before Ramon dragged himself out of bed and came down to the dining room, his dark hair matted over to one side. He stood and looked at me.

"What?" He rubbed the sleep from his eyes and yawned.

"Did you do this?" I opened my arms and extended them in the direction of the dining room table.

He turned his head and studied the room.

The dining room was not as I had left it the previous evening. Half of the chairs had been moved from the table and scattered to different parts of the room, and on the table, which I had set so carefully the night before, plates, silverware and wine glasses had been moved around. And the best part: several of the napkins I had folded in the shape of the fleur-de-lis had been unfolded and lay crumpled on top of the respective place settings. It almost looked as if people had just gotten up from a meal at the table, where someone had been having a dinner party—without me.

"I didn't do that," he said matter-of-factly. "I haven't gotten out of bed since we came down, and it was fine then." Then his eyes narrowed suspiciously at me. "You sure you didn't do it?"

"Yeah, right," I retorted. "I'm going to mess up the table I spent so much time setting yesterday."

Off in the distance, a rooster crowed and Ramon walked to the window, opened the shutter and looked out. "Why the heck is there a rooster crowing in Old Louisville?"

In the fading darkness, several rosy fingers of light crept behind the bare outline of a tree, an eerie confirmation that the sun would soon be up.

"I don't know why there's a rooster crowing in Old Louisville," I said. "Maybe we're turning into Key West and before you know it we'll have wild chickens scratching all over the place and six-toed Hemingway cats sleeping on the rooftops but I don't really care because all I'm concerned about at the moment is finding out who messed up my dining room table, thank you very much."

"Maybe you were sleep-walking or something." Ramon yawned, still gazing out into the back alley.

"I don't think so. I've never been known to sleep walk before." I surveyed the disorder in the room and went to join him at the window. "And besides, I didn't really get any sleep. I'm sure it has something to do with those weird noises before."

"Well, I'm going back to bed. Maybe someone's playing a practical joke on us." He padded across the floor and into the foyer before disappearing up the steps.

As I stared out the window, Ramon's footsteps creaked overhead and I was left alone to ponder the possibilities. Actually, we did have friends who would pull such a prank, but none of them had keys to get inside. In addition, there was no evidence that anyone had gained entrance to the house, either. Besides, who'd get up in the middle of the night when it was cold and blustery outside and make the trip to our place for a joke? I wondered if the animals could have disturbed the table, but the dogs had never left the second floor and the little black cat was still hiding inside the tiny bathroom closet most of the time. Even if she had ventured forth, the doors to the dining room had been closed. It didn't make sense.

The strange dining room antics proved to be a lively topic of conversation when it came time for the dinner party. More than one person was convinced the Widmer House was haunted. "If there's a ghost here and it wants me to believe," I said, "it had better show up and introduce itself. Otherwise, I don't plan on believing in ghosts."

Later that night, after all the banter and speculation died down, we all sat around the table in the dining room and nursed glasses of port. The dinner party had been a huge success, and we all vowed we wouldn't touch another morsel of food for a month. Or at least till the next time we got together. Once the dessert was finished, we got up from our chairs and walked into the parlor for a bourbon nightcap before everyone headed out into the cold weather.

As she approached the warmth of the fire, Laura stopped dead in her tracks and looked out the large arched window into the front yard. "Who is *that*?" She raised her finger and pointed at the patch of grass outside. A black silhouette hovered, outlined by the eerie glare of the streetlamp.

"What the–" I bumped into her and almost dropped the decanter of bourbon I had snagged from the console in the foyer. "What are they doing in the front yard?" I said, craning my neck to better see the figure outside. I maneuvered my way around the others, who were backed up behind us, and walked to the front door and opened it. From the porch, I walked down the steps and slowly approached the form in the front yard. It appeared to be an elderly woman in long skirts with a shawl draped over her shoulders. Something like a turban sat on her head. I couldn't be sure, but it looked like the person I had seen in the back alley shortly after moving into the house. Mesmerized, she stared into the front window.

"Can I help you?" I asked.

Startled, the woman jumped back and looked at me. Without a word, she raised the crook of her arm to shield her face and bounded away over the hedge. Although dead leaves and frozen grass covered the yard, she didn't make the slightest sound as she ran away. Watching her disappear from sight, I went back up the steps and returned to the warmth of the house.

"Who was that?" Wendy met me in the foyer and gave me a quizzical look. "Was it another panhandler?"

"I don't know," I said. "It looked like some voodoo lady or something." In the parlor, Beth held out a tumbler of bourbon, which I gratefully accepted.

"What did she want?" asked Laura.

"I don't know. She didn't say anything." I took a swallow and enjoyed the warmth searing the back of my throat. "I asked her what she wanted and she raised her arm like she was a vampire who had just seen a crucifix. Then she bounded over the hedge and ran down toward Oak Street."

"Well, she'll fit right in on Oak," said Skippy. He drained the last of his bourbon and held his hands out to the fire. "She's probably heading over to the corner of Fourth and Crazy to see what other nut cases are out and about tonight. Maybe they can get a musical act together and take their show on the road."

"Maybe it's Josephine," said Laura.

"Who the heck is Josephine?"

Laura looked out the front window for signs of any other visitors before hugging her shawl tighter around her neck. "I was talking to one of your neighbors before I came in tonight, and they were telling me about some of the interesting characters that live around here. She's supposed to be one of them."

"Josephine?"

"Yes. From what they say, she's an old voodoo lady who grew up in this area. They said her name is Josephine." She returned her attention to the small crowd in front of her and smiled. "Maybe it was her."

"Voodoo in Kentucky?" I swirled the remaining bit of bourbon in my glass and then raised it to my lips. "Did we even have voodoo in these parts?"

"Of course we did," said Skippy, the amateur historian. "Back when people still got around by steamboats, anything that New Orleans had eventually ended up in Louisville. Around here they used to call it 'hoodoo' though."

"Oh, great." I reached out for the bourbon. "Now we've got to worry about witch doctors and voodoo queens in addition to all the people who are plain crazy around here." I went to stand with Laura at the window and we looked out across the front yard. A tall African-American man came walking down the middle of the street. He wore a long black coat and carried a violin case at his side.

"Oh, who's that?" said Laura. "I've seen him around before."

"I forget his name," I said, "but I used to see him at the University of Louisville a lot."

31

"You talking about Micah?" Wendy took a drink of bourbon and swirled the ice cubes around in her tumbler. "You see him all over town. Always with his violin case."

"Yes, that's it," I said. "Micah." I left the window and plopped myself down in an armchair by the fire. "Not quite sure what his story is, but you really do see him all over the place." I stretched my feet out toward the fire and smiled. "I don't know about the rest of you, but I sort of like the fact that we have a guy with a violin regularly strolling around our city. It adds a bit of culture and I hope we see him down here a lot in Old Louisville." I sighed. "If you ask me, we can always make do with another interesting character or two."

Beth laughed a bit and nestled into her corner of the sofa. "Well, you guys can't say you didn't pick a colorful neighborhood, can you?"

"Never a dull moment down here." I filled my glass and passed around the bourbon for those wanting a refill, which was everyone. It was cold outside, but whiskey was keeping things nice and warm at Widmer House.

The Corner of Fourth and Crazy

The good thing about February is that it only lasts 28 days. Most years, that is. March finally arrived in Old Louisville and with it, the anticipation of spring. Although patches of ice and snow still crusted the ground, residents could taste the end of winter, and they nervously paced their warm parlors and paneled libraries like caged animals. They longed for a warm breeze and a bit of green grass. So did the people who were often found near the corner of Oak and Fourth streets.

Old Louisville is a unique neighborhood to say the least. Aside from civic-minded residents and spectacular architecture, it has its fair share of problems as well. Part of it is an image problem that goes back to the 1960s and 70s when many considered Old Louisville a seedy and unsafe part of the city. So, despite the gentrification that has taken place, many old-timers still think of it as a bad part of town today. Granted, Old Louisville is almost downtown, so it does have the normal troubles you'd find in the center of any larger city in the country, but in Louisville, people's perceptions don't always match up to reality. The purported crime rate is sometimes higher than other parts of town—a fact that is hardly surprising given the higher density of residents in a single square block compared to other Louisville neighborhoods—but a lot of the criticism has to do with the panhandlers and loiterers who sometimes prowl Oak Street after hitting up one of the many charitable social service agencies located in Old Louisville or after trying to find day jobs at a local employment agency. Often, they congregate at the corner of Fourth and Oak streets.

Back before my time, right as the hippies were petering out of existence in Old Louisville, locals called the corner of Fourth and Oak "Fourth and Fellini" because at any given moment you might come across a scene straight out of the famous Italian director's films. Or maybe something totally unexpected, like a group of men dressed as nuns or a woman in a purple sleeping bag with two armholes cut out standing up and playing *Claire de Lune* on the saw. But most call it the corner of Fourth and Crazy nowadays. You'll still find the occasional man in a nun's habit—in fact, most of the populace at Fourth and Crazy still count as nothing more than eccentric—however, you'll also find a random hustler, aggressive transsexual prostitute, or a drug dealer thrown in the mix. It makes life in Old Louisville interesting, to say the least.

One day in March, as winter was loosening its grasp on the neighborhood, I was driving to work and noticed a man kneeling at the bus stop at Fourth and Oak. I couldn't figure out why he was hunched over the way he was. Then I saw that he was chewing on a corner of the long wooden seat that comprised most of the base of the bench under the little bus stop hut. When I drove back home later in the day, I noticed that a large chunk had been gnawed from the bench.

Another day, there was a corpulent man in a shamrock-print caftan playing the bongos on top of the little waiting hut. Don't ask me how he crawled up there. The next night three drag queens in tight-fitting sequined gowns were up there, apparently rehearsing for a Supremes number. I hoped it was *Baby Love*, but I had the windows up as I drove by so I couldn't know for sure.

Widmer House was right around the corner from Fourth and Crazy. If you walked out the back door of 1228 South Third Street to the alley and went down four or five houses and turned left, you were there.

Nonetheless I was still surprised when I drove by the corner on my way to the grocery store one day in March and noticed a very large man sitting on the infamous bench at the bus stop. He was totally naked and contentedly sat there, presumably waiting for the bus. I recognized him as a local artist who's known for his colorful streetscapes of different parts of the city, but I had never seen him unclothed at the bus stop before. Come to think of it, I had never seen anyone fully unclothed at the bus stop before.

The man just sat there and grinned at passers-by, his big eyes wider than usual. When I passed by the corner again fifteen minutes later, four squad cars had pulled up and an officer had draped an Army-issue woolen blanket over the man. With wide eyes, the large man kept looking back and forth at passing cars and smiled, even waving every now and then. The policemen scratched their heads and paced around.

The next day, when I drove by the bus stop on the way to the grocery store to get some things to test a new batch of recipes, Nude Fat Guy was gone, replaced by a tall individual with a beach ball-striped propeller beanie like little boys used to wear in the mid 1900s. He was keeping time with his left foot and appeared to be playing an imaginary set of drums.

Next to him stood Josephine.

Immediately, I slowed the car for a better look, nonetheless trying to be inconspicuous. A heavy brown skirt hung down below the woman's knees, leather sandal straps curling around her ankles. Although the air was warm, she had on a bulky knit sweater and wore the same turban from the night before. At least I thought it was the same turban. Truth be told, I wasn't even certain it was the same woman. She seemed to have a serene smile on her face, but that quickly vanished when she caught sight of my gaze. Again, she raised her arm and covered her face, quickly turning away from me and running down the sidewalk.

My eyes widened and I shook my head and chuckled. "What is going *on* with that woman?" I said to no one in particular. "I don't even know her but I guess I did something to get on her bad side."

Voodoo Days

Frankly, I found it odd that there was a supposed voodoo lady running around the neighborhood. Not because I was afraid she'd turn me into a zombie or anything but because once or twice a year, I'd experience something I call a voodoo day. I made up the name when I was in my adolescent years, and it has stuck ever since. As far as I know there's no actual voodoo involved, but voodoo seemed as good a choice as any to describe the weird kind of days where random coincidences always seemed to converge in large numbers in my life. They started right around age twelve for me and waned in their frequency the older I got, but nonetheless I could count on one or two full-blown voodoo days a year. When I moved into the Widmer House, the frequency of my voodoo days seemed to increase dramatically.

When I was a teenager, most of my voodoo days centered on the television, no doubt because all we ever did was sit around and watch TV at home. Typical shows involved were *Gilligan's Island* or *The Brady Bunch*. Sometimes *Hogan's Heroes* or *One Day at a Time*. The way a voodoo day would work is that I—out of the blue—would find myself thinking about something I had seen on TV, and then that very scene or episode would be on the television sometime in the next twenty-four hours. And not just that, either; the exact scene would be on as the television was turned on or when changing the channel. That would then be the precursor to something peculiar happening.

For example: I'd be lying awake in bed on a Saturday morning and for some reason the episode from *Gilligan's Island* where they find the gigantic spider in the cave would pop into my head, and I'd chuckle to myself, remembering how fake the huge spider looked, its big old phony legs stiffly moving up and down as it crawled to the mouth of the cave. Then I'd get up and get a bowl of Captain Crunch for breakfast, and what would be on TV when I turned it on? The very first thing to pop up on the screen would be the goofy spider thrashing its fake legs in the cave as it chased Gilligan around. Then, there'd be a knock at the door of our house and a gypsy man would be standing there. Not a real gypsy, but a man dressed up as a gypsy, who would ask if he could use the phone because his car had broken down. And his car would be a red, double-decker bus like they drive around in London.

We lived in the middle of nowhere in the backwoods of Wisconsin, and you never saw men dressed up as gypsies, much less driving double-decker buses down a remote gravel road at nine in the morning. What were the chances of that? And then later in the day, something else weird would happen, like I'd look out the front window, and there'd be seven black dogs of all different shapes and sizes sitting in a perfect row looking at me like they knew I'd be coming to the window at any minute. Maybe they wanted a treat.

Once I was sitting in Mrs. Norton's class at school and for some reason I started to think about a *Brady Bunch* episode, the one where they were on vacation in Hawaii and Greg wiped out on his surfboard and they all thought he had drowned. When I got home that afternoon and walked through the door, the TV was blaring and I saw Greg on his surfboard just a second before he wiped out. Two hours later the phone rang and it was someone in Ireland who dialed the wrong number and got mad and wouldn't believe me when I told her I really wasn't her nephew in Galway trying to play a practical joke on her with a bad American accent. Then, at suppertime, I was amazed to see that the first mouthful of alphabet soup I had spooned up advised me to BE A MAN, and the pasta letters were perfectly spaced and straight. Those were voodoo days.

The older I got, the less frequent my voodoo days became, due in no small part, I'm sure, to the reduced hours in front of the television set, even though others have told me that pubescent individuals are often the most susceptible to paranormal phenomena. I don't know if I'd describe my voodoo days as supernatural, but I do know they started increasing in frequency after we took up residence at Widmer House.

The first voodoo day I recall at the house on Third Street started off with a bundle of sticks. I had gotten out of bed late one weekend morning when the sun was shining and the day was starting to warm up a teensy bit after a very chilly night. Standing at the front window, I watched as a blond woman in black strolled by, perhaps headed to Oak Street. Several minutes later another female figure passed in the same direction, this one wearing all black as well, and also sporting a head of long blond hair. The next two people who walked by, not as a pair, but separately, also were women in black slacks and black tops, and both had very, very long hair. The fifth person to pass was a neighborhood character known as Tina, famous for the head of long bleached blond hair that went all the way down to her ankles, and she was dressed all in black as well. What were the odds of five people passing by, all in the same direction, all wearing solid black, and all having extremely long hair? I chuckled and walked into the foyer.

Coffee cup in hand, I opened the front door and prepared to step out onto the porch to better survey my domain. As I took my first step, something down on the tile floor of the porch caught my eye and I had to swerve to the right to avoid stepping on it. When I reached to pick it up, I discovered a small bundle of sticks tied together with a willow branch. The sticks were maybe twelve inches at the longest, and there might have been twenty or thirty of them in all. It looked like the perfect little bit of kindling, so I took it up to the big room with the wood-burning fireplace on the second floor. It would come in handy for the next fire. It never crossed my mind to wonder why someone would leave a bundle of kindling on our front steps. It wasn't until later that I thought about Josephine.

Later on that day, when I made myself some lunch, something surprising happened when I took the cap off a bottle of beer. When I tossed the bottle top down onto the counter, it landed on its side and balanced in a vertical position while it skidded across the counter. That doesn't happen too often. Then, the phone rang and I went to answer it. A woman on the other line asked to speak to David and when I replied that he was on the line, she just guffawed. By the sound of my voice she quickly concluded that she had dialed the wrong number, confiding that she was trying to reach a tall blond guy with schnauzers who taught foreign languages at the university. When I told her she had reached the right person, she laughed and added that the man she was looking for drove a black car and lived in an old house on Third Street. Only when she gave the last name of the individual, who was indeed a different person, did we realize a strange coincidence had occurred.

When I hung up the phone and returned to the kitchen, the same thing happened after I ate my lunch and when I opened a second bottle of beer: when I tossed the top down onto the counter it landed upright on its ridged side and stood there till I knocked it over. I guess it shouldn't have been surprising that the day's odd events would herald the beginning of a year of very bizarre occurrences at Widmer House.

Spring finally took hold in Old Louisville. It started slowly, in late March, with the jonquils and crocuses, which soon wilted and made way for the redbud trees. But when April finally arrived, it seemed as if spring had come overnight, and the neighborhood just as quickly transformed into a garden of fresh greenery and heavily laden branches ready to erupt. The tulip poplars dropped their huge blossoms and the azaleas and dogwoods started blooming. The smell of new grass and damp soil permeated the air.

It was a beautiful sunny morning and I was in the kitchen, getting ready to test some recipes for a column I was writing for *Kentucky Monthly* magazine. I took out the needed utensils and from the refrigerator I removed several blocks of cream cheese and some English cucumbers. From the vegetable baskets under the window by the stove I got several huge onions and proceeded to chop them. I was writing a piece about benedictine, a local specialty invented in the late 1800s by Louisville caterer Jennie Benedict and I had four different recipes to compare. Part spread, part dip, it's something that tends to show up on Louisville tables during the holidays and special events, and the Kentucky Derby was right around the corner. Once I had fed the onions into the food processor, I used a cheese cloth to extract all the moisture and then proceeded to combine it with the other ingredients.

The antique phone I had refurbished rang and I went to the front of the house to answer it. A high-school friend was calling from her new home in Texas and she had tracked me down after losing contact several years before. We started catching up and before long I had told her about the recent move. An archaeologist, Mindy was thrilled to hear about the Widmer House and the historic neighborhood I now called home. She wanted more details and asked if I had found anything left behind by the original families, but the only thing I knew about was a 1907 inspection sheet from the Louisville Electric Company I had discovered taped to the door in an old-fashioned fuse cabinet on the second floor.

"Do you have any ghosts?" she inquired. I chuckled and told her about the odd noises, the pictures falling, and the several times I had come across the unexplained smell of coffee in the kitchen, but quickly disavowed myself of any real belief in the supernatural.

"I'm more concerned about the bats here," I confided. "It seems like they're flying around at all hours, even during the daytime. Isn't that strange? I thought they only came out at night, and when it was warm. I've seen them flying around when it's cold out, too."

"Hmmm. Don't know. I'm an archaeologist, not a bat expert."

Mindy listened as I recounted some of the details of the strange occurrences from the weeks before and soon we were laughing and recalling our penchant for telling ghost stories during our high school days back home in Wisconsin. We talked for another half hour or so and I was getting ready to say good-bye and hang up when I suddenly caught my breath and gasped. Up on the third floor, one of the doors had slammed shut.

"What?" Mindy stopped talking while I told her to wait and be quiet for a second. Trying to make as little noise as possible, I went over to the railing and listened. Distinct footsteps had started, and they seemed to be making their way down from the top floor. I looked around and spied a large glass paperweight on the telephone table. With my free hand, I picked it up in case I found myself face to face with an intruder and needed to defend myself.

"I think there's someone in the house," I whispered into the receiver. The telephone stood on a small table under the main stairs and I stretched out the cord to position myself closer to the balustrade to see up into the stairwell. I could see up to the third floor, but all I could see was darkness until the scrolled brass lamp hanging over the topmost landing caught a bit of light and reflected it. It seemed to gently sway in and out of the dim stream of light coming from the door to my office.

Ramon was at work, but thinking that perhaps he had come home early or maybe he had come for a quick lunch break as he sometimes did, I called out his name. But I got no answer, so I called out again. The only thing I could hear was distinct footfall, tread by tread, as the steps continued and approached the landing between the second and third floors. Plain as day, it sounded like someone was walking down the stairs, and the ground floor was the destination.

"What's going on?" asked Mindy. "Do you need to go?"

"Hang on a sec. Someone is coming down the stairs." I paused as the steps made it to the second floor and then started coming down to the last landing. I looked up to the first landing, where a shaft of sunlight had illuminated the two stained-glass windows, and waited.

The stairs from the ground floor to the second floor doubled back midway at the landing, obscuring a portion of it from sight. It sounded as if the invisible steps had reached the last landing and I was waiting for a pair of feet to materialize as they rounded the bend and came down the final section of steps. I held my breath and waited, but the footfall simply faded away, the unknown source concealed in the shadows. I had the distinct impression that someone had just walked all the way down the stairs and stopped on the very last step necessary for him or her—or whatever it was—to stay out of view.

With a clatter, I put the handset down on the little telephone table and flipped on the light in the stairway. "Who's there?"

There was no response, so I said it again. When I got no answer, I charged up the stairs, flipping on random lights all the way to the third floor, where all the doors were wide open. Finding no one, I trudged back down to the first floor.

"Is everything okay there?" Mindy's anxious voice crackled from the handset. "Tell me what's happening!"

I picked up the phone and gave her an update. "I'm fine. But I could swear someone was on the steps." I told her I had seen nothing at all and had no idea where the footsteps could have originated, other than on the third floor, where it clearly sounded like someone had slammed a door. Shrugging my shoulders, I finally said it must have been something with a perfectly reasonable explanation. Maybe the timbers expanding and contracting with the warmer weather had caused it. We had hired men to do some odd jobs around the house, so maybe that could have had something to do with it.

"Hmmm. Maybe your ghost doesn't like what you're doing to the place," suggested my friend. "Remember that old haunted farmhouse off Highway 54 we used to sneak into after theater practice? They said a ghost chased the family off because they inherited the home from a relative and when they moved in they started changing things around too much."

A slight shiver ran up my spine as I remembered the warning Margaret had given me. I gave a nervous laugh and told Mindy she was not the first one who had come up with that idea. We spoke for several more minutes and then said our good-byes. I hung up the old phone and even though it was bright and sunny outside, I made sure to leave the light on in the dark stairwell.

Lewis

That year in Old Louisville, spring was exceptionally beautiful, albeit short. By the start of the Kentucky Derby Festival at the end of April, the early tendrils of summer had already taken hold, and the humidity and warmth in the air hinted at the many sultry evenings that lay ahead. Azalea bushes danced with hundreds of animated blossoms in scarlet, crimson and fuchsia, and dogwood trees displayed delicate petals of pink and ivory at every turn. Tender sprigs of mint seemed to shoot up wherever a neglected patch of moist soil would permit—around the gas lamps on Saint James Court, where the wrought-iron legs of old benches dug into the damp earth of Central Park, at foundations and through the cracks in cobblestone and brick courtyards. It seemed that mint was growing everywhere.

For most people in Louisville, fresh mint in April means one thing: the Kentucky Derby is right around the corner and mint juleps are in store. It's a time when people pull out rare silver cups and cocktails shakers, long-necked spoons passed down from one generation to the next, and secret family recipes, all in anticipation of the one time of year when even the strictest of teetotalers have been known to allow themselves this one indulgence. Mint juleps and the Kentucky Derby were two of the many things that I had come to love about my move to Louisville in 1993.

There was still a lot to do on the house, but the rooms on the bottom floor were presentable, so like many homeowners in Old Louisville, we decided to have a Derby party. The small yard at the front of the house, on the other hand, was a wreck, and it needed a good bit of landscaping to enhance the curb appeal. Instead of hiring a professional, Ramon one day asked the first guy who walked by if he'd be interested in doing some landscaping work.

The man he hired was named Lewis, and it turned out that Lewis was a familiar local panhandler. He had hit me up for money several times as I walked to the store and I recognized him right away when Ramon introduced us. "Why don't you call someone from the Yellow Pages?" I asked later, when I got him alone in the kitchen. "I think Lewis has some problems. I've seen him passed out at the bus stop at Fourth and Crazy two or three times already. Hate to break it to you, but I don't think he's a qualified landscaper."

"Oh, all he needs to do is plant some things and pull some weeds," said Ramon. "I don't think it will be that hard. And we can help him out."

"I know it's not that hard, but garden work might be something of a challenge when you're a drunk," I said. "He reeks of alcohol. Didn't you smell it on him? He probably has a drug problem, too. What if he's a crack whore?"

"Well, I asked him and he said he doesn't do drugs. He only likes a drink or two now and then, he said." With that, Ramon left for the nursery to get some of the things for the yard makeover.

"I have a feeling he likes more than a drink or two," I called after him.

Lewis started landscaping the week before our Derby party. But after five days of work, it seemed that little progress had been made. In fact, it seemed like no progress had been made. Several holes had been dug and a number of plants in plastic containers stood at the ready, waiting for someone to transplant them, but other than that, the front yard looked much the same as it did the day Ramon had hired Lewis.

"What should I do with this?" Lewis asked one sun-filled morning, motioning with his head at the bag of mulch slung over his shoulder.

I had already told him three times to spread the mulch over the beds with the newly planted boxwoods along the sidewalk, but I quickly learned the man's short-term memory left a bit to be desired. "Spread it around the boxwoods in the front," I repeated. "There are ten more bags in the back yard." Then I walked into the house to do some work in the kitchen. I had come back from the grocery store and needed to start on the food for the party.

Half an hour later, the doorbell rang. I put down a tray of lemon tarts I had taken out of the oven and went to open the front door. Lewis stood there and asked what he should do next. I walked outside to see how the mulching had gone and was surprised to find that absolutely no mulch had been scattered around the boxwood hedges. When I looked over at Lewis, I noticed he had taken a swig from a bottle wrapped in brown paper. After wiping his mouth with the back of his hand, he stowed the bottle in his pants pocket.

"Where's all the mulch?" I asked. Out front on the sidewalk, there was some movement, and I looked up to see Micah walking by. Clad in a red Louisville Cardinals sweatshirt, he happily swung the violin case at his side and didn't seem to notice us in the front yard.

"Up there, around the boxwoods," he said, pointing at the azalea bushes at the front of the house. He smiled, seemingly satisfied with the job he had done.

"Well, those are actually the azaleas," I explained. "But no big deal. They needed mulch, too." I guided Lewis over to a large flat of Manhattan bushes and gave him his next task. "There are two dozen Manhattan bushes here," I said. "Plant a row of twelve to make a border for this side of the yard and then another dozen in a row to make a second border over there. That way the whole yard will have a hedge around it." I took several of the plants and laid them out so he could see exactly what I was talking about.

"Okay, Chief," he said. "And those?" he asked, pointing at two dozen hosta plants on the sidewalk.

"Once you have the Manhattans planted, do a row of hostas next to them, on the inside." I grabbed several hostas and positioned them to give him a visual guide. "Does this make sense?" I asked.

"Sure thing, Boss." He picked up a Manhattan bush and started to work.

"The Manhattan bushes on the outside, and the hostas on the inside," I said, simplifying the instructions for good measure.

Back in the kitchen, I started grating Cheddar for a batch of pimento cheese. When that was done, I mixed in a bit of mayonnaise and chopped red peppers. I was debating whether or not to add a dash of Worcestershire sauce when an uneasy feeling came over me, so I decided to check on Lewis.

He already had sunk a good portion of the plants into the ground, but it immediately became apparent that Lewis had not understood the instructions. Instead of a row of Manhattan bushes next to a row of hostas, he had started to plant a single row of Manhattan bushes alternating with hostas. "No, no, no," I said, using a trowel to remove the hosta plants. "Not like that, like *this*." I transferred Manhattan bushes to the recently vacated holes and started a parallel line of hostas. "When you're done with these two rows, do the same thing over there." I indicated the boundary of the yard on the other side of the walkway.

"Okay, I see." He bent over and continued to work. "No problem, Chief."

I went back inside and added a dash of Worcestershire to the pimento cheese; then I started a batch of benedictine. After grating the cucumber and mixing it with cream cheese and parsley pureed with olive oil, I stirred it all together and put it in the refrigerator. I had scooped flour out of the canister to whip up a batch of beaten biscuits when a hunch impelled me to check on Lewis again.

He had finished the rows he had started on, but, instead of a mirror image on the other side of the yard, he had planted the remaining plants alongside the house. He was sitting on the front steps, the paper-wrapped bottle in one hand. When he saw me, he stood up and put the bottle back in his pocket.

A slight groan escaped my lips. "Um, that's not quite what I wanted." I pointed to the edge where the plants should have gone. "I wanted them in rows, over there." I was going to explain it to Lewis once again when I noticed his bloodshot eyes and saw how he had begun to sway back and forth.

"Never mind," I said. I started uprooting the hostas and Manhattan bushes and transplanted them myself. Lewis grabbed a broom and started sweeping the sidewalk. On the street, a beat up old Chevy slowly drove by the house. A red-headed woman was leaning out the passenger-side window and she took a picture with an old Polaroid camera. As the car crept on its way, I saw something else lean out of the window behind her. It was an enormous pig, splotched with patches of pink and black, and it stuck its nose out into the air and snorted loudly.

"You sure do got some oddballs in this here neighborhood," said Lewis. He stood next to me and shook his head. Together we watched the car disappear from view.

Ramon and I had scheduled the party for the next day, and by noon the front yard was in presentable condition. Mounds of purple phlox tumbled over the raised edge of the curb, and the Manhattan bushes formed two neat rows on either side of the yard. A tidy row of boxwood hedges stood at the front, welcoming those who came up the walkway. Although the hedgerows added a great deal of character to the small front yard, the individual bushes seemed tiny and inconspicuous. I wanted to have one of those border hedges that were eight or nine feet tall, like the ones I saw down the block. It would take years before the hedge at Widmer House reached those heights, so I resigned myself to the wait. If I had learned one thing during that first half year we were in the house, it was that you needed to have patience if you wanted to live in an old house. Things generally didn't get done overnight.

I gave the front yard a final once-over and went back into the house. Ramon was off running errands, and Lewis said he would return in a couple of hours to get some money for his labors. I went up and took a shower. Several hours later, I had put on a linen jacket and everything was ready. At the bar we had set up in the front parlor I made myself a quick mint julep before the first guests arrived. Sipping the sugar-sweetened bourbon, I wandered from room to room and inspected the trays of hors d'oeuvres one final time. In addition to beef tenderloin with Henry Bain sauce, there were beaten biscuits with country ham and little silver dollar rolls with bacon and benedictine for the real meat eaters. I had also made up trays of sweet potato biscuits with pecan chicken salad and pimento cheese finger sandwiches, using recipes from the cookbook that had just come out. And of course, there were lots of sweets. I was setting out a vase with fresh roses next to a dish of pecan fudge when the doorbell buzzed. I went to open it, and Skippy was standing there in a seersucker suit.

He zoomed by me and made a beeline to the mint juleps, fluttering a scrap of brown paper in his hand as he walked by. "This was stuck in the iron grate of your front door." After setting down the paper, he filled a glass with crushed ice and added some bourbon.

"What is it?" I examined the scrap and wrinkled my nose. A large grease spot stained the center and illegible handwriting had been scrawled across one side. It looked as if someone had found part of an old grocery bag in the garbage and written a message on it. "Where'd you say you found this?"

"It was stuck in your front door. Probably that old Josephine leaving a voodoo curse for you or something like that." Skippy used a large stalk of mint to stir his drink and took a swallow.

"Well, I don't have time to figure out what it says." I squinted to decipher the words. "The house is going to be full of people in a quarter hour and I need to make sure there's enough ice for the bar." I crumpled up the paper and tossed it into a cardboard box I had set aside for trash.

He shook his head and took another drink. "Josephine's not going to like that."

"Whatever. She'll have to get over it."

An hour later the house swarmed with people, most wandering about with mint juleps. In the foyer, I stopped to chat with a group of neighbors who had stopped to admire my latest bit of handiwork, several large gold panels with the word "welcome" stenciled in different languages over several entryways. The idea had come to me, I explained, after discovering a pencil tracing of the German word for "welcome" on one of the panels. Wondering if it wasn't perhaps a remnant from the first inhabitants, the Widmer family, presumably Swiss speakers of German, I had decided to keep the greeting—misspelling and all—and embellish it to make it part of the décor. In Edwardian script, I had traced out black letters on a gleaming gold background and the result was very eye-catching. The greeting was then repeated in French, English, Arabic, and Esperanto on the neighboring panels.

I excused myself to make the rounds and offer bourbon balls to anyone with a sweet tooth when a terrible shriek echoed in the foyer. "Oh, my goodness!" cried a woman. She pointed through the window to the sidewalk that ran between our house and the neighbors. "Who is that?" A spate of concerned murmurs spread through the house, but it soon turned to relieved chuckles when I spied the source of the disturbance and explained that there was no need to worry. It was only Lewis. Standing outside the window in the clothes he had worn the last five days, he stared mutely through the window into the foyer like a man in a trance. From the way his body swayed back and forth, I could tell he was under the influence.

I ran through the back door to the side yard and pulled him out of view. "What is it, Lewis?" I said. "Why were you standing there, staring into the window? You could have knocked or come around to the back door."

"Okey dokey, Chief," he said, his words slurred together. A slight grin formed on his lips, and that's when I saw how dilated his pupils were. At his sides, his hands had started to fidget and twitch.

"Did you get my bill for services rendered?" He shuffled his feet and looked away.

"Bill? No, I don't recall getting a bill," I said. "No need for a bill anyway, since all you need to do is tell us the hours you worked."

"I left it on the front door for you. My invoice." His eyes started to dart back and forth, as if he expected someone to come up and startle us.

A light bulb went on somewhere. "Oh, that piece of brown paper on the front door? Hang on a sec and let me get it." I ran into the house to retrieve the crumpled mess from the trash box. Smoothing it out on the railing around the porch, I leaned over it and studied the writing a bit more intently. I was able to finally decipher the word "invoice" at the top and followed several jagged scrawls down to what appeared to be a series of numbers.

"Yep, that's my invoice, Boss." Lewis smiled and then swatted at something in the air.

Rubbing my eyes, I handed to note back to him. "Sorry, but you're going to have to read this because I can't make it out." I chuckled. "All I see is something that looks like $3,000."

"That's right, for services rendered. $3,000 is the bill for landscaping your beautiful house."

"Are you kidding? *Three grand?*" I hoped he was joking, but the petulant look on his face indicated otherwise.

"Yes, that's right. For services rendered you owe me $3,000." Lewis crossed his arms, which did nothing to help maintain his equilibrium. He lost his balance and had to throw out his arms to balance himself and remain standing.

"Okay." I took a deep breath to remain calm. "There is no way you did $3,000 worth of work. You've only been working for five days!"

"My services don't come cheap," he said. "$30 an hour is what I charge. Good help is hard to find nowadays."

"In the first place, $30 an hour is outrageous! And besides that, you did not work 100 hours."

"Yes, I did." Lewis crossed his arms resolutely and pouted. "I rendered service." Once again, he lost his balance and started to stumble backward, but I reached out and steadied him before he fell.

"Thanks, Chief," he said. He took the invoice from the railing and studied it.

"100 hours? Five days?" I tried to keep my voice down. "There is no way you worked 20 hours a day."

"Yes, I did," he said. "I rendered service, Chief."

I was going to bring up the topic of the quality of his work, when I thought of a better way of dealing with Lewis. I went back to the house and pulled Ramon into the kitchen. When we were alone, I said: "Thank you for hiring a crack whore who wants $3,000 for his landscaping services." I pointed out one of the side windows at Lewis, who was staring up at us. "Go out and take care of it. By my calculations, it can't be more than $500."

Ramon wrinkled his forehead. "Why's he charging so much? He only did half the stuff right and he took more breaks than he worked."

"Because he *rendered service*." I went to the sink and washed my hands.

"$3,000? You're kidding, right?"

"I wish." I returned to the dining room and passed around more bourbon balls.

Another Voodoo Day

Although we had been in the house for only half a year, it already felt like we had lived there much longer. Within several months we had developed new routines, and my favorite involved taking the dogs to the park on Saturday mornings. Generally an early riser, I would get up around 8 and spend a couple of hours doing things around the house until Ramon woke up around 10. Then, we'd grab the dogs, load them in the car and head off in search of coffee before ending up at Cherokee Park for a long walk. Most often, we'd go to Day's on Bardstown Road.

It was Saturday morning, and I had spent an hour testing a recipe in the kitchen. Outside, the bright sun hinted at a beautiful day ahead. Another hour passed and I listened for signs of life up on the second floor. Sure enough, someone stirred ten minutes later and I started preparing the dogs for the ride to the park. After I buckled on their harnesses, I opened the door and let them run around the back yard in anticipation of the walk to come, knowing they'd be eagerly scratching at the back gate within a quarter of an hour.

I returned some items to the refrigerator and listened while Ramon putzed around in the bathroom above. Soft footsteps shuffled along the hall and made their way to the linen closet on the other side of the back stairs, and then a loud scrape echoed as one of the large storage bins built into the original cabinetry was pulled out. Hmmm, I wonder what he's looking for, I thought. Since we kept a lot of summer clothes in that little room, I figured he must be looking for a pair of shorts or something to wear to the park. I closed the door to the refrigerator and washed several dishes in the sink while I waited for him to get dressed and come downstairs.

As I rinsed the plates and placed them in the rack to dry, I listened as the huge wooden drawer in the linen closet closed with a dry, raspy scratch. Drying my hands, I went into the butler's pantry. Then, the other storage bin was slowly pulled open, the same annoying grate of wood on wood resonating down the back stairs. I debated whether I should go upstairs and help Ramon look for the desired item, but in the end I decided instead to wipe down the counters and tidy up the rest of the kitchen. As I passed in front of the window overlooking the back yard, I could see the dogs pacing back and forth in front of the gate separating them from the car that would carry them to the park.

I walked back into the butler's pantry and yelled up the stairs. "Ramon! What's taking you so long? The dogs are ready to go!"

Overhead, I could hear more loud scraping as one of the drawers was opened and closed. It was followed by the same sound as another bin was pulled open and pushed shut. What the heck was he looking for? I decided to go upstairs and see what was causing all the delay, but then, the front doorbell rang, and I went and accepted a package from the mailman. When I returned to the kitchen and opened the box, I could still hear the sounds of someone rummaging through the linen closet, but I pushed the noise out of my head and devoted my attention to the package. It was a shipment of spicebush berries from the eastern part of the state, and I needed them for a pork recipe I was developing. I took one of the dried berries and crushed it between my fingers before lifting it to my nose. From the pungent aroma, it was easy to see why many cooks referred to it as wild allspice or poor man's allspice. I inhaled once more and that's when a door closed loudly somewhere and caused me to jump.

Not sure if it came from upstairs or not, I went back into the butler's pantry and listened. Once again, opening and closing noises seemed to echo from the small space of the linen closet, however, this time they sounded quicker and more intense that before.

Finally, I couldn't stand it any longer, so I ran up the back stairs to see what Ramon was looking for. "Good grief! Let's make a little more noise while we're at it!" I stormed over to the open door of the linen closet and placed my hands on my hips. "What the heck are you looking for?" I opened my mouth to issue another reprimand, but I realized I was staring into thin air: the linen closet was completely empty. The only indicator that anyone had been in the small room was that the cabinet doors had been flung wide open and the two huge drawer-like storage bins had been pulled out as far as they could go. And the two small risers for stepping up to reach the highest shelves had been pulled out below the bins, although we hardly ever used them.

I mumbled and cursed as I wrestled the large drawers back into place. Closing the cabinet doors, I went back to the hallway and headed to the second-floor living room. I pushed open the door and expected to find Ramon getting dressed in front of the TV, but nobody was there. Not seeing him in the adjacent room, I flung open the door to the front bedroom and found him, asleep in the bed, a light snore buzzing around him.

He opened an eye when he sensed me standing there. He slowly pulled himself up and fumbled for his cell phone on the nightstand so he could check the time. "Time to go to the park?"

"Were you rummaging around in the linen closet? Just a couple of minutes ago?"

"Me?" He looked at me as if I had gone crazy. "I haven't been out of bed since last night." He got up and pulled open the drapes to look out the window to the back yard. "Looks like the dogs are ready to go," he said. "I'll be ready in five minutes."

He started for the door, but then turned and looked me up and down. "Put on some different clothes," he said. "You look like a hobo again."

"Whatever."

He disappeared into the hallway and walked into the bathroom, leaving me to scratch my head.

I looked across the hall into the linen closet, where the drawers and risers had been pushed back in place. Nothing looked out of the ordinary, but I feared something strange indeed was going on at Widmer House. Could there really be paranormal activity afoot?

Drunk Cooking

One morning in late May, after a terrible windstorm, we awoke to discover major damage on the roof. The wind had jostled the branches on the nearby maple tree so much that they had broken off—and almost toppled—the large finial ornament on the northeast corner of the house. The base had been dislodged and had started to crumble as well, leaving hundreds of pounds of broken brick and terra cotta precariously teetering at the roofline. That's when we decided to step up the plans for the restoration of the façade. If we had to fix the damage from the storm anyway, we might as well go ahead and do the entire façade. The problem was that we knew very little about the restoration of old houses, much less the intricacies of general masonry that would be required to complete such a project. Not only was there tuckpointing to be done, bricks had to be re-laid and a number of decorative features needed to be rebuilt before the façade could be repainted.

As we soon found out, it was hard to find anyone to even give an estimate for the repairs or the restoration work. The two men who did show up stood in the front yard, looked up to the roofline to survey the damage, and then shook their heads and walked off. Several others offered to give us estimates for the restoration of the façade, but nobody wanted to take on the task of rebuilding the finial and its broken three-foot base. When most heard the damage centered on an ornate piece of decoration on a steeply pitched roof above the third floor, they immediately declined the challenge. My cousins, Pat and Mark, on the other hand, were not daunted by the job.

During the first summer in Widmer House, Pat and Mark were out of work and in need of a place to stay. What was I to do—tell them they couldn't stay with us? They had been houseguests before, and although tensions had started to rise toward the end, it usually worked itself out. We had six bedrooms, after all, so Ramon and I made a deal with them: in exchange for their services as handymen around the house—they could do practically anything—we would provide them with food and lodging, and the occasional bit of spending money.

In many respects, it started off as an ideal arrangement. Pat and Mark were both expert tile layers, so we soon had beautiful floors laid down in the kitchen and butler's pantry. They both had worked as professional painters before, so that came in handy as well. When they surveyed the damage from the windstorm, they were relatively confident they could rebuild the brick pedestal and remount the finial with the proper scaffolding and supplies. Restoring and painting the façade wouldn't require too much extra effort, they said. Ramon and I put on work gloves and got ready to help.

Within a couple of days a cherry picker had been rented and Pat and Mark began rebuilding the broken piece at the roofline. Scaffolding went up across the front of the house and for a week we scraped off all the old gray paint. After that, we spent another two weeks scratching out the old mortar from between the bricks and tuckpointing the entire façade. Then, we had to rebuild and recreate various pieces that had broken off. During that time, if there were oddities and weird occurrences such as invisible footsteps and things moving around on their own, they went unnoticed—no doubt because of all the noise and activity in the house.

A month and a half later, we were ready to start painting. But when the day came to start, my cousins were nowhere in sight. To mark the end of the tuckpointing phase of restoration I had given them each a chunk of money, and they headed out the back door, saying they were going to the bar around the corner for a beer. Ten days later they called collect from the Black Hills of South Dakota, where their truck had broken down, wanting us to wire them an advance on their next allowance so they could get the truck fixed and have gas money to return to Kentucky. As tempting as it was to leave them stranded in the Mount Rushmore State, we sent the money, and three days later Pat and Mark were back in Louisville.

A couple of days after their arrival, the painting of Widmer House began. We had rented a cherry picker again, to get to the tricky spots that were out of reach of the scaffolding, and the first week was spent applying a Pepto Bismol-colored coat of primer. This caused more than a few raised eyebrows in the neighborhood, because many feared we were planning on painting the house pink. But when we started applying the real colors, people stopped worrying.

From the minute the first bit of paint went on the front of the house, it was obvious that the results would be magnificent. Soaring some forty feet above the street level, my cousins started with the decorative peak of the gable and worked their way down, applying splashes of honey yellow and voodoo green to the stone trimming and railings, and rosy brick red to the exterior walls. Burgundy and hunter green rounded out the trim over and under the windows. The numerous acanthus leaves and garlands would be finished in gold leaf or metallic gold paint. As more color was added to the front of Widmer House, word traveled through the neighborhood, and most days there were small crowds of onlookers on the sidewalk out front. By the time the restoration and painting of the façade were completed at the end of the summer, the house at 1228 South Third Street had become something of a local conversation piece and cars were regularly pulling up to the curb so people could snap pictures.

Some finishing touches remained, and the front yard still needed more work, but all in all, the exterior had come a long way in the short time we had been there. With the cooler weather around the corner, it would be the perfect time to return my attention to the inside of the house.

Pat and Mark, however, had other plans; several months of regular work had increased their appetite for wanderlust and the open road was calling. Despite all the great work they had done around the house, they were starting to wear out their welcome.

Although Ramon and I had established some basic ground rules as to what constituted an acceptable curfew for houseguests, Pat and Mark never felt the need to abide by the rules. My cousins tended to be night owls, which wasn't a bad thing in and of itself, however, they were not capable of silent late-night comings and goings. Rarely a night passed without them waking up the rest of the household when they came back from their carousing, which was often around four, when the bars closed in Louisville.

Early one morning, I awoke to find Ramon standing at the foot of the bed, baseball bat in hand. "What?" I pushed myself up on my elbows and squinted against the light he had switched on.

"I heard something downstairs." He moved to the doorway and peered out into the dark hallway.

"I didn't hear anything, and I'm the light sleeper." I listened, but other than the sound of the dogs rustling on the bed, there was nothing.

"It sounded like breaking glass." Ramon edged out into the hallway and stopped to listen.

I collapsed back into a prone position. "Good luck finding out what it is. I've been there, done that before. I'm staying in bed."

"I think someone broke a window." He entered the stairwell and disappeared into the darkness without saying another word.

"And don't mess up my dining room table!" I called after him. Bess grumbled in her sleep, as if to second the motion.

After several minutes of hearing Ramon go from room to room in search of the mysterious noise, guilt got the better of me. I crawled out of bed, grabbed a Louisville Slugger, and joined him on the landing of the stairs. We crept down and cautiously checked all the panes in the windows on the first floor, but none of them had been broken. I looked under the dining room table and Ramon stuck his head out the back door. We found nothing.

"I know I heard something break down here." Ramon strode purposefully toward the little door under the back stairs that led to the basement. "And I know it was a window somewhere." He flipped on the light and descended the steps to the dank rooms under the house. I joined him in a large room we used for storage. The ceiling bulb had burned out in the adjacent room, where shadows seemed to creep across the floor and up the cold stone walls, but other than that everything seemed to be in order.

After checking the laundry room we walked into the next area and examined the two small windows high up in the wall that normally let in a bit of light from the ground level outside, but they were both fine. Dirty, but fine. There was only one room left to search: the small room on the other side of the laundry that we used to store things like lawn furniture and pool supplies during the colder months. It was also the only room in the basement that had a door that led outside. You could open the door, walk up half a flight of stairs, and you'd be in the back yard. Given its location at the back of the house and the heavy door that sealed it off, I doubted that Ramon could have heard anything breaking in that room.

But Ramon pushed open the door with a loud scrape and flipped on the light switch. There stood Mark, in the middle of the room, illuminated by the stark light of a lone bulb. A nearby window was noticeably devoid of a large chunk of its glass, much of which lay in glittering piles on the cement floor. A slightly crazed look had painted itself on Mark's face and his eyes darted back and forth. From one of his hands, a dark cut generously dripped blood to the floor.

"How did you break that window?" Ramon surveyed the scene and then walked over to the gaping hole in the pane.

"I don't know." Mark had suddenly become sheepish.

"What do you mean, you don't know?" I grabbed a broom and started to sweep up shards of glass. "What are you doing down here anyway?"

"I don't know." He lifted his good hand and scratched his chin.

"Are you insane?" I stabbed the broom at the floor and tried to round up all the stray bits of window. "Just what we need, one more thing to fix." I bent down and swept the debris into a plastic dustpan.

"I didn't want to wake you up, so I came in through the basement."

"Oh, well, you did a bang-up job of not waking us up." Looking at Mark, I came to the realization that he wasn't processing my sarcasm as readily as he usually did. My cousin lifted his head and gave a paranoid sweep of the room with his eyes.

"What'd you do, break the window to get in?" said Ramon. "We've told you a thousand times to ring the doorbell."

"I was trying to get out."

"Get *out?*" Ramon and I both spoke up in unison.

"Didn't know where I was and thought I was trapped in here." Mark lifted up his hand and studied the gaping wound.

"You've got to be kidding, right? You didn't know where you *were?*" I looked at my cousin, and he just shrugged his shoulders. "Okay, let me get this straight. You broke into the basement..."

"I didn't break into the basement. I left the cellar door unlocked before we went out tonight."

"Whatever. So you *entered* the basement here and then all of a sudden forgot where you were?" I looked at Ramon, who had started to leave but decided to stay when he heard the conversation getting interesting.

"I couldn't help it. When I turned the lights out, I didn't know where I was," Mark said. "It was dark."

"Of course it was dark, numbskull. That's the way it gets in the middle of the night." I shook my head. "Maybe you need to return during daylight hours next time so you don't get lost and forget where you are."

"Well, maybe I couldn't help it."

"Just forget where you are all of a sudden?" With a flip of the light switch, I plunged the dank cellar room into darkness and cried out in an exaggeratedly shrill voice: "Oh my goodness! Where am I? Where am I?" I shuffled around like a ninny and bumped into the hot water heater for added effect before turning the lights back on. "Oh, pardon me," I said. "The lights went out and for a moment I totally forgot where I was."

Mark stood there, sullen.

Ramon moved into my line of vision and I saw him lift his finger to his nose and replicate a snorting gesture as a possible explanation for my cousin's altered state of awareness. Good grief, I thought. Just what we needed.

"Come on upstairs so we can bandage your hand," I said. "You need to stop bleeding or you'll attract zombies."

After that, Mark swore that he and Pat would be in well before the bars closed and if the doors were locked they would ring the doorbell and not try to gain entry into the house through unconventional methods. That arrangement worked out for less than a week.

One night, a strange metallic clanging and rattling woke me from a deep sleep around half past three. Ghosts? Images of spectral Victorian chain-rattlers danced in my head. Just as I was about to stop straining my ears and fall back asleep, another ringing clatter echoed from the front of the house. I pushed myself up on my elbows and cursed.

Suddenly, the floor above shook with a hard thud, and I was immediately out of bed, grasping the baseball bat. I slid open the pocket door to the little room next door and listened in the darkness. Overhead, another thump made the floorboards groan. Then, something banged against a wall and tumbled down a flight of stairs before crashing onto the landing below.

"What the heck was that?" Ramon had stuck his head through a door and spied me in a solitary shaft of moonlight as I slowly pulled open a door to the hallway. "Wait a minute," he whispered. "Who knows what it could be? It might…" He was cut short as something heavy scraped on the hardwood floors and thumped against a wall. After some scuffling on the stairs to the bottom floor, another loud crash reverberated through the house.

Ramon in tow, I exited through to the hallway and turned on the light in the stairwell. Bats raised in the striking position, we quickly snuck to the landing and peered down the final set of steps to the foyer.

I flipped on another light . . . and there lay Pat, sprawled on his back in the middle of the floor. Upon realizing he was the object of speculation from our perch up on the landing, he slowly pulled himself to a semi-sitting position. "What's up?" he said, rubbing his hands together.

Several pictures had been knocked from the walls in the stairwell and I stooped to pick them up and return them to their spots. One of them had a crack in the glass and would need to be reframed. I slowly exhaled and took a deep breath. Pat, I realized, had climbed the scaffolding outside, all the way to the third floor, and forced open one of the windows in my office rather than come through the front door. Then he had stumbled and tripped most of the way down the stairs to the bottom floor.

Ramon shook his head and went back to bed. "Your cousins..." he muttered.

"Sorry, man. I was going to get something to eat before I went to bed." Pat rose and massaged a spot on his back. "I tried to not wake you guys up." He rubbed his hands on the front of his pants and looked around.

"Well, here we are, *awake*. If you had rung the doorbell, at least only one of us would have needed to get up."

Pat turned and staggered off toward the kitchen, leaving me in a wake of alcohol vapors. "I need to eat something. Sorry, man, I'm just tryin' to survive."

"Oh, so you're trying to survive by climbing three stories of scaffolding while inebriated?" I called after him.

"Sorry, man. I'll knock next time." He slurred the words over his shoulder and disappeared.

"And eat one of the sandwiches I already made for you guys in the refrigerator!" I yelled. "No more late-night cooking for you jokers," I said. "You pass out and leave stuff burning on the stove and it wakes Ramon up. He's gonna snap and kill you both one of these days."

Upstairs, I crawled under the covers and soon fell back to sleep.

Later that morning the tantalizing aroma of fried eggs and bacon tickled my nose and roused me from my sleep. Then the smell of buttered toast made my mouth water. I turned over in bed and smiled to think that someone was making breakfast for me. But when I opened my eyes, I saw that it was still pitch black outside.

I looked at the clock on the bedside table, and I discovered that not even a half hour had passed since leaving Pat downstairs. Quietly, I bolted for the backstairs, praying that I could make it to the kitchen and work some magic with a fan and a can of air freshener before Ramon came to.

I was getting ready to creep down the hallway when Ramon's calm voice cut through the darkness: "I'm going to kill your cousins. Both of them. Any day now."

I ran down to the kitchen, where Pat sat at the table, preparing to tuck into four eggs sunny-side up and what looked like a whole pound of bacon. Nearby stood a plate stacked high with buttered slices of toast.

I resisted the urge to clobber him while I turned on the exhaust above the stove. "What did I tell you? *Eat the stuff that requires no cooking!*" I yanked open a window and then theatrically opened the door to the refrigerator to reveal a glut of ready-to-eat contents. "Look! Food for days, and none of it has to be cooked." I pointed out an entire cold pizza and a basket with three different kinds of wax paper-wrapped sandwiches inside. There was a plate of cold fried chicken. Then I threw Tupperware containers full of potato salad, macaroni salad, and marinated vegetable salad onto the table in front of him. I also hauled out a huge chocolate cake and a dozen blueberry muffins I had made earlier that day. "Why do you feel the need to cook so late at night? Especially when you know it smells up the whole house and when there's tons of stuff ready to eat?"

"Sorry, man, I'm just tryin' to survive." Pat speared several pieces of bacon with his fork and made himself a folded-over sandwich with a piece of toast. "Had a craving for bacon and eggs, man."

I reached for a can of Lysol and liberally sprayed the kitchen. "No more cooking at night. Eat the stuff I make for you, please!" I looked back and saw Pat's eyelids drooping as he polished off the rest of his early-morning breakfast.

A week later, Ramon and I had gone out to dinner at 610 Magnolia, an Old Louisville favorite around the corner, and when we retired about midnight, we were relatively confident of a good night's slumber. Pat and Mark were ensconced in the back bedroom, sound asleep for all intents and purposes, so we assumed they were in for the night.

But several hours later my eyes flew open when I felt the dogs stirring on the bed. After squinting in the darkness, I realized they had gotten up because somebody was standing near the fireplace mantel. It was Ramon, who walked over to a window and slid up the sash. "Someone is cooking downstairs." As soon as he pointed it out, I became aware of a spicy aroma permeating the house.

"I can't believe your sense of smell," I said, rubbing the sleep from my eyes. "You sleep through everything else, but food will wake you up in two seconds flat."

"I'm going to kill your cousins." He walked into the next room to open more windows and let in the fresh summer air. That's when the smell of something scorched hit my nose.

I raced downstairs, the dogs gamboling along behind me. Evidently, they thought it was morning and time to go outside and I opened the back door and let them out. On the stove, a large saucepan with messy ribbons of red dripping down its sides sizzled over a low flame, the remainder of the contents slowly burning to the bottom. I turned off the stove and walked into the next room, where Pat slouched on the couch in front of the little TV. In his lap was perched a humongous bowl full of steaming chili.

"What the heck is the matter with you? You're a first-rate knuckle-head, you know that?"

Pat opened his eyes wide and looked around, probably only just coming to the realization of his surroundings. "What? Where am I?" He straightened up from his hunching position and the large bowl tottered precariously between his knees.

"Seriously?" I put my hands on my hips and stared at him. "You two dingbats seem to be forgetting where you are an awful lot lately." I walked to the doorway into the kitchen and pointed at the charred mess on the stovetop. "Remember where you are now, Julia Child?"

Something registered in his eyes and a hangdog expression settled in over his features. He looked down at the bowl of chili and frowned. "I wasn't cooking," he stammered. "I was just heating up the chili you made for us."

"Same thing." I opened a window and turned on a desktop fan. "See this?" I said, yanking open the door to the refrigerator. Inside were containers of homemade ham salad and pimento cheese and half an apple pie I had baked the previous day. There was also a big plate of bratwurst, a bowl of peeled hardboiled eggs, and three leftover rib-eye steaks that we had grilled for dinner the night before. A large pepperoni pizza with one slice missing rested on the top shelf. I had also baked buttermilk biscuits, peanut butter cookies, and two loaves of whole wheat bread that morning, and it was all out on the counter in plain view.

Pat sank back against the cushions. "Don't worry," he said. "I'll eat my chili and go to bed."

"Get up then and eat it over there." I pointed at the kitchen table. "I don't trust you to eat it in here. You'll pass out and drop the bowl of chili, I know you."

At that moment there came a scratching at the back door and I went to let the dogs back in.

"Man, I'm fine," Pat said, settling back as if he'd already won the argument. "Chill out."

"Whatever. You two are wearing out your welcome really fast," I said under my breath. As I went past the stove to the door, I put the scorched saucepan in the sink to soak.

Rocky and Bess ran in as soon as I opened the door, but Fritz was nowhere to be seen. While peering out over the back yard and into the alley, I spied him standing stock still against the back fence. When he didn't respond to my calls, I went out to see what was keeping him. As I approached, a low growl rumbled in his throat and I noticed that he had his nose up against the slats as if he were trying to get a whiff of something on the other side. I reached down and picked him off the ground and when I stood up, a motion near the dumpster caught my eye. It appeared to be someone leaning over the edge and rooting around inside, and when the form righted itself, I saw that it was a woman with billowy skirts and a bandana or a turban on her head. The light on the back alley had burnt out so I couldn't really tell for sure, but it looked like Josephine.

Before I could study the figure, the woman deposited something in an old grocery cart and started pushing it down the alley to Oak Street. The wheels bumped and rattled over the uneven bricks as her dark form faded from sight. A light breeze rustled the branches of a nearby tree, and although Josephine was lost from view, it seemed that a soft melody trailed behind her, borne aloft every now and then by the wind. I couldn't make out any of the words, but the lines she sang sounded French to me.

I carried Fritz back to the house and locked the door behind us. Chin drooping, Pat was still sitting on the sofa, and Rocky and Bess were sitting on the floor, looking up at him with bewildered expressions. "You better not be falling asleep," I said.

"No, man, I'm not falling asleep." He shifted languidly in his seat. "Gonna eat my chili and go to bed." The bowl that rested precariously on his knees, however, showed no signs of any chili having been eaten.

"Ramon is really going to lose it one of these days, and he is going to kill you." I started back up the stairs, but then I turned back and found myself standing over my cousin again. "You *promise* me you're not going to pass out?"

"Yeah, man. I promise. I'll be done and up in bed in five minutes."

I narrowed my eyes and retreated. Behind me, the dogs' toenails clicked on the wooden stairs as they followed.

It was after four in the morning, and I was exhausted. Ramon, thankfully, had gone back to sleep right away and as I entered the hallway on the second floor, I could hear him snoring loudly. Looking forward to at least three hours of sleep before I had to get out of bed again, I put the dogs up on the bed and crawled under the covers. The first five minutes I lay there, my muscles tensed for the inevitable disaster, but when nothing happened, I finally started to relax. After ten minutes more, I was breathing a bit easier and, hoping for the best, I closed my eyes. Ten minutes later, all was silent, so I convinced myself that Pat—out of courtesy—had very quietly mounted the back stairs and disappeared into his shared room at the back of the house. I sighed deeply and let myself drift off.

Not too long thereafter, a crash echoed downstairs.

The dogs jumped up at the foot of the bed. Cursing, I slowly pulled the covers back and put my feet on the ground. In the hallway I stopped for a moment and listened. Ramon, by some miracle, still snored away, and I was grateful for that as I stole down the front stairs to see what had happened. On tiptoes, I crossed the dining room and pushed the swinging door open into the butler's pantry.

Before me was a sight almost too terrible to bear. Surveying the disaster around me, it was easy to see what had happened. When he passed out, Pat's legs had relaxed and come apart, and the uneaten chili had plummeted to the tile floor and the antique bowl had volcanoed its contents up and around the entire room before shattering into dozens of small pieces. I put a hand to my mouth and gasped at the magnitude of the destruction done by a single bowl of chili.

From the ceiling, which had been covered in gold anaglypta and hundreds of hand-applied gemstones, globs of ground beef and tomato sauce rained down around me. Practically every inch of the apple green walls and hand-stenciled fleur-de-lys in the tiny room was covered in chili spatter, as were the cream-colored wainscoting and the wooded trim. On the nearest jacquard curtain, three kidney beans slid down the fabric in a gloppy rivulet. Two months' worth of tedious work was now drenched in a chaos of beans and chili sauce. It had even splashed into the kitchen, covering a swath of green and blue tiles in a streak of messy red.

Pat, on the other hand, hadn't been touched by the mess, save for a solitary smear of chili in the middle of his forehead.

"You said you wouldn't pass out!" I shouted it so loudly a blood vessel popped somewhere in my left temple.

But from Pat there was no response, save for a long, drawn-out snort as one of his arms fell from his lap and landed on a chili-spattered cushion.

Just then the door from the dining room swung open. Ramon entered the butler's pantry, but when he saw the disaster area, he immediately spun around and exited the room, all in the same motion. "Good luck cleaning up that mess," he called over his shoulder. "And when your cousin wakes up, tell him I'm going to kill him."

I lowered my face so Pat could better hear me. "Wake up!" I said.

But Pat had entered an even deeper sleep and began to snore loudly.

Careful to avoid the puddle of chili in the middle of the floor, I ran into the kitchen and grabbed two banged-up soup pots. I crashed them together right in front of his face. "Wake up!" But Pat continued his loud snores.

I realized then my stocking feet were covered in chili and I had by some miracle avoided cutting myself on the random bits of ceramic scattered throughout the two rooms. I carefully hopped over to the coatroom, removed my socks and grabbed a pair of hard-soled slippers. I returned with a long-handled, old-fashioned mop and poked Pat in the leg with it.

Finally, he opened his eyes. "What?"

I put the head of the mop on the floor and tried to clean a path through the chili. "I knew you were going to pass out. Look at what you did."

Pat's head and body remained perfectly still as he rotated his eyes in their sockets and scanned the environs. "What happened?" Pat pushed himself up and took another look around the room.

"You did exactly what I said you were going to do. You passed out and dropped your Jethro Bodine-sized bowl of chili on the new tile floor." I made a dramatic outward sweeping gesture with my arms and faked a big smile. Then I pointed at the floor, the walls, the ceilings, the curtains.

"Oh, man—" Pat tried to stand up but fell, mashing chunks of tomatoes and chili beans into the fabric of the couch.

"Get up and start cleaning."

"But, man—" He stood for a moment and then slipped and fell, more beans and tomatoes smashing onto the tile.

I pointed the handle of the mop at him so he could grab it and pull himself to a vertical position.

"Man, I just—" After taking several steps, he slipped on a large, succulent chunk of ground beef and crashed to the floor in the kitchen. He managed to pull himself up right away, but he slipped again and stumbled back into a clean section of kitchen wall. The chili riding on the back of his flannel shirt smeared itself along the new paint job, the bright red of the tomato sauce contrasting nicely with sunny shades of yellow.

"On second thought, maybe you should go to bed," I said. "I'll do the cleaning."

Pat trudged upstairs and slowly made his way to bed.

Two hours later, after I had cleaned up the last of the con carne, I would find one long chili smear on the wall in the stairwell as I went back up to bed.

Before crawling under the covers, I went to the front room on the second floor and opened the shutters on the windows looking out onto Third Street. I don't know why I felt the need to do this, but when I did, I stopped for a moment and gazed out onto the street below. There, under the cone of weak light coming down from one of the street lamps, stood a lone figure. He appeared to be standing there, looking up at the house. The lights weren't on in the room I was in, so I'm not sure if he could see my silhouette or not, but after a moment or two, he seemed to shake his head and shuffled away down the sidewalk.

It was a Friday night, and Ramon had spent the entire day waxing the hardwood floors downstairs in preparation for a visit from his mother in Texas. I had had a full day of teaching, so we were both beat when we turned in for the night. Pat, somewhat subdued by the chili affair, had decided to spend a couple of nights at a friend's house. Mark, on the other hand, had found cause for celebration and was out at one of the neighborhood bars with some friends. To prevent him from breaking into the house and smashing out all of the windows, I had reluctantly told him I would leave the back door unlocked.

I slept fitfully until about two in the morning, when I heard Mark come in the back door and stumble up the stairs. My fingers crossed that Ramon would not wake up, I listened as my cousin softly shuffled down the hall and disappeared into the back bedroom. After five minutes, I breathed a cautious sigh of relief and let myself fall back to sleep.

Sometime later, maybe a half hour or so, I came to the realization that Ramon was awake and standing in the doorway. "I heard water some place," he said, head turned slightly to better make out a sound I could not hear. "There's a dripping noise coming from somewhere. I wonder if we have a leak."

I got up and sat back on my elbows. "Is it raining?" I listened intently, but heard nothing that sounded like water. In the back hallway, however, I thought I could hear a slight shuffle as someone retreated to the room at the back of the house.

"Are you sure?" I said. "I don't hear anything drpping. Should I go outside and look?"

"It's not outside," Ramon answered. "It's inside somewhere. There must be a leak."

I cocked my head and listened intently, but there was nothing. "I don't hear a thing," I said. "I hope it's not the ghost or whatever was making all those odd noises before my cousins got here."

He concentrated for thirty seconds and said nothing. Then, he inched through the hallway to the stairs at the front of the house. "It's stopped already," he grumbled. "I'm going to go see what it was."

I fell back onto my pillow and pulled Rocky and Bess close to me. Fritz, on the other hand, jumped from the foot of the bed and followed Ramon.

I pulled the covers up under my chin and listened as they made their way downstairs. I could visualize Ramon checking the kitchen and walking through the coatroom and then examining the sink in the little bathroom under the front stairs. Then I could see him opening the door and checking the cellar before mounting the servant's stairs to see if anything was wrong in the bathroom on the second floor. Afterwards, I could hear him trudge up to the third-floor bathroom, where, I speculated, he found nothing as well.

Back in the hallway outside the bedroom, he scratched his head and rethought his strategy. "I know I heard water coming from somewhere. It sounded like it was down in the foyer, but I didn't see anything."

I sat up. "It was probably outside." I punched my pillow to fluff it up.

"No, it was inside, and it was dripping water." He walked down the long hallway and started a thorough search of the other bedrooms on the second floor.

Realizing that I wouldn't get any sleep until Ramon discovered the source of the noise, I dragged myself out of bed and joined him on the front stairs as he descended to the foyer. I flipped on the light, which caused the slick floors to sparkle and shine, and we searched the parlor and the dining room. There were no signs of water anywhere.

Ramon scratched his head again and did a complete 360 of the room, convinced that he had to be missing something. "I know it came from down here somewhere." He started moving from corner to corner in search of the culprit sound, careful not to slip on the newly waxed floorboards.

Then, as he approached the area between the base of the stair and the small bathroom underneath the landing, a glint of light on the smooth floor caught our attention. At first, it appeared to be a reflection from a gleaming patch of hardwood, but from a new angle, we could see the light from the stairs now completely illuminated the shimmering surface of a large puddle that had previously gone unnoticed. Stretching out from the bottom step to the grandmother clock, the source of disturbance measured at least four feet in diameter.

"What the—" In his stocking feet, Ramon almost slipped on the polished wood as he tentatively approached the pool. Catching himself on the balustrade, he got down on his hands and knees to inspect the puddle. I carefully made my way to the other side and looked up to see where the water could have come from. Everything seemed dry overhead. I got down on all fours as well, and we both eyed each other across the glittering surface of the puddle.

"Maybe a pipe broke somewhere?" I looked over my shoulder at the nearest plumbing, in the small bathroom under the stairs.

Ramon, on the other hand, slowly shook his head. "I don't think it's from a broken pipe." Then he fell silent as a look of disgust swept over his features. He cautiously lowered his face to within inches of the surface of the puddle and took a short whiff before exploding. "This is PEE!"

I was about to test the feel of the water, but I jerked my hand back and lifted my head as Ramon shot up the stairs. "Wha—what?" I stammered.

"It was your cousin Mark and I'm going to kill him!"

I quickly backed away from the puddle in the middle of the beautifully waxed hardwood floor. "Gross."

Loud footsteps pounded down the hall overhead, and I listened as Ramon threw open the door to the little room at the back of the house. After what I assumed to be a series of mumbled curse words that started in English and transitioned to Spanish, I heard his first identifiable words. "What did you do?" He was yelling at my cousin, who was evidently fast asleep. "Wake up and come downstairs!"

"He's just like Pat," I half-heartedly called out into the ether. Shaking my head, I began to trudge up the stairs. "Good luck trying to rouse him. It's easier trying to wake up a cadaver with a cup of coffee."

From the end of the hall, I heard some random jostling and a smattering of swear words as Ramon tried to rouse my cousin. After a few seconds, I heard a groan that emanated from Mark.

"What?" said a slurred voice heavy with sleep, or whatever.

"What did you just do?" said Ramon.

"I don't know," said Mark. "Went to the bathroom?"

I emerged at the top of the stairs and walked back to the bedroom Mark and Pat shared. Ramon stood over Mark, who sat on his bed and glumly rubbed sleep from his eyes.

"Oh, yeah?" said Ramon. "So you went to the bathroom. Where'd you go?"

"I don't know. The bathroom down the hall?" Mark closed his eyes and fell back onto his pillow.

Ramon shook Mark until he sleepily opened an eye. "What? Where am I?" he said, casting a suspicious glance around the bedroom.

"Good grief. Here we go again with the not knowing where we are." I shook my head.

Ramon reached down and pulled Mark out of bed. "You went pee on the landing, and now it's all down on the hardwood floors I spent all day polishing. Get downstairs and clean it up."

A soft clack-clack-clack echoed behind me as Fritz trotted down the hall and nosed his way around my legs and walked into the bedroom. He sat on his haunches and studied the sight before him.

My cousin closed his eyes again and tried to slump down on his bed, which caused Fritz to bark once. "Don't even think about going back to sleep," said Ramon, dragging Mark to his feet. I picked up Fritz and stood aside as Ramon shuffled down the hall; Mark was in front, aided by the hand grasping his collar in the back.

They stumbled along the hallway and down the front stairs. In the foyer, Ramon pointed to the door leading down to the basement. "The shop vac's down there," he said. "Get moving."

Fritz was getting antsy, so I put him down and got his leash on. I opened the front door and took him out into the yard. During all the commotion, Rocky and

Bess had come down to the landing and watched from a safe distance, but when I tried to get them to join us in the front yard, they only stared at me like I was crazy. Simultaneously, they turned around and padded back up the stairs, no doubt to the comfort of my bed.

Outside, the air was damp, and the moon appeared to be almost full. Only a few thin strips of cloud stood out against the purplish sky. Inhaling a lungful of cool air, I stood on the front steps and watched as Fritz moseyed over to an ivy patch and started to root around. That's when I noticed a shadowy form standing on the sidewalk out front.

At first, I assumed it was a person walking past the house, but then I saw that the figure was stationary. Whoever it was only stood there, apparently staring up at the house. I was considering whether or not it would be a good idea to speak to the person, but before I could make up my mind, the form turned and started walking down the sidewalk toward Oak Street. From the silhouette and gait, it appeared to be a slender man. From the safety of the steps, I watched him disappear down the sidewalk, and then tugged on Fritz's leash. We went inside and I quickly closed the door behind me.

Ramon and Mark had emerged from the cellar stairs, and Ramon stood watch as Mark glumly pulled the shop vac into the foyer. Fritz and I looked on as Mark plugged in the machine and started to vacuum up the puddle, but it was slow going. After several minutes, I took Fritz and we went back upstairs to join Rocky and Bess.

Several days later Mark and Pat moved out.

Nighttime Visitors

Not too long after my cousins left, I was pleased to discover that a company was still making Sugar Babies candy, a childhood favorite of mine I thought had gone out of existence. When I spied them one day at the drugstore, I snatched up several bags and brought them home. I put the little caramel bits in a nice silver bowl in the kitchen, smiling to myself whenever I saw them over the next several days.

One morning, however, I was alarmed to discover that someone had been sneaking them out of their little silver dish, which I kept on the counter in the kitchen. Not only that, they were being messy about it and leaving Sugar Babies scattered all around the bowl. I asked Ramon if he had been eating them, but he swore he hadn't, adding that he didn't even like them. Although I was puzzled by the theft of my Sugar Babies—not to mention scandalized by the fact that Ramon did not love them as much as I did—I soon forgot about it and began keeping the little silver dish in one of the cupboards at night.

About the same time, we started to hear faint scratching noises in the kitchen walls and the ceiling in the butler's pantry. But with all the odd things that had been going on in the house, I was willing to chalk the strange sounds up to more unexplained phenomena—until a week later, when I went down to the kitchen for my morning coffee.

The night before, I had forgotten to put the bowl of Sugar Babies away in the cupboard. It was still early, before sunrise, when I got out of bed. Although there was plenty of light to see by, the interior of the house had been cast in a milky, gray pallor that seemed to make everything glow in a dark and silvery sheen. I entered the kitchen, and my hand reached out for the light switch, but I stopped short of flipping it on, debating whether or not I could make do with the natural light afforded by the two large windows in the kitchen. In my hesitancy, I became aware of a soft noise that reminded me of marbles or small stones being gently moved around on a plate. I let my eyes roam the kitchen, scanning the new tile on the floor and searching out something in the cupboards, and then my gaze shifted to the sink. I saw nothing, but again I heard the soft clink-clink of something small and solid being moved around on a hard surface.

That's when I looked over and saw the rodent, a foot away from me on the kitchen counter. It sat up on its hind legs and was greedily devouring one of my prized Sugar Babies, almost like a squirrel going at an acorn. It was no doubt enjoying its sugar fix so much that it hadn't heard me sneak up on it. I was horrified to no end, especially when I saw its fat belly paunching out over the edge of the silver candy dish.

"Leave my Sugar Babies alone!" I yelled, turning on the lights. Then I yanked open the nearest drawer and extracted a large wooden spoon. Only mildly startled, the rat looked up and dropped the half-gnawed Sugar Baby. Seeing me waving the wooden spoon, it dropped down on all fours and rattily scampered away to the relative safety of my KitchenAid stand mixer. After several seconds, it darted out from behind the stainless steel bowl, and as it weaseled its way along the groove where the counter and backsplash came together, I furiously slapped at its tail with the wooden spoon. Of course, I missed every time. Slap! Slap! Slap! Slap! Slap! I followed as it took cover behind the flour and sugar canisters. Slap! Slap! Slap! Slap! Slap! I chased it around the sink and pounded at it until it reached the stove and dove behind it.

When I pulled the stove away from the wall, I discovered a large hole had been chewed through the plaster, right above the baseboard. I pushed the appliance back into its spot and started hatching a plan. I had to protect my Sugar Babies from the rodent.

Later that day, I found Ramon upstairs. "We've got rats," I told him. "Or maybe they're just big mice. What should we do?"

"Buy some poison." He was watching TV with the dogs and didn't appear to be too concerned.

"That's so inhumane," I said. "I'll feel like a murderer. Maybe I can find some of those humane traps where you catch them and let them go."

He rolled his eyes and said nothing. There was a pot of burgoo simmering on the stove, so I turned down the heat, put on my shoes and told him I was going to run around the corner to Lee's Hardware. "Put on a different shirt," he called after me. "You look like a hobo."

If I looked like a hobo, the cashier behind the counter didn't say anything about it. When the woman heard my predicament, she cheerily walked me to an aisle that catered to the likes of exterminators and other people charged with the riddance of vermin. Poised and smiling like a game show model, she stretched out an arm and showed me a lovely assortment of traps and poisons. "There you go. One of these will do the trick."

I looked around for a few seconds and picked up a package of traps. "All I see is poison and traps. Don't you have the nice traps that catch them but don't kill them? I don't want blood on my hands."

She looked at me like I had a screw loose. "So, what are you going to do once you finally catch them?" She pursed her lips and crossed her arms.

"I'll let them go free outside," I said.

She laughed. "And you don't think they'll find their way back inside?"

"But, I'll plug up all the holes so they can't get back in," I said, cautiously eying the box of poison she was shoving in my direction.

She laughed so hard she snorted. "And you don't think they know how to chew new holes? They'll be back inside in a week, and they'll be bringing their babies and their cousins along. Here, take the poison and get it over with." She shuffled back to the counter and resumed her seat on the stool. "Rats are nasty. They deserve poison."

I turned the box of poison over and studied the instructions, but then returned it to its spot on the shelf. Shamed, I bought some paintbrushes and left.

On the way home, I had a brilliant idea. I didn't have to let them loose right outside my house—I could drive them somewhere far, far away and set them free there. But it had to be somewhere far enough away that their mousy radar wouldn't guide them back to Old Louisville.

I knew the perfect place: the East End! I could drive them all to Lake Forest or any one of the well-heeled subdivisions out that way and set them free amidst the cookie-cutter splendor of suburban America and its manicured lawns and tidy hedges. The East End needed more vermin, and I was ready to help.

Several days later—and after numerous unsuccessful trips to the exterminator sections of local stores—I located a set of humane mousetraps on line and ordered them. Within days, they arrived and I was ready to make my first express delivery of rodentia to the East End. I placed two traps—each baited with Sugar Babies—behind the stove and the other two I placed on either side of the silver candy dish on the counter where the initial transgression had taken place. I waited throughout the day, and nothing happened. When I went up to bed, I was sure I'd awake to full traps the next morning.

Every single trap was empty, though, and most of them looked as if they'd been moved around a bit; one of them next to the silver bowl had even been tipped over on its side. The worst part was that the number of Sugar Babies in the bowl looked significantly diminished. Undeterred, I filled the silver bowl and returned it to the refrigerator, where I had been storing it while I worked out my strategy. That night, before I went up to bed, I put the bowl back on the counter and repositioned the traps.

When I came down the next morning, the same sight awaited me: considerably fewer Sugar Babies and traps that had been moved around. I also discovered a hole chewed through a cereal box in one of the cupboards and a half-eaten potato dragged across the floor and abandoned in plain view. They were taunting me.

Time for plan B. I got in the car and drove to the store. I had heard about sonic repellants that you plug into an outlet and *poof!* no more rodents, so that would be the next course of action. The only problem was how to round them up outside and capture them so I could still deposit them in the front yard of some

East End McMansion. Maybe I could look around outside and locate the Grand Puba of mouse holes that had allowed them access to the interior of my house in the first place, and then set up the deathless traps nearby. It was worth a try.

Two hours later, I was back at home, three of the electronic devices in a plastic bag swinging at my side. I read all the instructions and warnings after extracting them from the packaging, and I plugged them in. One went in the outlet above the baseboard right next to the stove; I plugged a second one into the socket above the counter, inches away from the spot where the silver bowl with the Sugar Babies rested when it wasn't stashed away in the refrigerator; the third ended up sticking out of the wall, under the little table in the butler's pantry. I went up to bed that night, relatively confident that my rodent problem had been solved. So confidant, in fact, that I neglected to put the silver bowl and the Sugar Babies in the refrigerator before retiring.

When I dragged myself downstairs the next morning and entered the kitchen, I was made painfully aware that these electronic repellants were a load of bunk. Almost all of the Sugar Babies were missing from my silver bowl, which had been upended in the sink, and several half-chewed specimens had been scattered across the surface of the counter. Two potatoes had been dragged out of the basket on the floor by the refrigerator and lay, uneaten, in the middle of the doorway. Above the microwave, one of the cupboard doors was ajar. Inside I found a tipped-over box of rolled oats with a hole chewed through its bottom and the contents spilling out. Two plastic-wrapped packages of microwave popcorn had been thoroughly decimated, one of them a crinkled-up, twisted mess that had gotten stuck in the hole at the back of the cabinet where the rodents had attempted to carry it away. Had they gotten together for a party or what?

Okay, time for plan C, I told myself. Now I wasn't so concerned about the creatures dying—but it had to be a humane demise. No sticky traps where they languished in mouse purgatory for days before the Grim Reaper came to carry them back whence they came—no, they needed to die right away. Only slightly annoyed that the East End would not enjoy the fruits of my labors, I made for the front door and soon found myself back at Lee's Hardware store on Oak Street.

"You want a plain old trap this time or you want poison?" The woman behind the counter fairly beamed at me. "I say go with the poison. That'll get 'em good."

"Let's try the traps and see how that goes," I said reluctantly. "Traps are the tried and true way, aren't they?" I headed to the vermin aisle and grabbed four traps.

"Yeah," she nodded her head. "Nothing like a good old-fashioned snap trap to do the trick. Get the little bastards good." She rang me up and I headed through the door into the pleasant weather outside. I walked to the store to get more Sugar Babies and then went back to Widmer House.

Before I reached the kitchen, the traps had been unpacked. I had to teach that afternoon, so I quickly baited each trap with a plump Sugar Baby before setting it in what I considered a most enticing location. Then, I left.

I returned late that afternoon and walked through the back door, anxious to see the devastation wrought by the traps. But not a single mousely corpse did I find. Instead, I noticed that all the traps had been sprung and all of the Sugar Babies had been spirited away. I felt my ire rising. How did they do that?

I reset the traps and let the dogs outside. Then I took up a spot on the couch while we watched TV, all the while keeping an eye out for the kitchen. From where I was sitting, I could see the corner of the counter where the silver bowl usually sat, and I was sure to spy any rodent that had the temerity to venture forth.

One hour passed, and then another as darkness fell, but nothing happened in the kitchen. I was suddenly bored with the television, so I decided to run up to the third floor and do some work in my office. Just then, a loud *snap* echoed in the kitchen.

Wringing my hands in anticipation, I tiptoed into the kitchen, praying that I would find a dead rodent in one of the traps. The two devices on the counter hadn't been touched, so I moved over to the stove and peered over the side to the floor. Sure enough! There, on the blue and green tiles lay a limp critter in the deadly grip of the trap. I clapped my hands together, only slightly remorseful to have the death of the rodent on my conscience. At least I would finally be rid of the things, I told myself. And more important, my Sugar Babies would now be safe.

I studied the flaccid piece of gray fur while I decided what to do with the carcass. Should I remove it from the trap for recycling purposes or should I throw the entire thing away, rodent and all? I decided on the latter and pulled a pair of barbecue tongs out of a nearby drawer.

Carefully, slowly, I aimed for the rodent corpse and grabbed the trap with the cold, metal pincers. Holding it out at arm's length in front of me, I opened the back door with the other hand and prepared to walk through the back yard to the trashcans in the alley. It was balmy and warm, and several stars twinkled overhead as I made my way around the swimming pool. Suddenly, the tongs started violently bouncing up and down as the rodent kicked its back legs and came to life.

"Wheeeeee! Wheeeeee! Wheeeeee!" It made the most blood-curdling, pathetic squeals as it thrashed to and fro in an attempt to free itself from the trap. "Wheeeeee! Wheeeeee! Wheeeeee!" The neighbors must have been able to hear it a block away.

As the thrashing and squealing continued, I looked up and at the back door I saw Rocky, Bess, and Fritz, who had come to see what all the commotion was about. On the other side of the screen door, they stood with their heads cocked. Pangs of guilt stabbed at my soul as I realized what I had done and I rushed to the large city garbage can in the back alley to get rid of the evidence. I lifted the dark plastic lid, tossed the trapped creature inside, closed the lid and then scampered back to the house.

However, when I reached the back door, I could still hear the muffled squeals coming from the garbage can. As the thing continued its pitiable shrieking I knew I couldn't just toss it away and let it suffer. I'd have to put it out of its misery, so I turned around and went back to the trash container. My stomach a nauseous pit, I considered my options. Stomp on it? No, it would probably manage to bite me and give me rabies. Squash it with a big stone? No, that would be too messy. Hurl it against the wooden fence? No, too unreliable; the thing might not die. Little by little the squealing was starting to subside as the rodent was overcome with exhaustion. But all of a sudden, the big aboveground pool in the back yard came into focus. Yes, I thought to myself. I would drown it!

Quickly, I threw back the lid and leaned over into the half-full container. But when the creature saw me, it started squealing again and tried burrowing into a mound of rotting vegetable peels. Only after it seemed that I pushed half my body into the container did I manage to seize the trapped creature with the tongs and extract it from the trash heap.

Running back through the gate, I tossed the struggling rodent over the edge of the pool and watched it hit the water with a splash. It floundered a bit, momentarily buoyed by the little wooden raft clamped to its neck, and then plummeted to the vinyl blue depths below. Relieved, I sat down on the deck and reassured myself that death would be soon in coming. The dogs were still at the back door, looking at me, and seemingly waiting for an explanation. I told myself to ignore the drowning creature in the depths, but after a moment's reflection I gave in to the urge and peered over the side of the pool.

There, at the shimmering bottom, I could see the little guy with the trap still around his shoulders, pushing himself toward the nearest plastic wall in an attempt to exit his watery grave.

What have you done, you monster? I thought to myself. The guilt too much to bear, I grabbed the tongs and heaved myself over the edge of the pool, plunging my upper torso headfirst into the cool water while my feet kicked up into the naked air. Underwater, I opened my eyes and spied the creature as he spotted me and turned to scuttle off in the opposite direction. I inch-wormed forward with my arms and reached out with the tongs, managing to grab him at the last possible second. With a thrust from the arm that wasn't holding the trap, I heaved myself backward and exited the water with a gasp, suddenly aware that I had lost both contact lenses during my water aerobics.

"Wheeeeee! Wheeeeee!" The water had apparently revived the rodent and he started squealing twice as loudly as he had before. I was starting to get afraid a neighbor might hear and call the police. "Wheeeeee! Wheeeeee!" Now the dogs were barking at the back door.

Let him go! Release him from the trap! I told myself. Then maybe he would stop making so much noise. Water cascading down my face, I leaned against the side of the pool to steady myself. Then I grabbed the wooden base of the trap, careful not to get my fingers near his mouth or claws, and somehow, I managed to raise the wire snap a tiny bit, and the rodent was able to dislodge its body from the trap. It fell.

But, instead of falling to the ground below, he hit the edge of the pool and bounced back into the water.

Good grief. Was this really happening? I watched as a little snout poked up from the surface of the water and his legs started kicking. He paddled across the surface of the water to the other side of the pool. But unless I helped, his only options were to end up at the bottom of the pool again or in the strainer basket. Both of them involved drowning.

I ran to the opposite side of the pool to render assistance, but when the creature saw me waiting for him, he turned around and swam back to his initial point of entry. So I ran back around again, but once more, he steered himself in the other direction when I came into his field of vision. I guess I couldn't blame him, since I no doubt represented a great deal of bodily harm in his little rodent mind. Remembering the long-handled skimmer with its mesh catcher, I dislodged the implement from its horizontal spot along the fence and managed to scoop the creature out of the water. I walked down several steps and then deposited him in the lettuce patch, not more than two yards from the side of the pool.

I expected the rat to be paralyzed or mangled from his injuries, but given that I had misjudged him a mouse and had bought a mousetrap, the larger rodent was only stunned. I collapsed next to him in a patch of arugula. Out of breath, I studied the wet, panting form and waited. He coughed and spat up a mouthful of water. Then, he raised himself up and gave himself a good shake. He slowly crawled to the fence, eyeing me warily as he looked back over his shoulder, and inserted himself in a two-inch knothole in the wood.

"Please stay away and don't come back," I wheezed as the last little bit of rat tail disappeared through the gap in the fence. "Because it's time to revert to plan D. We're getting rat poison."

That's when I heard a crash in the house.

After grabbing a towel that had been left to dry, I patted the moisture out of my hair and hurried inside. Nobody else was home, so I could only wonder at the loud crash. It sounded like something heavy and solid had fallen and caused the whole house to shake. Although previous crashes had invariably yielded no visible explanation for their causes, I still expected to find something broken—or at least out of place—when I entered the house. But once again, a thorough search of all three floors, the basement, and attic yielded absolutely nothing to account for the strange noise. I returned to the foyer, prepared to chalk up the sound to settling timbers.

The evening weather forecast had warned of high temperatures for the following day, so I decided to close the shutters to keep out the sun in the morning. As I approached the large window in the foyer, I jumped back, startled by a figure standing outside the window. Trying to stay out of view, I pulled back a bit of lace and peered into the darkness. A narrow shaft of light from the nearest street lamp cast a soft glow around a dark silhouette in the space between the houses. Trancelike, someone was staring into the house.

Lewis, I thought to myself. The grizzled old man kept showing up for odd jobs around the yard—although Ramon usually had to haggle with him to get his quotes reduced by at least nine hundred percent—but he always refused to come to the door. Instead, he'd take a position outside the foyer window and wait till somebody spotted him.

I walked out onto the front porch and looked around the side of the house. "Lewis? Is that you?"

Silently, the form approached me and came to stand in the light. It was a grizzled old man, but it wasn't Lewis. "No, but Lewis sent me," he said. "I'm Frederick. He can't come no more and told me to come and look after the yard work at your beautiful house here."

"Oh," I said, wondering if Frederick would show the same tendencies to gouge as his predecessor. "Well, Ramon's the one in charge of the yard work and stuff, and he's not here. Come back tomorrow and talk to him." I said good-bye and turned to go.

"This house is pretty, but it's mad at someone," he quickly called after me.

"Huh?" I stopped short of pulling open the door and looked back at him.

Frederick took a couple of steps toward me and repeated his observation.

"Ah. And why is that?"

"She is talking to you, and you are not listening." He crossed his arms and nodded his head wisely.

"Talking to me?"

"Yes." He nodded once. "Like she do before you came into the house tonight. "She make a big boom to get your attention."

"Oh, that," I said, remembering the reason I had come into the house. "I thought it was the house settling or something like that."

"When a house settles," he confided in a low whisper, "she don't go *boom!*"

"Oh, I see." I paused to consider the rationality of his statement.

"When she make a big boom, she is telling you something." He reached into the breast pocket of his shirt and pulled out a small canvas pouch. "You need the voodoo to understand what she say." He shook the cloth bag and the contents produced a hollow, rattling clatter. I hoped they weren't dried chicken bones or anything like that.

"Well, I personally try to avoid voodoo and any other religion involving zombies," I said.

His brow wrinkled in an irritated scowl and one of his hands slapped the empty air. "No need to fear the voodoo, only the bad people who do the voodoo," he said. "My mama and grand mammy both practiced the voodoo and they was good women. Their people came here by way of New Orleans."

"Funny, I didn't find out till recently that they even had voodoo in Kentucky."

"We don't have as much as way down south," he said, "but it's here. They calls it 'hoodoo' in many parts."

"Say,"—something suddenly occurred to me—"have you heard of this woman who runs around in a long skirt and turban? They say she's a voodoo queen and her name is—"

"Josephine?" Frederick narrowed his eyes slightly and studied me.

"Yes, that's the one. Do you know anything about her?"

"Everyone on the streets know Josephine." He turned and gestured to Third Street. "She was around back in my mama's day. She live over by the tree over where the old floral gardens used to stand. The places where the witches used to gather. The Witches' Tree."

"What's the Witches' Tree?"

"The old tree where all the witches used to meet," he explained impatiently. "And still do."

"Wait a minute," I said. "You're telling me we've got voodoo queens *and* witches down here in Old Louisville?" A smile started to creep across my features as I pondered the dark side of the neighborhood.

"Course we do! Even had lots of gypsies back in the day."

"No way! Gypsies?" I couldn't believe my good fortune. "Kentucky had gypsies, too?"

"Sure thing!" He stood up straight and picked something off his sleeve.

"What about vampires and werewolves?" I asked hopefully.

"Blood suckers we got. Werewolves, I'm not so sure, though there's a really hairy guy who lives in the park." He narrowed his eyes again and studied me for a brief period before continuing. "You'd be surprised at some of the things you see down in this neighborhood," he said.

"Well, I'm not so sure about that. I've seen some pretty crazy things down here." A woman pushing a shopping cart loudly along the sidewalk passed out front and I watched her stoop to pick up an abandoned aluminum can and toss it inside. "But gypsies, huh? That's a new one on me."

"Place used to swarm with 'em." Frederick turned to the side, reached into an interior pocket and took a long swig from a silver flask. Then he held it out toward me. "Want some?"

"No, thanks," I said. "I'm fine." On the sidewalk, the retreating shopping cart faded from view with a squeak and a rattle. "So, what do you know about this Josephine?"

"Well, she's not a gypsy," said Frederick. "She's voodoo."

"Yes," I said, "but does she do the good kind or the bad kind? She's not going to turn me into a zombie or anything like that, is she?"

"Depends on you," he said after taking another dram from the flask, "cuz she does the good and the bad kind."

"So, are you saying she'll do the bad kind if she doesn't like you?"

"Yeah, she's like the Stick Witch that way. Make her mad, and you better watch out. But," he said, "when she's your friend, there's nothing to worry about."

"Stick Witch? Now who's this?"

"You been down here in Old Louisville how long and you don't know about the Stick Witch?"

"Afraid not," I said sheepishly.

"She's that old witch who runs around with the Kroger cart full of sticks," he explained. "She got another cart, too. A smaller one. Scours the neighborhood looking for broken branches and twigs for her fire. Probably brews her potions and stuff over under the–"

"—the Witches' Tree?"

"Yeah, the Witches' Tree." Frederick looked up into the sky and rocked back on his feet. He closed his eyes and seemed to tilt his head to the side, as if hearing an unseen voice.

I wracked my brain trying to conjure an image of the Stick Witch. Strangely enough, I recalled seeing a woman who fit that description on several different occasions. "Have you had good or bad experiences with her?"

"I leave her alone and she leaves me alone," he said. "But I hear she can get mean."

"What kind of stuff does she do?" I asked. In the front yard, there was a rustling as something moved around among the Manhattan bushes.

"Piss her off and you find a bundle of sticks at your front door." Frederick lifted the flask to his lips and took another drink.

I recoiled when I remembered the small pile of twigs on the porch earlier in the year.

"You get a bundle of sticks and that's when all the weird shit starts to happen."

"Like what?"

"You name it, it happen," he said. "Watermelons falling out the air and hittin' you in the head. Wakin' up in the morning and finding a yellow monkey eating your tomatoes in the back garden. Findin' a mule eatin' from the candy dish down in your living room in the middle of the night. That kind of stuff."

"I see." I thought back to the bundle of twigs and wondered what I had done to incur her wrath. "You know, I found a bunch of sticks on my front step several months ago. You think I did something to make her mad?"

"You had weird stuff happening here?" He squinted his eyes at me.

"Well, I don't know," I said. "You're the one telling me my house is talking to me and saying I need to use voodoo. I'd say that's pretty odd."

"No, no, no." Impatience welled in his voice. "Ghosts in your house is natural. Spirits are all part of the world," he said. "But cakes fallin' out of the sky and roosters wearin' birthday hats is freaky!"

"I guess so."

"Who knows?" Frederick drained the last swig from the flask and wiped his mouth with the back of his sleeve. "Maybe she likes you."

"She doesn't even know me." I watched as he stashed the empty flask in his pants pocket and retrieved the canvas pouch.

"That's how she is, the Stick Witch," he said. "If she likes you or you do something nice for her, you find a bunch of sticks at your door too." He shook the pouch at me and its contents rattled.

"And then what happens?" I asked.

"What you mean?" He stared at me and then started to move toward the sidewalk in front of the house.

"Well, what kind of stuff happens when she leaves you the bundle of sticks when she likes you? You win the lottery or something like that? Get a promotion at work?"

"No!" he scowled and slapped again at something invisible in the air.

"Same kind of stuff happens. Like I said before, a cream pie falls out of a tree and hits you in the head when you're walking to work or you find a jackass eating bonbons out of your Aunt Sallie's crystal candy dish!"

I gasped, suddenly remembering the rat hunched over the silver bowl of Sugar

Babies. "Oh my god," I whispered. "Maybe it was the Stick Witch." I looked at Frederick. "Does a rat eating my Sugar Babies count?"

Frederick stood there and stared. "Maybe so, maybe not." He turned and started to shuffle down the front walk to the sidewalk. "I'll come back tomorrow and talk to this Ramon about doing your yard work."

"But wait!" I ran after him and grabbed his sleeve. "What's so good about finding a yellow monkey in your back yard eating your tomatoes?" I said. "Or finding a donkey with a sweet tooth in your living room?"

He stopped and turned to look at me. "Well, what's so bad about it?" he asked. "It's all in how you look at it."

"A yellow monkey eating tomatoes in your back yard could be good?" A slight chill tingled the night air and I rubbed my bare arms to generate some warmth.

"Yes!" he rasped in a throaty laugh. "How many people you figure ever wake up in Old Louisville and find a yellow monkey eating tomatoes from their garden?"

I stopped and did a mental tally, quickly arriving at a very low number.

"I've never seen one!" he said. "But I tell you what. I walk out and find me a yellow monkey eating tomatoes in someone's garden one day, it gonna make me grin nice and big." A large smile revealed a mouthful of startlingly white teeth. "You know why?" he asked. "I'll tell you why. Because that's something you don't see every day now, is it? That's something special."

"I guess I see your point." A smile formed at the thought of the rat hunched over the silver bowl on the counter.

"Now some cranky people, they'd get all bent out of shape at something like that and probably get out a gun and shoot the poor monkey," he said. "Others would try to pet the monkey and give it a root beer."

"Yes, it all depends on how you look at things."

"Exactly," he whispered. "Same thing with this here house." He raised a hand to sweep an outline around the façade of Widmer House. "Whatever this house is trying to tell you depends on how you listen to it."

"I guess I'll try to listen better next time," I said.

Overhead, there was a soft chittering sound and when I lifted my eyes, the form of a large bat swooped down between the houses and quivered through the columns of the front porch. With a flutter, it vanished around a corner. My eyes were drawn to the stretch of sidewalk in front of the house, where cottonwood fluff had collected on the grass like a thin layer of fresh snow.

Without a sound, Frederick shuffled down the walkway, crossed the street, and disappeared in the shadows on the other side.

Frederick ended up doing a good deal of work for us, and his prices were considerably more reasonable than those of Lewis, his predecessor. Apart from yard work and gardening tasks, Frederick proved adept as a handyman as well. Little by little, we were able to tackle the remaining projects associated with the exterior of the house. By the time summer officially arrived, the restoration of the façade at Widmer House had been completed. The cherry pickers were out of the front yard, the scaffolding had been dismantled, and the new paint job gleamed. It was Tuesday night, and—glasses in hand—the gang stood in front of the house and admired the lavish façade.

In addition to tuckpointing the entire front of the house, we and my cousins had managed to rebuild a number of crumbling window ledges, several ornamental acanthus leaves, and an eroded piece of terra cotta decoration above the third floor windows. At the base of the soaring gable, where we discovered two pedestals that had lost their sculptures over time, we had mounted two large plaster finials. Ramon and I found the two-foot-high pieces one day at a local antique mall, and when we learned that they had come from an old château in France, it seemed to be the perfect fit for a Châteauesque house. After using mortar to secure them in place, we painted the scrolls and curlicues to match the rest of the house and then touched up the façade.

Standing there, studying the front of the house, we all agreed that—despite the aggravating nights of drunk cooking and tomfoolery—my cousins had done an incredible job of painting. Most of the surface had been covered with a layer of bright brick red, but the window ledges and surrounds were done in a deep burgundy, as were many of the flat, raised trim pieces. Elsewhere, the pilasters and lengths of molding sported two contrasting shades of green while the window frames and pieces of terra cotta tracery at the roofline had been painted a deep honey yellow. Flanking the steep gable above the third floor were two intertwining pillars, which had been painted yellow and green, and at the second-floor level was another set of these pillars; however, their alternating twines were painted burgundy and light green. Atop each pillar was a small stage where two strange creatures dug in their claws and bared their fangs. They were about two feet in length, and each had a large tail that tapered up and curled along the wall while the head was down close to the base of the pedestal.

At first I had thought they and the other lizard-like figures found on houses throughout the neighborhood were some type of fierce sea serpents or mythological beings, but after doing a little research I discovered that they were most likely stylized representations of salamanders.

It seems that King Francis I of France, the originator of the Châteauesque style in the 1500s, had chosen the salamander as his personal emblem and later architects had seized upon this connection when looking for ornamental symbols in their Château-inspired designs in this country. In Old Louisville, I had discovered at least four other homes that had salamanders in some form or other on their façades, and architects had described each of the designs as being heavily influenced by the Châteauesque style.

Salamanders were something that always fascinated me, and although Kentucky had almost three dozen varieties of the creature, I had never really seen a real live one up close and personal. Salamanders have long been associated with the occult and Egyptians had a Salamander hieroglyph which signified a man dead from cold. Ancient authors often ascribed mystical abilities to these animals and believed they were able to survive a blaze. Many identified salamanders with the element of fire and thought they could even extinguish flames with the frigidity of their bodies. This association with fire probably came from the fact that salamanders had been reported living in volcanoes, where the constant moisture on their skin served as protection. In medieval iconography the salamander represented someone who never lost the peace of his soul and remained confident through all difficulties. It was also a symbol of loyalty and for the alchemists the salamander symbolized a stone fixed in red, or sulfur.

Before the two terra cotta salamanders on the façade of the Widmer House were painted, they were a deep red. Covered in gold leaf, now they sparkled in the early evening sun, as did the numerous wreaths, garlands, floral swags, and acanthus leaves that had also been gilded or painted metallic gold. As I stood there and studied the fierce golden salamanders from below, it somehow seemed reassuring to be living in a house guarded by two such creatures.

Towering over it all, a small golden figure caught a glint of gold in the fading sunlight, and my eyes were drawn to the very peak of the highest gable. There, on an ornamental pedestal, crouched a tiny little gargoyle, all but invisible to those who knew its story. Ramon and I had found the sculpted stone image at the Louisville Antique Mall one day on an outing several weeks before, and I immediately realized it would make an ideal topper for the empty platform at the pinnacle of the house. After purchasing the small monster, we had had it gilded in gold leaf and then cemented in place so it kept watch from the highest point of the house. I had named the gargoyle Silvia, in honor of Ramon's sister, but she didn't seem to appreciate the gesture as much as I did.

I chuckled, and, behind me, there was some movement. I turned to discover our neighbors coming up the front walk to say hello. "It's official," said Anne. "Yours is without a doubt the prettiest house in the neighborhood." After thanking her I got her something to drink and we stood there for a moment while I pointed out the details.

"Hey, look. It's Micah!" Wendy rushed up and pointed to the opposite side of the street. Sure enough, there he was, in a trench coat and shuffling along with his violin case. Without stopping, he looked up and saluted, then turned his head back to the sidewalk and made his way down Third Street.

"The house looks fabulous!" said Allen and Kris, walking by with their two English bulldogs. "I can't believe you guys got it restored so fast." They paused to study the front of the house and nodded their approval. "It's amazing to see all the detail now," one of them said. "We've passed this house hundreds of times and never really noticed how elaborate the façade is. It's really incredible."

I thanked them and invited them up to the tiny front lawn for a drink. "We've still got some work to do inside and in the back yard, but the façade is definitely finished," I said. They eagerly accepted and joined us. Just then, Dale and Bill from the next block came down the sidewalk and called out a greeting, so I waved them up to join us as well. Suddenly, we had a neighborhood party and we ran inside and brought out several small tables and chairs. Some people sat, others stood, but the front lawn soon filled with laughter and lively chatter. Over the next hour, other passers-by stopped to pay their compliments as well, and the front yard was packed with well-wishers nursing glasses of wine or cocktails and nibbling on canapés passed around on trays.

Out on Third Street, a number of cars had slowed down as they passed, their windows rolled down so they could study the goings-on in front of the house. From one of them, an arm reached out the passenger side window and waved in an attempt to get somebody's attention. It was a reporter from the *Courier-Journal*, the main Louisville newspaper, and she wanted to know if it was true that the house was haunted. Chuckling, I told her people had said it was haunted in the past but that I had never seen any ghosts myself. When she pressed for more details I had to admit that some strange things had been happening in the house since we moved in, but I quickly added the disclaimer that there were probably perfectly logical explanations for the occurrences. When I mentioned that I had begun to talk to other people in the neighborhood about their houses and the stories associated with them, and that I was planning to write a book about it, the reporter quickly grew excited and insisted on talking more about it. She said it would make a good article for the newspaper and we made plans to meet the following week.

As her car drove away, I noticed someone standing out of view behind a tree on the other side of the street. When I looked up, she seemed to step back and disappear in the shadows under the branches. That's when I noticed the figure had on an ivory-colored turban and a brown, billowy skirt. I walked several feet down the street to get a better view, but when I did, it seemed she backed up to stay hidden behind the tree. I was contemplating whether or not I should cross the street and try to engage her in conversation when a large white Mercedes slowed down and pulled up to the curb. Two middle-aged women with dark glasses and bleached hair sat in the front seat, and they were chatting back and forth. Another woman with streaky blond hair sat in the back seat, her face pressed up against the window. Slowly, the windows on the passenger side went down and their conversation drifted out to the sidewalk, where I had returned.

"…but the house looks fabulous! How much do you think it cost?"

"Oh, it couldn't have cost that much. Nobody wants to live down here in Old Louisville."

"But I heard it's really turning around in this neighborhood. People are buying these old places and fixing them up."

"I know. They say Old Louisville is going to be the next Savannah or Charleston. I love it here, especially over by the park. A lot of people say St. James Court and Belgravia Court are better than the Garden District in New Orleans."

"I know what you mean, but I could never live in this area. It's too close to downtown. All those weirdoes and so many poor people. Eww."

"Yeah, I suppose. And I'm sure the upkeep on old houses is outrageous. You think they even have central air in these old mansions?"

"Maybe you should tell Steve to buy a place on this street. Rent it out or something."

"I don't think he'd be caught dead here. He's totally an East End kind of guy. Once in a while he'll let us go to Bardstown Road to eat at Lilly's or Jack Fry's, but he avoids downtown like the plague."

"They sure did a nice job on this house. I wonder what it's like on the inside."

"Looks like they're having a party or something. Maybe we should get out and see what it's all about."

"Good heavens, no! I'm not getting out in Old Louisville."

"Yes, we better stay in the car. Anyway, they're expecting us at the Jefferson Club in a quarter hour, so we better head that way."

I was about to walk over to the car and invite them up for a drink, despite their annoying comments, but the windows on the passenger side suddenly buzzed up and the car sped off.

I was tempted to chase them down and tell them lots of people, in fact, did want to live in Old Louisville and that the upkeep on an old house probably wasn't any worse than it was for their houses in the East End and that yes, most of the places in Old Louisville did have central air, but I decided against it. Anyway, I had an unfinished glass of wine waiting for me on the table where I had left it, so I went back and the festivities resumed.

"Hey, would you look at that?" Somebody on the steps pointed up where several bats flapped and tumbled in a formation over the front yard. "Not even dark yet, and you've got bats flying around."

"I see those three bats all the time," I said. "Not sure what their problem is, but they're always fluttering around the house. I think they live up under the highest gable. Maybe they're friends with Silvia the Tiny Gargoyle."

Over the next half hour, even more people stopped by and joined the party. Skippy went inside and brought the dogs out on their leashes and they enjoyed a great deal of attention as people stooped to pet them. By the time the sun started to set, so many people had commented on how *fabulous* the house looked that an idea suddenly occurred to me. I went inside and returned with a bottle of Champagne. Gathering everyone together at one corner of the house, I thanked them all for coming and then gave a brief rundown on the history of Widmer House and the work that Ramon and I had done on the place in the short time we had called it home. To a huge round of applause, we smashed the bottle of Champagne against the side of the house and officially christened it La Casa Fabulosa, or "the fabulous house" in Spanish. At last, I had found a name that did the house justice.

Several minutes later, the sun disappeared and darkness descended over the neighborhood. The day before, Frederick had helped us install a series of floodlights in the front yard, most of them hidden among the fledgling Manhattan bushes on either side of the house, so we turned them on and illuminated the façade of La Casa Fabulosa. There was an audible lull in the conversation as people stopped what they were doing and beheld the glittering gold leaf and bright colors before them. Then, someone raised a glass and made a toast, and the celebration resumed and carried on till the wee hours of the morning.

Pat and Mark had been gone for a couple of weeks, but we had more visitors at Widmer House. I kept meaning to call the glazier to fix the smashed window in the basement, but somehow I managed to keep putting it off, so most of our visitors were the four-legged creatures that squeezed themselves through the pane that had been broken out. Although my suspicions had been aroused on several occasions when I had gone down to do the laundry, I had ignored the telltale sounds of scampering feet as I turned on the light. The fact that we had a possum living in the basement was ascertained one day when Victor walked into the kitchen with a puzzled look on his face. Victor was a Cuban friend who was staying with us for a while and he was sleeping in the guest room on the top floor.

"Why don't that funny kitty cat downstairs like me to pet her?" he asked as he poured himself some orange juice. "She don't like me?"

"What are you talking about? We don't have cats anymore." The month before, our little black cat had bolted through the back door as I opened it to let out the dogs. Without so much as a look back, it bounded over the fence and disappeared into a neighbor's back yard. Although I had searched for hours and put flyers up all around the neighborhood, Ramon and I were not able to find the little cat.

"You don't got the kitty cats no more?"

"Nope. Only dogs, and none of them lives in the cellar." As if on cue, Rocky, Bess, and Fritz trotted into the kitchen and sat at my feet, a clear indicator that they expected a doggie treat.

"Well who's that big mean kitty with the long pointy nose who live on top of the dryer then?" He elongated his fingers in a cone at his nose to provide a bit of visual clarification. "Every time I reach out to pet his fur, she open up and growl at me." He opened his mouth and made chomping motions. "She got the long pointy teeth."

"Oh, my god, you tried petting it?" I said as I walked over to the basket where we kept the treats. "That's not a cat. That sounds like a possum!" After giving each of the dogs a biscuit, I went to Victor and turned his hands over for inspection. "And don't pet them. They could bite your fingers off."

"What kind of kitty is this . . . possum?" He drew out the new word and tried it on for size. "I do not think we have this type of kitty in Cuba."

"It's not a kitty," I said. "It's more like a big greasy rat that's going bald. Sometimes they curl up and play dead but other times they'll bite your fingers off."

"Well what you got a big hairy rat living on top of your clothes dryer for then?" he said.

"Ask my cousin Mark."

Victor knitted his brows in vexation. "Why? He collect the big and greasy rats?"

"No, he made the hole in the window and that's how they're getting into the basement now." I went to the counter and checked on some bread dough that was rising in a covered bowl. "Which reminds me," I said, "I need to quit procrastinating and fix it once and for all." I punched the dough down and turned it out onto the surface, where I began dividing it into small rolls.

"Well, you no want rats in the house, is time to put the poison in the cheese."

"No poison!" I said. "That's so inhumane." The rats were another story, but I refused to kill the possums. "I'll see if I can borrow a live trap from Dale and Bill down the street. I'll catch the critters and then take them out to the East End where I'll set them free." A devious smile slowly formed as I envisioned a swarm of possums descending upon a tony neighborhood.

"The poison, she is better." Victor grabbed his basket of laundry and went back upstairs.

"But the live trap, she is more humane," I called out as he disappeared into the butler's pantry. Victor responded by informing me he was invited to a party and would be gone most of the evening. Humming the tune to "*Guantanamera*," he trudged up the back stairs and started to get ready.

Seeing they weren't going to get more treats, Rocky and Bess retreated into the butler's pantry and took up spots on the sofa. Fritz, ever the loyal companion, sat contentedly under the table and watched while I filled the dishwasher and wiped down the counters. When I finished, I slipped him another treat without Rocky and Bess seeing and then got back to the bread recipe. After brushing the slightly risen rolls with egg white, I turned them upside down and pressed the tops into a plate of poppy seeds before baking. When they emerged from the oven, each one crowned with a perfect dark circle of poppy seeds and filling the kitchen with a wonderful smell, I knew I had finally hit on the right recipe.

I buttered one of the hot rolls and shared it with the dogs, whose wagging tails indicated their approval. Afterward, I straightened up and went to the third floor to conduct some research. Ever since my conversation with Frederick, gypsies had been on my mind, and I endeavored to find out as much as I could about their presence in Louisville. But before sitting down at the desk in my office, I stopped, suddenly feeling drawn to the bank of three small windows. An odd feeling came over me and I had the sensation that somebody was watching the house.

I went to the window seat and looked out onto Third Street. Other than for random fireflies that flickered in the grassy areas, the road looked empty. I sat down for a moment and Fritz jumped up beside me and took a spot on a cushion. For several minutes, we watched in silence as the specks of phosphorescent green flashed on and off, but then a low growl came from Fritz and his ears perked up. Down below, there was movement on the sidewalk. Someone pushing a shopping cart emerged from behind a tree. I couldn't tell if it was a man or a woman, but the person looked up and stopped. The cart came to a halt, and after a long glance, the figure lowered its head and resumed its journey. I raised the middle window and Fritz and I listened as the cart bumped and creaked over the cracked pavement and then disappeared under a canopy of leaves near the corner with Ormsby. Silence followed but it was soon eclipsed by the electric din of cicadas, which seemed to crescendo from nothing and overtake the darkness where fireflies gently flashed. I lowered the sash to shut out the sound and scratched Fritz behind the ears.

We sat there another ten minutes, staring out the window, and then I went to my desk to start my research. I turned on the computer, typed in the word "gypsy" and hit the enter button.

That's when the lights went out and La Casa Fabulosa was plunged into blackness.

The Witches' Tree

In the darkness it was easy to hear the cicadas buzzing loudly outside and I sat for a moment in my office, hoping that it was only a temporary blackout. A thin shaft of light filtered in through one of the three windows where Fritz and I had sat and it landed on the soffit wall that jutted out over the fireplace. I had recently completed an art project on the green wall over the mantel, and specks of gold and red glittered where stenciled letters and faux jewels spelled out the words to a favorite Tennessee Williams saying of mine: "I love to visit the other side now and then, but on my social passport *Bohemia* is indelibly stamped, without regret on my part." It quickly became evident that the lights were not coming back on so I walked to the door.

Fritz trailing behind, I felt my way out of the room and to the steps leading to the lower floors, one hand gliding along the cool wood of the railing while the other skimmed the outer wall of the stairwell. For some reason, each step provoked a loud creak as I wound my way down to the foyer, and it seemed I passed through a very cold spot on the landing between the first and second floors. I quickly convinced myself that it was only a draft and navigated the last stretch of stairway.

On the very last step I almost tripped over Rocky, who had come to find me when the lights went out. I picked up both him and Fritz and deposited them next to Bess on the sofa in the butler's pantry. Then, I pulled a flashlight out of one of the kitchen drawers and went to the basement to check the circuit box. Fighting my way through cobwebs, I located it on a far wall and opened it. Although a quick sweep of the flashlight revealed that none of the circuits had blown, I flipped the switches on and off anyway. But the house remained in darkness. After several more attempts, I gave up and left the dark cellar.

In the kitchen, I peered through a window into the back alley and saw that lights shone brightly in all the neighboring houses. I decided to go to the front door and see if Third Street had any light. Approaching the door, I was somewhat comforted to see the glare from the street lamps wash across the shiny floor in the foyer, but I shrank back when a hunched-over form arose in front of the door and blocked out most of the light. Because of the lace curtains hanging over the windows in the door, the shadow was somewhat obscured, however it appeared that someone had risen from a crouching position on the front porch. The form quickly ran down the front steps and disappeared into the darkness.

My heart racing, I inched my way to the door and pulled back the curtains. When I had ascertained that nobody was in the immediate proximity, I walked outside and looked around. The street in front of the house was empty, but down near the corner at Oak Street, under the hazy glare of the streetlamp, I saw a bit of movement on the sidewalk and realized it was someone pushing a shopping cart in my direction. A faint creaking sound arose as it neared and it got louder the closer to the house it got. There were several shopping bags of groceries in the cart and if the woman pushing it saw me watching her from the porch, she didn't show it as she bumped the cart down the rest of the block and disappeared from view.

Even after she was gone, I could still hear the faint rasp of the metal cart as it continued down Third Street. Shaking my head, I turned to go back into the house, but something caught my attention. There, on the tile floor in front of the welcome mat, was a small pile of sticks. But unlike the bundle I had found before, this was a little mound that could have been the beginning of somebody's campfire. One by one, twigs had been stood upright so as to lean in and form a small teepee shape. It was directly in my path from the front door to the steps and I couldn't figure out how I had so completely missed it when I first came out of the house. I must have stepped right over it.

Irritated, I used my foot to sweep the mound of sticks into the nearest flowerbed, and I sauntered down the steps to the end of the walkway and looked both ways down the street. Although random shadows seemed to skulk about here and there, lurking behind bushes and creeping along the curbs, none of them appeared to be the Stick Witch. Or Josephine. Or anyone else who might have left a pile of sticks on my front stoop. Maybe it was Frederick or Lewis playing a prank, I told myself. The neighborhood and all its weird characters, I realized, were starting to annoy me. Bohemia was one thing; Crazy Town was something else altogether.

I scratched my head and decided to return to my darkened house and find out what had caused the blackout. But when I turned to go back up the front walkway, there was a surging kind of click and all at once I saw that blazing light shone through every single window of La Casa Fabulosa. In the foyer stood Rocky, Bess, and Fritz, their fuzzy silhouettes outlined against the bright light flooding through the iron grill of the old security door. For a moment, my jaw dropped and I stood there trying to take it all in. How had all the lights come on when most weren't turned on in the first place? Only a few of the lights had been turned on before the power went out, but could I have inadvertently hit some of the light switches as I fumbled my way through the darkness?

I pushed through the door and walked back to the butler's pantry, where the dogs joined me. I gave them each a treat and settled them in on the couch in front of the television, which had also come on, although I hadn't used it even once during the day. Then I made my way to the upper floors to turn off the unnecessary lights. And as I feared, every single light had been turned on. Well, every one except for the light in the little room at the back of the second floor, which sat dark and quiet behind the closed door. When I went inside, the room seemed unnaturally cold, so I quickly closed the door and left.

In the butler's pantry, the dogs were getting antsy and looking forward to their evening stroll. But I was somewhat leery about leaving. Ramon would be getting home from work soon, and as I debated whether or not it would be best to wait, the landline rang in the foyer. I went to answer it.

"Hidy ho," said a somewhat gruff voice from the other end. It sounded like an older woman.

"Hi?' I said with a note of hesitancy.

"Hidy ho," repeated the voice. "You know you got a bum out in your back alley, don't you?"

"Who is this?"

"You heard me right. You got a bum in your back alley," she said. "I saw him snooping around your black car. Better go on and check now."

"But..." I wanted to argue with this woman but the sense of urgency convinced me to go check on the car and get more details later. "OK, give me a second." I headed through the kitchen to the back alley. For security, I grabbed a rolling pin on the way out, but when I crossed the raised deck and found myself looking at my parked car, there was nobody in sight. I opened the gate and went out into the alley, but I couldn't see anything. I looked both ways down the alley and, save for a car passing on Oak Street, there was nothing to see.

"You were too slow," the voice reprimanded when I picked up the phone. "He got away. Skedaddled across the alley and into the backyard of one them houses facing Fourth Street where it was all dark and shadowy."

"I thought I was moving pretty quickly, but not quick enough, I guess." I was getting ready to ask who she was and how she had my number when she cut me off.

"Yes, and he was a gimp, too, so you should have caught him." At the other end there was a phlegmy cough, which was followed by a cackle. "It's like he sensed you coming the minute you put the phone down and he hightailed it out of there, but like I said he can't move too fast."

"You mean he's handicapped?"

"Yep, he's a gimp. Call it whatever you like, but he needs a cane to get around. Probably one of them bums at the corner of Fourth and Crazy pestering people for handouts. Maybe a truck rolled over his foot. Maybe he was born a gimp and got the club foot. God only knows." There was another bout of coughing and it sounded like she was holding the phone away from her mouth. "Hang on a bit, hon," she said and resumed coughing. When she came back on the line, there was a sharp intake of breath and she spoke in a low voice. "Hold on now. It looks like that bum is headed down Fourth Street now, maybe for the park."

"You can see him? How can you see him? Who are you, by the way?"

"Sure I can see him. I can see practically all the neighborhood bums," she said. "Hang on a sec while I watch him gimpin' his way down the street. Yeah, it looks like he's going for the park."

"Well, that's nice to know," I said, "but I still have no idea who you are and how it is you can see all the neighborhood bums."

"I'm Loretty, your neighbor, but you don't know me." She coughed once and chuckled pleasantly. "I've lived in this neighborhood for years."

"If you're my neighbor," I said, "how is it that we haven't met? And how come you know my phone number and who I am?"

"That's easy. I looked you up in the phone book." There was some shuffling on the other end and it sounded like she was slurping a drink of something. "And I know your name because I asked around after you started fixing up that house. We've been watching your progress ever since you started painting all them pretty colors."

"There's more than one of you? Who are you anyway?"

"I told you already, hon, I'm Loretty. Hang on a sec while I get another swig of my bourbon." There was a long pause after which came another slurping sound and the smacking of lips. "I'm Loretty, your neighbor across the street."

"Across the street?" Tugging the cord of the phone along behind me, I walked into the darkened parlor and looked out the front window. A good section of the block on the other side was occupied by a 16-story residential high rise built in the 1960s known as the Hillebrand House. Many considered it a sort of eyesore but I had come to disapprove of it only when I saw a photo of the beautiful Peabody mansion that had been demolished to make room for it. In any case, it seemed like fire trucks and EMS vehicles were there at all hours of the day tending to the residents' various emergencies, which often involved elderly tenants falling and not being able to get back up. "You're not in the Hillebrand House, are you?"

"Yes siree, bob, yes indeedy," she said. "That's exactly where I am. Been here a number of years now and don't get out much anymore. My living room window looks out onto Third Street."

As she coughed and took another loud drink I moved closer to the window and raised my head to get a better look at the building, most of whose windows had gone dark. "What floor are you on?" I said.

"I'm way up top," she said. "Got a bird's eye view up here. Wait, can you see me?"

I was about to tell her there was no way I'd be able to see her when a light went on in one of the windows at the top of the building and it quickly flashed on and off several times. "Ah, is that you flipping the light on and off?"

"Yes siree, bob, yes indeedy," she said. "Here I am. Loretty of Hillebrand, at your service."

"Well, Loretty, nice to meet you," I said, turning on a light so she could see me. I waved and then extinguished the light.

"Alrighty then, I see you," she cackled. "That's a pretty blue shirt you got on there."

"You can see what kind of shirt I'm wearing from all the way up there?" Looking up at the dark window where she sat, I wondered if Loretty would hit the lights again, but she didn't.

Instead, there came another round of coughing before she spoke again. "Well, that's because I got a little extry help up here. I got a pair of field glasses my daddy brought back from dubbya dubbya two. Got 'em off a dead kraut, and they're the good kind, too. I can see real far." She laughed.

"And you'd be surprised how much I can see up here. And how much of the neighborhood." She paused and took a swallow of her drink. "I can see for blocks and, so you know, I've been keeping track of your gimpy bum as we been talking. Looks like he's over by the Witches' Tree right now."

"You can see the Witches' Tree from up there?" At the back of the house, the dogs started barking but quickly stopped. Ramon must have come in the back door, so I decided to wrap up the conversation, and before she had a chance to respond, I changed the subject. "Say, you didn't see anyone on my front porch before you called, did you? I saw someone out there and when I went to check I found a pile of sticks. You think it was the guy snooping around in the back alley?"

"Sticks?" said Loretty. "No, I didn't see anyone on your front porch, but I don't think it was the gimp that did it. That sounds like the Stick Witch. She's that crazy old bat who pushes around her shopping cart full of sticks."

"She's a real person?"

"She's been around forever, probably longer than I have," she laughed. "I see her all over the neighborhood and at all hours of the day." Loretty coughed then and told me to hang on for a minute. When she was done she got back on the line and took a drink of her bourbon. "Listen, hon," she said. "I need to let you go so's I can go and watch my program. I'll call you the next time I see that gimp or any of the others bums snooping around your back alley."

"Thanks for calling," I said. "It's been nice talking to you." And just like that, Loretty was gone.

I walked into the dining room as the swinging door opened and in walked Ramon from the butler's pantry. "What are you doing?" he said.

"Talking to a lady who lives across the street in the Hillebrand House." I walked into the kitchen for a piece of blackberry pie and between bites I filled him in on what Loretty had told me. After the last mouthful I washed it all down with a huge glass of cold milk. Then I told him about the lights going off and the pile of sticks at the front door.

"Probably one of the bums from down on Oak Street," he said. "Maybe we should get a security camera for the back of the house."

"Maybe. But it sounds like Loretty is as good as any security system. She said she'll call if she sees anything."

Shrugging his shoulders, Ramon went upstairs to watch television. The dogs were prancing about at the kitchen door, so I hooked them to their leads and we left through the back alley for a nice long walk.

A half hour later my head had cleared as we strolled down Third Street and through Belgravia Court. Although the evening was warm, a bit of chill tinged the breeze that rustled the leaves near the gaslights around the fountain on St. James Court. On the green, at the south end of the boulevard, there was an assemblage of a dozen people or so and I smiled to see that they were playing a round of nighttime croquet. They were attired in light colors and pastels that made them stand out in the darkness. That's when I noticed that they were all in Victorian attire. The women wore bustled dresses and some sported lacy parasols; the males had on striped jackets, pleated white slacks, and straw boaters. Fascinated, I watched them for several minutes. Save for the clacking of ball and wooden mallet every now and then, the group made very little noise.

Shadows fluttered across the front of a white Georgian mansion with blue shutters. Built around 1901, it was once home to famous Kentucky poet Madison Cawein; now it was home to another local literary figure, celebrated author Sena Jeter Naslund. As we passed, an unseen hand drew back a lacy curtain from a window on the second floor, and a dark form peered down at me before receding into the darkness.

The wind picked up as we cut through Central Park on our return home, and I realized that we were only a couple hundred yards from the Witches' Tree. Instead of taking the path to the right, we veered left and headed for the corner of Sixth and Park. If a witch was leaving sticks on my front porch I might as well go and see where she hung out. I was also curious if I'd see the limping man Loretty had warned me about.

A gibbous moon hung low in the sky as the dogs eagerly tugged their way to a new destination. We passed under a wisteria-laden pergola and picked up the path that exited the northwest corner of the park. After crossing the street, I took up a position along the brick wall of a large residence that had formerly served as a cloistered monastery and studied the adjacent corner, the corner where the witches' tree stood. Other than the soft tunes from a radio wafting through an opened window, all was quiet.

The tree in question stood along a thin hedge, and the reason locals referred to it as the witches' tree became apparent as soon as we left the shadow of the brick wall and approached the patch of ground illuminated in the glare of a nearby streetlamp. A solid, knobby trunk shot up into a mass of tangled limbs, and spindly black branches pointed downward in a thick canopy that cast a glum shadow over gnarled roots poking through the bare earth at its base. Green mold and whorls covered the bark, and a multitude of wart-like burls and knots blistered and extended the surface, transforming the tree into a living mass of wooden growths and gnarls. A tree for witches indeed.

I had done a little snooping since hearing Frederick mention the tree and managed to piece together the legend behind it. Despite the scientific and technological advances of the 19th century, it seemed that many parts of Kentucky's largest city held on to old superstitions, and belief in curses, black magic, and witches was commonplace. Given that the riverboat and rail connections to New Orleans and other points in the South ensured a constant stream of followers of the occult, voodoo practitioners kept the neighborhood that is Old Louisville today hopping with supernatural action. The Witches' Tree emerged as a meeting point for many of these dabblers in the black arts.

According to local lore, the tree known as the Witches' Tree started its life as a majestic, towering maple that sprang up practically overnight in the 1800s when the Dumesnil family still owned the land. Famed for the lovely flower beds and hedgerows that graced the grounds of their estate, the Dumesnils once maintained an adjacent tract of land dedicated to the cultivation of ornamental shrubs, myriad rose bushes, and a wide variety of flowers. Locals named it the Dumesnil Botanical Gardens, and it became a popular destination for visitors in search of a bit of rest and relaxation from the hustle and bustle of life in a 19th-century metropolis. During the warm months of the great Southern Exposition from 1883 to 1887, the garden's shady pathways and fragrant blooms provided welcome relief from the Kentucky sun to thousands of visitors from around the world.

When word later got out that the Dumesnils planned to sell their beautiful gardens and that planners would develop the land to construct houses, many people in the neighborhood were heartbroken to think they would lose their treasured botanical gardens. The most distraught of all, however, was a coven of local witches. The imposing tree, with its perfectly straight trunk, had become the preferred gathering spot for nightly rituals where they mixed potions and cast spells on those who incurred their wrath or curried their favor. They had almost lost it once before, and they weren't ready to risk it again.

By most accounts, problems began in the spring of 1889 as locals began preparations for their annual May Day celebrations. Given their connection to the hardwood industry, it fell to a family of lumber barons, the Mengels, to organize the neighborhood May Day celebrations every year. With tons of logs at their disposal, they usually sent their employees to pick out the tallest and straightest one to be erected and decorated as a maypole; but in 1889, Clarence Mengel decided to cut down a local tree instead, the beautiful maple at the corner of Sixth and Park. Of course, the local witches were less than thrilled to learn that their beloved maple had been singled out for its flawless shape and impressive height.

At the end of April, the witches learned, their tree would be cut down, shorn of its branches and then festooned as a maypole. The witches got together and posted a parchment note on their tree. Addressed to Mr. Mengel, it warned that a terrible calamity would befall the city in exactly eleven months if their wishes were ignored and the tree cut down.

But on the last day of April, two woodsmen from the Mengel factory cut down the great tree, and the next day, the lovely maple was resurrected in a different location, decorated with fresh flowers, colorful ribbons and boughs of greenery. Mr. Mengel officiated at the ceremony and the celebrations went off without a hitch.

After the May Day festivities, the trunk was dried, cut, and burned in a great Whitsuntide bonfire. By the time the heat of summer arrived, most had forgotten about the witches' warning and the beautiful maple tree. When the winds of fall and winter started whipping through the neighborhood, rumors had it that the coven had moved to a distant forest where they had resumed their nightly gatherings and castings of spells. When townspeople began planning for the next May Day celebration in April, the witches' curse had slipped from memory.

But exactly eleven months later, on the evening of March 27, 1890, the most destructive tornado in the history of Louisville roared in from the west and destroyed a large portion of the city. Within five minutes, more than 600 buildings—including some 500 homes, 10 tobacco warehouses, three schools and the downtown train station—had been shattered like kindling. It was also reported that the winds had wreaked havoc at the Mengel's lumber works.

In the end, upwards of a hundred lives were lost, several of the victims from the Mengel family. And eyewitnesses reported something curious: before the winds of the storm had subsided, the tornado had made a strange righthand turn and roared from downtown into the neighborhood around the Dumesnil Botanical Gardens. As the twister passed the stump where the lovely old maple tree had stood, a mighty bolt of lightning shot out and struck the stump, and a gnarled and twisted old tree magically sprouted up on the spot—one that replaced the one taken from the witches.

Rumor had it that the coven of witches soon returned to resume their nightly rituals at their old spot, but with a new tree. And to this day, people say the gnarled old tree violently rattles its dead and twisted branches in warning whenever a tornado threatens the neighborhood.

A low wind surged just then, and, as if sensing my thoughts, the jagged branches of the spooky old tree clattered a brittle admonition while the dogs and I came to stand underneath. It stood in the corner of a small plot of land that served as a front yard for a large brick apartment house from the early 1900s, and I wondered how many of the residents knew the story behind the eerie-looking tree. Probably not too many, I concluded, studying the balconies where several unconcerned tenants sat at small tables looking out over the yard.

There was a slight commotion under the tree and a dark form fluttered around the trunk and shot through the hedge. The dogs went crazy and tried to chase it, but I managed to keep them under control as it skittered along Park Avenue. At first I thought it had to be a dog or a cat, but as it passed under the light of the next street lamp, I saw that it was a wild turkey. With a loud screech and a throaty gobble it jerked and raced into a backyard where it disappeared.

Wild turkeys in Old Louisville? I was about to turn and head back to the house when a light went on over the doorway of a darkened balcony above. From a slamming screen door emerged a woman in brightly colored skirts and a green turban. *Josephine.* Ample hips swaying, she walked to the railing and leaned against it as she gazed down at the gnarled old tree.

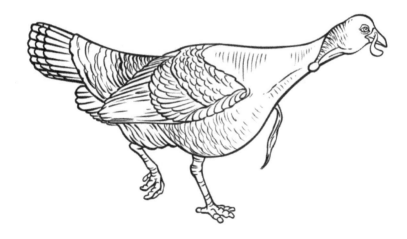

The Kroghetto

I quickly yanked the dogs out of sight and crouched behind the hedge. Through a hole in the foliage, I watched as Josephine raised a hand that had been dangling at her side and lifted a huge cigar to her lips. As she inhaled, the white ash at the tip flared in a blaze of intense orange and a thin wisp of smoke snaked its way to the balcony above. She exhaled a lazy, billowy puff that scrimmed over her face and dissipated in a hazy cloud that drifted out over the courtyard below. While the sweetly acrid smoke tickled my nose, I shifted my weight and eased myself down into a sitting position on the curb. After another long drag on the cigar, Josephine reached over and grabbed a large silver goblet she had placed on the railing and took a long drink. After setting the ornate container back on the railing she turned her head and called over her shoulder to a vague form that hovered in the light of the room behind her.

"André, you got them ingredients?" Her speech had a slightly French accent to it. Cajun or Creole, perhaps? She took another long drag on her cigar and exhaled. "The full moon, she is coming." Overhead, a low-flying UPS jet sliced its way across the sky as it came in for a landing at the airport.

"No," a deep male voice said in response. "I ain't had the time. You stop at the Kroghetto tomorrow after work and get them."

After another dram from the goblet, she put the cigar to her lips and blew out a long stream of vaporous white. "Broke dick man," she cursed. "Always havin' to do things myself." The screen door slammed behind her as a shadow retreated and disappeared into the dim glare of the apartment. Several moments later, someone extinguished the lights and all the windows went black.

What was Josephine going to buy? With the dogs eagerly responding to my movement, I rose slowly from my sitting position and brushed dried grass from the seat of my pants. Taking one last glance at the Witches' Tree before I left, I followed the dogs as they pulled me along.

The dogs were still energetic so we took the long way home and walked over to the corner of Ormsby and First Street. From a hedgerow of fragrant olive, the sweet scent of apricots filled the air. Over on the southwest corner loomed a large Gothic church constructed of red brick. Up near the crown of the squat corner tower, illuminated by floodlights, a series of gargoyles seemed to glare down at us. In front of a large brick house festooned with an abundance of terra cotta ornamentation, the dogs became fascinated with something and I stopped while they rooted around in the corner of the yard. When I went to see what they were sniffing and snuffling at, I discovered something I had never noticed in all the times I walked by. There, nestled in the ivy, was a remnant of the days when they still used horses in the neighborhood. It was a hitching post, but this one appeared to be made of poured concrete. After moving some of the vines to the side I was able to get a better look. The really interesting thing was that it had been poured in the shape of a large, flat tree stump. Grooves along the trunk simulated bark and the flat part of the stump, where the solid iron ring had been attached, even had visible concentric growth rings. Immediately, I recalled the story about the Witches' Tree and how it had sprung up from the trunk of an old maple tree and I had to wonder at the coincidence of my coming across another stump minutes after leaving the other tree. But it was getting late and I had to get back home and hit the hay. In my mind, I was already formulating plans to go looking for Josephine at the Kroghetto the next day.

Most people will tell you a minor problem with Old Louisville is the lack of decent supermarkets. Aside from a couple of tiny neighborhood grocery stores, there still aren't many supermarket selections in the immediate vicinity to this day. When I moved there, there was a Winn-Dixie at the corner of Fourth and Crazy, but that ended up closing and the only supermarket left was the Kroger store several blocks away on Second Street, not too far from downtown. Many in Old Louisville call it the Kroghetto, and only go there when they don't have time to drive somewhere else like the new Kroger out by the track or the Dirty Kroger over on Brownsboro Road. Incidentally, I never really understood why they insisted on calling that one the Dirty Kroger because it always seemed clean and sparkly to me, in fact much cleaner than the one on Second Street, the one known as the Kroghetto.

Since I always tried to patronize neighborhood establishments, I tended to shop at the Second Street Kroger more than most in Old Louisville. Nonetheless, when I closed the front door behind me the day after I overheard Josephine's plans and walked the three blocks down to the supermarket, I was reluctant to make the trip. It seemed that every time you shopped there, you had to plan on spending at least three times the amount of time you'd spend at any other normal grocery store. And most of the cashiers back then were possessed of attitudes that could be described as lackadaisical at best, and plain grumpy at worst. If they weren't waiting for a manager to come and void an order they had rung in wrong because they couldn't remember the correct produce codes, they were ignoring patrons and telling their neighbor cashier about the party they went to the night before.

Granted, the customers were no doubt a source of their grumpiness. When they weren't arguing with the cashiers, they were holding up the line deciding which of their items to throw back because they had gone over budget and didn't have enough to pay for all of their purchases. Or else they were having problems trying to figure out how to use the credit card swiper or copping an attitude because the cashier had to send someone back to the meat department to check on a price because they had picked up the one package of baloney or chicken thighs that didn't have a price tag on it.

The first time I shopped at the Second Street Kroger I only bought five items, but I was in the store for almost an hour because it took me that long to go through the line. To start with, the woman in front of me got into a spat with the checkout girl about whether or not Juicy Juice was covered under food stamps. (It was.) Then she had to decide which to return—the sour cream coffee cake or the jumbo-sized bag of frozen mixed vegetables—because her total came to $53.29 and she only had $50.00. (She returned the vegetables.)

Then, when I finally got to unload my shopping basket a quarter hour later, there was a problem with each of my five items. First, the cashier mistook my new red potatoes for radishes and we had to wait five minutes before a manager arrived to void off the price for radishes ($1.79 for a one-pound bag). After that, the scanner wouldn't read the barcode on the ruler I needed for a crafts project at home and after five minutes of failed attempts she gave up and rang it in manually as only ten cents (a savings of $1.09). Then, she rang up my cilantro as parsley and we had to wait another five minutes for the manager, although it really wasn't necessary since they both cost the same amount ($.79 a bunch). By the time the man with the mop and pail cleaned up the mess she made after dropping my jar of dill pickles on the floor, another ten minutes had passed, and she still had to go and get a replacement jar. I thought we were home free when she rang up my last item, a Baby Ruth bar, however, it came up as $99.00 instead of $.99 and we had to wait another five minutes to get it voided. She manually rang it up and only charged me ten cents for it in the end, but it still got on my nerves.

Although most trips to the Kroghetto didn't take that long, they still tended to involve more problems than trips to the Kroger stores in other parts of town. So, when I walked through the sliding glass doors into the dim interior that day in search of Josephine, I prepared myself for the worst. Even though I had come to spy on somebody, I needed to buy something as a pretext and I was sure that whatever it was, it would invariably involve trouble at the cash register. Therefore, and out of nostalgia, I decided to buy a Baby Ruth, and nothing else. I would take it home and see how long I could wait before eating it. Two days, I was hoping.

As I went to peruse the candy aisle, I made sure to keep an eye out for Josephine. It was about five. Assuming that she worked until five, she could show up at any moment. After tossing the candy bar into the basket, I needed to kill time so I moseyed over to the meat department and checked on the price of rib eyes and then went to the bakery section and looked longingly at a tray of frosted chocolate brownies. Eventually I tore myself away from the baked goods and walked through the produce department to the aisle with household cleaners—all without any sign of Josephine. A half hour later, I had walked every inch of floor in the store and I started to worry that my solitary candy bar might arouse suspicion.

I decided to make one last sweep of the store when I ran into Cookie.

Cookie was a man I had met several years before when I was a grad student at the University of Louisville, and I tried to avoid him. Unfortunately, he always managed to spy me before I saw him, and escape usually proved impossible—as it was this day in the Kroghetto. He saw me and smiled, and zoomed over with his cart.

"How you doin'?" he asked.

"Oh, I'm fine, thanks." Cookie was always friendly enough, but a little creepy. I'm sure it had something to do with the lascivious grin that was always on his face. Other than his basic greetings and farewells, I could hardly understand a word of what he said, so I preferred to make our encounters as brief and painless as possible. The only word I was ever able to make out was the word "cookies," which he tended to use in abundance, and for that reason I called him Cookie. He had told me his name at one time, but, of course, I wasn't able to understand what he said.

Surreptitiously, I tried to maneuver around his cart, but he had parked it sideways so it blocked most of the aisle.

"Howboutsommadatgimmedatsommadatcookie?" He said with a big grin and a wink.

In response, I politely rolled my eyes and prepared myself for the same conversation that played out every time Cookie cornered me in Old Louisville. "Excuse me?" I said, my shoulders drooping slightly.

"Howboutsommadatgimmedatsommadatcookie?" His eyebrows arched in eagerness.

"What?" I protested meekly. "I can't understand you."

"Youknowwhatasays," he said. *"Yougonnagimmedatsommadat? Cookie?"*

"I don't know what you're saying. All I understand is 'cookie.'"

He nodded his head eagerly. *"Cookieswhenwegongetem?"*

"What about cookies?"

"Timeagetsommadatgimmedatcook-aaaays!" He rubbed his hands together and smiled.

"I still don't know what you're talking about. I don't have any cookies! There," I said, pointing to the cookie aisle, "go get some there. There's a ton right there."

He furrowed his brow and frowned. *"Wandem-cookiesoverhere."* He pointed at me and grinned. *"Gooooodcoook-aaays!"*

"Oh, well, then, nice talking to you. Try the bakery section. I saw some nice cookies over there." I took advantage of his newfound good humor and scooted around his cart. I had lost my sweet tooth, and the cash register lines looked exceptionally long, so I returned the Baby Ruth to the white, blue, and red box where I had found it and I beat a hasty retreat out the door. I had had enough of the Kroghetto and would have to find Josephine later.

And Another Voodoo Day

The next day Loretty called me as I was testing a recipe for spare ribs and onion gravy. She informed me that in the morning twilight, before the sun had fully risen, several possums had been creeping along my fence and that the neighbor from three doors down had surreptitiously stowed one of his full garbage bags in our trashcan before the sanitation trucks rolled through the alley on their weekly rounds. "No sign of the gimp," she reported.

The day after, I had another voodoo day.

As I lay in bed that morning, for some reason my mind started wandering to the time Julia Child dropped a turkey during the taping of *The French Chef* and then confided to the camera that the good thing about being the only one in the kitchen is that no one has to know what goes on there before she returned the turkey to the roasting pan. When I went downstairs and turned on the little TV in the butler's pantry a half hour later, what was on? A documentary about Julia Child on A&E. And, as it turns out, the scene with Julia dropping the turkey was the very first thing I saw as the picture came into view after turning on the television set.

I watched the biography through to its end, and then I thought back to the days when I studied in Santa Barbara, California, which was where Julia Child resided in her final years. One afternoon, after returning from the downtown farmer's market where I happened to see the large woman happily fondling a Japanese eggplant, I was walking to class when a surfer dude with a surfboard strapped to his back sailed by on a skateboard, playing a Peter, Paul & Mary song on a guitar.

Wait a minute! I thought to myself. Old Louisville's got lots of weirdoes, so how come I've never seen a surfer dude sailing by on a skateboard, playing a Peter, Paul & Mary song on a guitar here? All of a sudden, a prickle of goose bumps rose on my arms and I had a strange but familiar feeling.

I got up and walked to the front parlor and looked through the large arched window. And what did I see out on the sidewalk in front of my house? A young, ratty-looking guy with long bleach-blond hair standing on a skateboard rolling down to the next corner. A guitar strap over his shoulder, he strummed away on the instrument, barely noticing the old lady he almost ran off the sidewalk. I couldn't hear what he was playing, but I'm fairly confident it was something by Peter, Paul & Mary. And even though he didn't have a surfboard strapped to his back, it was enough of a coincidence to let me know I was in for a voodoo day.

An hour later, I was standing in line at the Kroghetto, kicking myself for not having gone somewhere else as the disheveled woman in front of me argued with the cashier. When I finally got to unload my cart and wait for the grand total, I surveyed the contents and hazarded a guess: Looks like $122.79 worth of Kroghetto merchandise, I thought to myself. Sure enough, when the cashier scanned the last item and gave me the final tally, it came to $122.79, her words echoing in my head as the digital numbers flashed on the screen of the cash register.

As I rolled the cart to the exit, I shrank back with a start. The electric door popped open with a squeaky whoosh and in walked Josephine, a golden turban with an emerald brooch snugly encasing her scalp and a lacy, loose-fitting blouse hanging from her shoulders. Her skirt billowed out as she sailed past me and headed for the produce department. A wicker basket swung at her side.

I resisted the urge to squat and hide behind my cart and turned around so she wouldn't see my face. To add to the ruse, I put a coin in the nearest gumball machine instead. *Jackpot!* And out rolled *thirteen* huge gumballs and not just the single one that a dime was supposed to get you. (Voodoo days had their advantages every now and then.) I greedily stuffed them into my pockets, hopeful that store security hadn't noticed my unjust enrichment, and when I lifted the metal flap, out rolled another thirteen, although I hadn't fed the machine a second time. I was debating whether or not I should lift the flap and press my luck for another thirteen when I remembered that Josephine had entered the store. Quickly, I ran my purchases out to the car, stowed the gumballs, and soon found myself back in the store, inspecting a head of red cabbage while Josephine conversed with an employee several yards away.

I couldn't really hear what she said, but in her hands she held a bunch of something green as she peppered the employee with questions. Giving Josephine a helpless, wide-eyed look, the young girl wrinkled her nose and shrugged her shoulders before backing up and walking away. Josephine tossed the bundle into her basket and walked over to the milk case, no doubt in search of some odd dairy substance to heighten the magical effects of the mysterious greens she had purchased. Throwing down the fresh pineapple I was pretending to scrutinize, I followed her.

The green shine of the brooch caught in the reflection of the glass door, Josephine snagged a pint of buttermilk and tossed it into her basket. Then she breezed on, past the butter and cheese, past the potato chips and snacks, past the canned vegetables and tomato sauce, and entered the aisle for baking needs. She sauntered forward and came to a stop in front of the spices. A free hand stroking her chin, she studied the selection of jars and vials and shook her head slightly.

I was relatively certain that there was nothing like broom tops, bloodroot or brimstone to be had in the Kroghetto spice aisle, but I did a quick mental rundown of the indispensable herbs and spices used in your everyday voodoo ceremony and soon realized that I knew next to nothing about voodoo. From a brief bit of research on the Internet, I knew voodoo botanicals included items with foreboding-sounding names such as nightshade, devil's shoestring, and goofer dust, but I knew little about the actual requirements for the ceremonies themselves. What was Josephine looking for? Mandrake, mistletoe, mugwort? Snake root, soap wort, sassafras? Whatever it was, she wouldn't find it here and would probably head over to Bardstown Road. Working with the choices at hand, I tried to figure out good substitutes in the event that I should get up the nerve and approach her with my suggestions. Allspice? Lavender? Anise? Cloves? They all seemed rather exotic but I doubted they'd be any good in raising the dead or turning enemies into zombies. So, I put my incredible powers of reasoning to use—voodoo came from Haiti and Haiti was in the Caribbean and so was Jamaica—and soon came up with the answer: *jerk seasoning!* Yes, she must be looking for a substance that could both flavor chicken *and* facilitate the rendering of curses.

I almost had a heart attack when Josephine reached up and grabbed the only jar of jerk seasoning on the shelves and put it in her basket.

Granted, I had reached my tongue-in-cheek conclusion through questionable deductive powers of reason, but voodoo days were powerful things.

Josephine exited the aisle and I scrambled to catch up to her without drawing any attention when none other than Cookie himself emerged from behind a huge pyramid of canned chicken broth.

"Howboutsommadatcookie?" he said with a lewd grin.

After our most recent encounter, I had slowly started to wonder if the cookie he always talked about really referred to the chocolate chip or oatmeal raisin (my favorite) variety, but I had my reservations. I decided to give him the benefit of the doubt, however, and pointed at a display of Pepperidge Farm products artfully arranged at the end of the aisle as I tried to make my getaway. "Cookies, yes," I said, "right over there. See you later."

"Nawwww . . . notdemdammcookies!" He crowed his indignation as I scuttled to catch up to Josephine.

But she was nowhere to be found. At the cash register, I saw only Nick, who lived two blocks down from me in a gorgeous Neo-Georgian mansion, so I ran back through the aisles in an attempt to locate Josephine. After five minutes I realized I had lost her.

"Youknowyouwannadatgimmedatcook-aays!" Cookie leapt out from behind a cardboard display stand of assorted nuts.

I rolled my eyes and prepared to lose him again, but then a thought struck me. "Say, do you know that woman who was just here?" I asked.

"Woman?" he repeated. *"Shegotdemcookies?"*

Although I wasn't sure I got the gist of his sentence, I said: "The woman with the gold turban and the long skirt. She had a basket on her arm."

"Josephine?" He narrowed his eyes to distrustful slits.

"Yes," I said, glad that I understood the whole utterance, "that's the one I'm talking about. You know anything about her?"

"Josephinegonnagetsommadatcook-ay?" He stood up straight and squared his shoulders.

"Well, I'm not sure what you said, but I don't know anything about Josephine's cookies," I said. "All I need to find out is if you know anything about her that doesn't involve cookies." We were in the aisle and I realized I needed a box of linguini, so I stooped down to compare prices while I waited for his answer.

"Josephinegonnagitsommadatproblems," he explained.

"Problems?"

"Shegonnadosommadatdeviltrick." He nodded his head when he saw my pasta selection.

"Did you say 'devil trick'?"

"Oh yes! Sommadatdeviltrick!"

"What do you mean by devil trick?"

"Sommadatderedeviltrick, dumbass!" His face scrunched up in a scowl. *"Devil trick! Voodoo!"*

"Really?" My tone shifted a notch toward disbelieving. "She's not really into voodoo, is she?" While I waited for his answer, it slowly dawned on me that he had called me a dumbass. I decided to let it pass.

"Datderejosephinewannagetsommadatdeviltrick!" he warned. *"Leaveoffadat.*

"Okay," I said. "What you said."

The lascivious grin returned. *"Whenyougonnagimmadatsommadatcookie?"*

I turned around and left.

Given that the day had been plagued with so many odd coincidences, when I turned in late that night I was hardly surprised that it would not be a quiet one.

Lying in the cool darkness of the bedroom, I suddenly awoke from a deep sleep. In the back of my mind, it seemed that I had heard a sonorous chime from the grandmother clock in the foyer or maybe a creak off in the distance, but I wasn't sure if that was the cause of my abrupt awakening. In the house, all was silent save for a gentle tick tock downstairs, but I had the distinct impression someone else was in the house. I listened for a moment and tried to figure out what was causing my sense of unease and then I realized that the light above the landing out in the hallway had been turned on. The bright light had no doubt caused me to wake up. Cautiously, I grabbed the baseball bat at the side of the bed and tiptoed through the door. I crept down the stairs and came to a stop in front of the grandmother clock in the foyer. The soft ticking subsided and even though the chain weights hadn't reached the halfway point, the pendulum came to a halt right before my eyes. The silver face of the clock read 3:30.

After pulling up the weights and setting the pendulum back in motion, I made the rounds of the house and ascertained that nobody had entered uninvited. Ramon had most likely risen in the middle of the night to go to the bathroom and had forgotten to turn the light off, I told myself. Nonetheless, I had developed a routine when I searched the house, and it always concluded with a look out over the front and back yards. I pulled open the front door and stood on the porch; no sign of anything unusual there. Then, I walked to the back of the house, opened the door and went outside. After a quick survey of the yard, I readied myself to return to the house, but something caught my eye. Through the wooden slats of the back fence, I noticed the gleam of a light that seemed out of place.

I studied it for several seconds and came to the realization that the light was coming from the interior of my car. The dome light. Somehow, I must have turned it on when I parked earlier in the evening, and now it threatened to drain the battery. I returned to the kitchen and grabbed my keys before leaving the security of the back porch for the carport on the other side of the fence.

The backyard consisted of a large aboveground swimming pool with a raised deck that enclosed half of it, and this wooden deck led from the back steps to the parking area at the rear of the house. As I approached the parked car, it became visible from my vantage point on the raised deck several feet above ground level, and I saw that the dome light had indeed come on. But not because I had left it on; the door on the driver's side was wide open, and a form in a camouflage army jacket leaned over the steering wheel, his hands furiously at work on the steering column. Behind the car, in the middle of the alley, a second man was standing lookout. When he saw me, he turned and hightailed it down the alley. When his partner in crime realized he was being watched, he reached down at his side, withdrew something and pointed it at me. It was a gun.

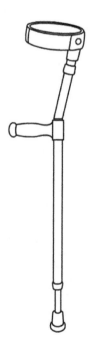

I immediately fell to the ground, shocked. I had never caught anyone in the act of hotwiring my car nor had anybody ever pointed a gun at me before. I rolled off to the side, found a knothole in the fence, and peered through it. I assumed the crook would race down the alleyway as fast as his friend had, however, he appeared to be in no hurry. Slowly, the man exited the car and quietly shut the door behind him. Then he grabbed something he had propped against the side of the car and started to walk nonchalantly down the alley.

He had a pronounced limp and walked with the assistance of a forearm crutch, the kind of crutch where the user slips an arm into a cuff and holds a grip for support.

"The gimp!" I said under my breath, quickly reprimanding myself for the lack of political correctness.

Muttering, I dragged myself to my feet. I debated running inside to wake Ramon but decided to yell for him instead. I didn't want to let the perpetrator get away after all. "Ramon! Ramon! Someone's trying to steal the car!" From somewhere deep inside I could hear Fritz franticly barking. At least he had heard me. I shouted several more times, but Ramon's window remained dark—a testament to his ability to snore through anything. Up on the third floor, there was no light or movement from Victor's room either. I'd be dead by the time they finally woke up.

Remembering the cell phone I had grabbed when I left the security of my bed a half hour before, I punched in the number for the police and exited the back gate so I could trail the would-be car thief. He had left the gun on top of the car when he grabbed the crutch, so I felt relatively safe following him. When the dispatcher answered and asked what the matter was, I told her two men had just tried to steal my car. After giving my address, I told her that one of them—a youth in his 20s with black jeans and a red basketball jersey and matching cap—was headed south on Fourth Street at that very moment. The police would no doubt see him when they rushed over from the substation in the middle of Central Park, about two blocks away. The other, I said, an older male, was still in the alley behind my house, headed for Ormsby Avenue.

"What's that one look like?" she asked.

"Well,"—I caught up to him and took a better look—"he looks to be in his 50s, white, gray beard and gray hair. He's wearing dirty blue jeans and kind of an army camouflage jacket that's zipped up all the way. He also has a black knit cap on and beat-up, brown boots with the laces untied."

"Ooie!" she said. "You got a good look at that one, didn't you?"

"Well, yeah," I said. "I'm right here walking next to him."

"What do you mean? He's still there?" I heard what I imagined to be heavily manicured nails clacking out a description on the keyboard.

"Yes, right here beside me," I said. Stoically, the man with the limp slowly made his way down the alley, pretending that I wasn't there.

"What? He not big into getaways? Only want to wait around and get caught?"

"Well, he can't really run away." I turned away from the man and lowered my voice a decibel. "He sort of has a bad limp and can't walk very fast."

"What?" said the voice at the other end of the line. "Is he crippled?"

"Yes," I said, "although I don't think the Americans with Disabilities would approve of your choice of vocabulary. He uses one of those Canadian crutches."

"Canadian crutch? What's that?" asked the dispatcher, her nails hammering out a set of instructions.

"You know, one of those crooked crutches they put their arm through and lean on. It's got a handle halfway down for them to grab and hang on to. His is red." I looked over and watched the man gingerly maneuver his way along a patch of rough cobblestones.

"Oh," she said. "One of them! Yep, he's a gimp all right."

I watched the end of the alley up ahead, thoroughly anticipating the wail of sirens and screeching wheels at any second. In the five minutes since discovery, the man had progressed about a hundred feet, and according to my calculations, it would take another five minutes before he reached the street ahead.

From the other end, the dispatcher barked out a series of commands. "Wait right there! Don't move. Stay by your car so the police know where to go."

"But what if this guy gets away?"

"Stay by your car," insisted the dispatcher. "He's not going anywhere."

"Well, he's trying awfully hard," I said. At my side, the car thief had picked up his pace, no doubt spurred on by the confirmation that the police were on their way. "And there are all kinds of places he could hide around here. All he needs to do is sneak between the buildings and they'll never find him."

"Stay by your car!" repeated the voice from the other end.

I hung up. Reluctantly, I ran back to my car and stood out in the middle of the alley to better keep an eye on the failed car thief. Valiantly, he was trying his hardest to escape; in another two or three minutes he would reach the end of the alley.

I paced back and forth and looked at the time on the cell phone. More than five minutes had passed since I dialed the police, and there was still no sign of screeching tires or wailing sirens. In the house, Fritz was still barking but there was no sign of movement or lights going on anywhere. Under the yellow glare of a street lamp at the end of the alley, I could see the car thief stop and contemplate his options. He was looking for a place to hide, and instead of limping all the way down to Ormsby Avenue, he turned left into a parking lot behind a large mansion that had been converted into offices. Within a couple of minutes, he had disappeared into the shadows.

Impatiently, I continued to pace in the alleyway until I could take it no longer. Another five minutes had passed and the police were nowhere in sight, so I sauntered down the alley to the spot where the crook had last stood. Off to the left, a row of imposing mansions with narrow strips of yard between them provided ample opportunity for cover. I was certain that the darkness had swallowed him and turned to return to my car when a voice from somewhere overhead got my attention.

"Pssst. He's over there." A man's voice came from a darkened third-floor window in the apartment building across the alley. Although I couldn't see anybody, I could sense the figure as it stood there and pointed. "Over there, behind that wall," the disembodied voice said. "He's crouched down. I woke up when I heard you screaming before and I've been watching him ever since."

"Thanks," I said. Over, beyond a low brick wall that connected two of the old mansions, a shadow shifted and revealed the hiding spot. "Sorry for waking you up."

"No prob," the voice whispered. "Lots of freaks here in Old Louisville."

At that moment, a line of four squad cars came barreling into the alley and out popped a total of eight officers.

After a quick run down, half of them went to inspect the car, while the others remained at the mouth of the alley with me. A tall officer with chestnut hair wrote down the particulars as I told him what had happened and when I pointed to where the crook had gone to hide, another went over and peered over the low brick wall. Then, almost comically, he reached down and pulled the reluctant man up to a standing position by the back of his collar. Holding the crutch, he helped the man over the fence and guided him over to an officer with a note pad.

While two officers questioned the man, the other two walked over to the car with me and we joined the others.

"Is this yours?" asked one of them, a short woman with a buzz cut, holding a gun out to me. It was the gun the man had left on top of the car when he fled.

"Uh, no, that would be his," I said, motioning with my head at the suspect.

"Not real, anyway," said the woman with the buzz cut. She pulled the trigger and out sputtered a flaccid stream of water. "Squirt gun."

"Well, that's nice to know." Sheepishly, I kicked the toe of my shoe along a patch of gravel in the cobblestone before looking the other way.

"This yours?" A heavy-set man with a buzz cut slid out of the driver's side of my car and held up a long, thin strip of metal for my inspection. The bottom portion had several notches and indentations in it.

"Uh, no, I assume that would be his as well." I motioned again with my head at the suspect. "I'm not an expert, but that appears to be a slim jim, right?"

"Maybe, maybe not," said the male buzz cut. "You sure you didn't forget to lock your car?"

"What's that got to do with it?" I said, my ire rising. "Even if I hadn't locked my car, which I'm not saying I did, that doesn't mean the general criminal public is invited to steal my car, does it?"

"Maybe, maybe not," said the male buzz cut again.

I pointed to the metallic device he held in his hand. "I think most rational people could safely assume that the thing you have in your hand right now is a slim jim and that the man over there"—I pointed—"used it to get inside my car."

"Hmmmm," said Mr. Buzz Cut.

I rolled my eyes. "Well, it's not mine."

At that point, the officer who had been questioning the car thief joined the others and they conferred for several minutes in a huddle. The one who had done the questioning broke away from the group and walked over to me. "So, what do you want us to do now?" He tucked the note pad away in his back pocket.

"What do you mean?"

"Well, what are we supposed to do now that we're here?"

"Well, why don't you tell me?" I said. "You're the police, aren't you? What do the police usually do when they find someone breaking into cars?"

"Depends," said the officer.

I bit my tongue and tried to tone down the sarcasm mounting in my voice. "You *arrest* people like this, don't you? And then you take them away, right?"

"No can do," he said.

"Why not? You're supposed to lock up the bad guys."

"No can do," he said. "We're not set up to take gimps downtown."

"What?" I was certain I had heard wrong. "Are you saying you're not going to arrest him because he has a limp?" And what was up with everyone using that word all of a sudden?

"Affirmative." He walked over to the car and laid the squirt gun and the slim jim on the hood. "We don't have the facilities to house those with disabilities."

"Good grief! So, what happens if he kills someone? He still get off because of the limp?"

"Depends," said the male buzz cut. Behind him, two officers, cheered on by the onlookers, had gathered around a portable video game and furiously worked the controls. The man who had tried to hotwire my car huddled in as well.

It was becoming painfully obvious that the conversation was going nowhere. I reluctantly made ready to go back to the house when a thought hit me, a memory from a lecture during my one year at law school that had somehow been triggered. I turned and stopped Mr. Buzz Cut before he joined the crowd around the video game. "Hey," I said. "Even if you're not going to take him downtown, I can still press charges, can't I?"

He stopped and turned around slowly, a clear lack of enthusiasm evident in the sour look gave me. "Yeah, I suppose."

"Good," I said. "That's what I'll do then."

"So what am I supposed to do now?" he asked.

"Well, not being the official from law enforcement here," I said, "I'm not sure, but I was hoping to get the man's information?"

"All right." The officer rolled his eyes a bit and looked to the side, but he gave no indication of getting the information and handing it over. This was worse than pulling teeth.

After a brief and awkward silence, I finally broke down. "Okay, would you *please* get his contact information and give it to me?"

"Yeah, sure thing." With a complete absence of gusto, the officer reluctantly walked over to the thief—who acted very put out to have to give any more information—and returned with a sheet of note paper with the man's name and address. He was living with his brother on Fourth Street in a house right across the alley. I thanked the officer and turned to go, but a snippet of conversation he exchanged with the others caused me to stop and listen.

"You see that crazy old gypsy woman over under that tree by the park?" asked one of the officers who had remained silent up to that point. "That one you hauled in last week for vagrancy?"

"That woman who looked like something straight out of the movies, with the big gold hoops in her ears and all?" said the short woman with the buzz cut.

"Yeah, that one. Drove by that tree near the corner of the park on the way over here and there she was, sitting under that tree like she owned the thing."

"Wait a minute," I said, approaching the throng. "Are you talking about that tree at the corner of Park and Sixth? The one they call the Witches' Tree?"

"I haven't ever heard it called that before," answered Mrs. Buzz Cut, "but that sounds like the tree. It's all gnarled and has these weird, jagged branches."

"Might as well call it the Witches' Tree, though," said the officer with the sandy brown hair. "There always seems to be a bunch of old hags hanging around there."

I turned around and approached the cluster of police people. "Say, have you ever heard of this woman they call the Stick Witch?" I asked, happy to have finally found some use for the local police. "She supposedly pushes this old cart around and collects branches and twigs from around the neighborhood, and they say she's been seen over by that tree a lot."

"Stick Witch?" The man with the buzz cut frowned as he said it. "Doesn't

119

sound like anyone I've seen around here."

"Well, what about Josephine?" I said. "She's this voodoo woman who wears a big, flouncy skirt and a turban. She lives over there in that same area, I think."

"*Voodoo* woman?" One of the policemen who hadn't said anything before looked at me askance. "You mean like zombies and killing chickens?"

"Yes, I guess." I opened the trunk of the car and threw in the slim jim and the squirt gun. Who knew? They might come in handy. Silence had fallen over the group and I realized most of them were studying me with crooked grins.

"You're telling us you see witches and voodoo ladies?" asked the female officer who didn't have a buzz cut. Her mouth twisted in a smirk as she tried to keep from laughing.

"You're the ones talking about seeing gypsies sitting under trees, not me!"

"Yeah, but she's not a real gypsy," said the officer with the brown hair. "At least, I don't think she is."

"She's a scam artist," said one of the others.

"Who knows?" I said. "Maybe she is, maybe she isn't." I looked down one end of the alley, where the slick glow of a street light lay reflected in the cobblestone, and then looked down toward the other end. That's when I realized the man with the limp had snuck off and was probably tucked away in bed already.

At that point, one of the walkie-talkie things strapped to Mr. Buzz Cut's shoulder squawked something unintelligible to my ears and before I knew it, they had all piled into their cars and squealed out of the alley, lights flashing.

Somewhere in the distance, an owl hooted, and I looked up at the starry sky and took a deep breath.

"What are you doing out there?" Ramon had come to stand on the back steps and was looking at me. "It's four o'clock in the morning."

"Thanks for the news flash," I said, closing the gate softly behind me. "What finally woke you?"

"Fritz kept barking. I guess he heard you out here. What were you doing?" He balled a fist and rubbed sleep from his eyes.

Fritz, who had bounded down from the porch when he saw me, looked up and panted his concern while furiously wagging his tail. "I was preventing people from stealing the car," I said. "It's a good thing one of us is a light sleeper."

"Did they break out a window or something?" He positioned himself to get a better view of the car parked out back. Fritz fell on his back and accepted my thanks for his loyalty—in the form of several vigorous belly scratches—before jumping to his feet and running into the herb garden.

"No, they used something to jimmy the lock." I watched as Fritz sniffed around the base of a large lovage plant.

"Who is this Jimmy and why he try to steal your socks?" It was Victor, standing at the back door with a confused look on his face.

"Never mind. Go back to bed. Someone was trying to steal the car, not my socks."

"But somebody come into the room and wake me up and tell to come downstairs," said Victor. "So I come down."

"I guess that was Ramon then." I stopped and looked at Ramon for confirmation, but he shook his head and said he hadn't gone up to the third floor. "You probably heard me yelling down here," I said. Victor looked like he wanted to say something in protest, but I mounted the steps to go back into the house. I stopped short of entering the house, however, when I heard Fritz's low growl from the side garden. It was a growl he used when he found something he didn't like.

"What's he got now?" Ramon asked. "Hopefully, it's not another possum."

"Ooh!" said Victor. "One of the mean kitties with the long and pointy noses and the sharp and pointy teethes?"

"Fritz! Come here, boy." I walked over to the area between our house and the next and called out again, but Fritz refused to come. Instead, another long growl issued from the darkness.

"Fritz, where are you? Come here!" Ramon followed behind as we felt our way in the darkness. Several steps later we found a thick shaft of light that sliced its way through the opened gate in the short expanse of fence that joined the front of the two buildings. Nearby, in the shadows, we saw Fritz, his teeth bared at a form leaning up against the wall.

"Hey, who let this dog in the bathroom?" asked an indignant voice. We both jumped back and Fritz lunged forward and grabbed the speaker's pant leg. Once our eyes adjusted to the semi-darkness, we were able to see it was a young man, in his twenties, and he was using the side of our house for a urinal. The bars had just closed, and I quickly surmised he must have gotten lost on his way home.

"Does this look like a bathroom, dumbass?" said Ramon, reaching down to detach Fritz from the man's pant leg. Fritz managed to get in a good nip before he was carried to the back porch.

"Hey," said the guy leaning against the wall. "Someone get that dog out of the bar before he bites me again."

"Is this the Jimmy who try to steal your socks? Or is she the person who walk into my room and wake me up?" Victor walked up behind me and studied the form standing there. "Why he like to pee on your house?"

"He thinks he's still in the bar," I whispered out of the side of my mouth. Then I raised my voice and spoke to the intruder. "You're not in the bar anymore, kid."

As if he hadn't considered the notion before, the young man looked around and observed his surroundings for the first time. "Hey, who turned out the lights in this here bathroom?"

I rolled my eyes. "That's the point we're trying to make," I said flatly. "You're not in a bathroom."

"I'm not?" He zipped himself up and took another look around. Then, he narrowed his eyes suspiciously before speaking. "Isn't this the bar?"

"Dumbass," said Ramon, looking down from the back porch. Shaking his head, he yanked open the kitchen door and went inside. Fritz growled his agreement.

"Ah, no. This is not the bar. This is our yard and you're peeing on our house." I walked to the gate he had left open and motioned that he should follow. He stumbled forward and scratched his head as I extended my arm. "This is Third Street," I said, pointing at the expanse of concrete out front. "That's where you want to go, I assume. And try not to pee on any of my neighbor's houses, please."

"Okay, man, thanks." He swayed several times, but he eventually made it to the sidewalk, where he struck up a conversation with an invisible friend. "Dude," he said, "I was just in the bathroom and this dog comes outa nowhere and bites me on the leg!" He reached down and pulled up his pant leg. "Look! It even left a mark." The conversation continued until he stumbled out of sight.

I secured the latch on the gate and returned to the kitchen. But instead of going up to bed, like Victor and Ramon had, I put on my tennis shoes and grabbed a light jacket. Then I called for Fritz and hooked him to his leash. If there was a gypsy sitting under the Witches' Tree, I wanted to see for myself.

Neptuna Petulengro

Fritz looked back at me as he tugged on the lead, happy to have scored such an early morning walk, and all by himself no less. Rocky and Bess were soundly asleep, and I left them curled up on the bed, so it was only Fritz and me out on the streets of Old Louisville at what was probably the quietest time of the night. At the end of the alley, we turned right onto Ormsby Avenue, crossed to the sidewalk and headed west, past a squat crepe myrtle tree mounding with panicles of purple flowers.

As we neared the intersection with Fourth, the Puritan, a large apartment-hotel built in the 1910s loomed on the right. Half a block down, we passed on the left an enormous orange brick mansion from the 1880s that had been home to J. T. S. Brown, the bourbon baron whose whiskey, Old Forester Bourbon, still enjoyed cult status as the bourbon of Louisville over 130 years later. Across from that stood the Mayflower, another snazzy apartment-hotel, built around 1919 and a hotspot of activity at a time when gangsters and bootleggers roamed the city. Across the corner from that was the J. B. Speed house, a rambling mansion from the 1880s. An artful collection of red brick gables and green trim, it cast a long shadow from the bright lights of the adjacent parking lot out across the street in front of us. At the corner with Sixth, we took a left, went down the street and passed a wrought iron gate at the entrance to Floral Terrace, one of the neighborhood's most hidden walking courts. Beyond that was the Witches' Tree.

As we approached the corner, the spooky, gnarled old tree emerged from the shadows behind a row of hedges. When we reached the street, we veered right and followed the sidewalk that led to Seventh Street. An hour must have passed since the policeman had seen the gypsy under the tree, so I assumed that she would have been long gone; nonetheless, I hadn't given up hope. As we rounded the corner, the spooky tree never left my sight, and I was startled to see an attractive young woman with long dark hair and large hoop earrings sitting under its twisted, knotted branches. I fought the urge to stop and stare, and kept on walking instead.

We went halfway down the block, and I made myself turn around and skirt the corner a second time. Again, I saw the female with a dark complexion and a long skirt under the tree, apparently unaware of any passersby. Out of the corner of my eye, I saw that she wore a white blouse with poofy peasant sleeves and delicate embroidery in pink and yellow thread around her neck. Her eyes, heavily outlined with mascara, were closed.

I let Fritz drag me halfway down the block, but at the entrance to Floral Terrace I made him stop and we turned around for another pass of the Witches' Tree. This time, however, we entered the gate into Floral Terrace and took an alternative route to get to the Witches' Tree. We walked down the court, where an alley led back to Park, but before we headed back that way, we stopped at the fountain in the center.

Amidst the tidy brick gambrels and American foursquare houses, water splashed in a small pool. According to neighborhood lore, another infamous tree had stood here for many years until residents felled it and replaced it with the fountain. This tree, however, was a tall cottonwood that reportedly had been used for lynchings and locals referred to the ghost that still haunted the site as the "man from the hanging tree." I had done some research on the subject, and although I was never able to substantiate that lynchings ever took place there, I was able to prove that a number of suicides had occurred at that location. The most famous took place in 1901 when a man by the name of Sam Turner decided to end his life. Under cover of darkness, he climbed the tall cottonwood, rope in hand, and sought the highest and sturdiest branch he could find. He shinned out to the end and tied one end around the branch and the other end around his neck. Then he jumped.

The next morning an early riser spotted his body swinging 40 feet up in the air, and a crowd of more than 500 turned out to watch as his corpse was lowered and taken away to the morgue. A chill ran down my spine as I realized that I was standing in the very same location as the crowd that turned out to watch Turner's body being cut down and carried away, so I tugged at Fritz's lead and we made our way back to the Witches' Tree. As we rounded the corner for the third time, I saw that the woman's eyes were open and that she anticipated my arrival.

"What do you want?" Tiredness edged her voice, which was not entirely unpleasant. "I'm not a hooker, if that's what you're thinking."

"Oh, no," I stammered, fighting the blush that heated my cheeks. "I didn't think that at all. Sorry. I was out walking my dog."

"Awfully early to be out walking your dog, isn't it?" She rolled her shoulders and reached a hand up to massage the back of her neck.

"I like walking around the neighborhood in the wee hours when there's nobody else around," I said. "I like to imagine what it was like back in the day."

"Hmm." She ran her fingers through her hair and stifled a yawn.

"Awfully late to be out sitting under a tree, isn't it?" I reached down and patted Fritz on the head. He stood with his front paws on the curb, his nose eagerly sniffing something new in the air.

"Not really," she said. "I guess you could say I'm a night person as well." With a hand heavy with gold and silver rings on its fingers, she motioned to a spot on the ground next to her. "Have a seat. Lots of room under my tree."

"Thanks." I walked a few steps up the rise and sat down on a patch of bare, dry earth between two exposed roots. It was the exact same spot where I had been sitting the previous night when I discovered Josephine on one of the balconies. Fritz, tail wagging, sniffed the woman's extended hand and sat between us. "By the way, my name's David," I said.

She smiled. "My name is Neptuna."

"Neat name," I said, rubbing Fritz behind the ears. Overhead in the branches of the Witches' Tree, something screeched and hopped from branch to branch.

"I was named after my father, Neptune. Neptune Petulengro." She leaned back against the mangled bark of the trunk and looked up into the jagged limbs.

"Petulengro? Very exotic. Is it Romanian?"

"It could be," she said, stifling another yawn, "but I'm not sure. It's the gypsy equivalent for Smith. My people used to make horseshoes."

"You're not really a gypsy, are you?"

"Damn straight." She brushed away a dead leaf that had fallen in her lap. "Born and bred."

"You know, I heard there were gypsies around here, but I didn't really believe it." I turned my head as a squirrel scampered out to the end of a branch and peered down at us. "You don't really think of gypsies in Kentucky."

"Oh, we're all over the place, trust me. We get around."

"You don't say." I was intrigued. "So, do you live here or what?"

"Not really," she said. "We pass through a couple times a year, though. And I make sure I come and visit my tree whenever we're in town."

"You know they call this the Witches' Tree, don't you?" I reached out and steadied Fritz, who had stood to growl at the squirrel above.

"Yeah, I've heard lots of stories about this tree. That's one of the reasons I like it so much." She scratched Fritz behind the ears and eased him back into a sitting position.

"Say, do you know Josephine?" I asked.

"Nope," she said, "who's that?"

"Some voodoo lady that lives in this building." I pointed to the balcony.

"Voodoo lady? They got voodoo in Louisville?"

"Supposedly." I shifted my position to make myself more comfortable. "I don't know for a fact, but she sure looks the part, in any case."

"How's that?" She closed her eyes and rested her head against the trunk of the tree.

"She's always wearing this turban and has a long, billowy skirt on." From my position, I watched as two shadows skulked along a pathway in the park.

"Sort of like this one?" she asked, her hand fluffing out the hem of her skirt.

"Yeah, sort of."

"Well, you have to be careful," she said. "Looks can be deceiving."

"Yeah, I know. Never judge a book by its cover." I picked up an interesting stone lying at my feet and turned it over for inspection. It was light green, almost jade-like, and flecked with bits of brown.

"What about me?" she asked with a wry smile. "Do I look like a gypsy to you?"

"Well, actually,"—I hesitated, worried that I might offend—"you do, to a certain extent."

"Good." She chuckled. "Because I try to look like a gypsy."

"Why's that?" I brushed a bit of dirt from the stone and rubbed its smooth surface between my thumb and forefinger.

"Well, most of us Roma dress like ordinary people nowadays, so you'd never know. I like to stand out, though, so I wear the long skirt and the hoop earrings." She reached up with a finger and flicked one of the golden hoops.

"The earrings do the trick." Off in the distance, the squeaky rattle of a shopping cart rumbled over the concrete of a walkway in the park. I conjured up an image of the Stick Witch out and about in search of twigs and branches.

Neptuna rose gracefully and brushed off her knees. "Well, I guess I should be moving on," she said. "Or else the cops might stop and make trouble for me again. We're leaving town in a few hours anyway."

"Well, it was nice talking to you." I got to my feet and waited while Fritz trotted over and said good-bye to her. "Maybe I'll see you the next time you're around."

"You'll know where to find me when I am in town."

"So, where are you headed to now?" I tugged Fritz away from her and stepped down to the sidewalk.

"Down to New Orleans," she said. "Louisville's half way there. North to south, south to north. That's how it's always been."

"That's how it's *always* been?" I repeated. "How long have you been doing this?"

"Oh, as long as I can remember." She joined me on the sidewalk and shook several blades of dried grass from her skirt. "And my grandparents and their parents used to do the same thing." She looked across to the park, reached out her arms and then yawned. "We've been around for a while. Go read up on it and you'll see. Take care." She flashed a grin at me and then turned and walked down the sidewalk. With her skirt swaying, she passed under the glare of a streetlight and disappeared into the darkness on the other side.

I stood there for a minute and listened to the sounds of the neighborhood. Then I turned to go, but found myself face to face with a huge beast covered in black hair.

Big Voodoo Day

I passed a plate of poached salmon with saffron potato salad to Laura and then served another for Beth. The weather was nice, so the Tuesday Night Dinner Club was eating outside on the back deck.

"You're kidding me!" said Beth. She took the plate and placed it in front of her. After pouring a bit of white wine, she passed a plate to Skippy. "It was a guy in a gorilla suit?"

"At five o'clock in the morning?" Wendy had finished her glass of wine and poured another. David McHugh and Ramon were sitting next to the pool, their bare feet soaking in the cool water. Rocky, Bess and Fritz sat at my feet and looked longingly up at the table.

"Yes," I said, "but it wasn't really a gorilla suit, it was Sasquatch." I grabbed a yeast roll, broke it open and smeared it with soft butter. "Remember that movie, *Harry and the Hendersons?*" I asked. "About the family who takes Bigfoot home to live with them?"

"Oh, the one with John Lithgow?" said Laura.

"Yes, that one," I said. "The guy I ran into was dressed up as that thing, goofy grin and all."

"What was he doing out so late in a monkey suit?" Beth picked up Bess and sat her on her lap.

"It was some frat guy from the University of Louisville." I laughed and shook my head. "He said they had been having a costume party and he wanted to swing by and scare his girlfriend because she wouldn't go with him. She lives in the apartment by the Witches' Tree."

"Did you ask if he knew Josephine?" Skippy unrolled a checkered napkin and put it in his lap.

I helped myself to asparagus salad. "It's a good thing he was wearing a heavy costume, though, because Fritz bit him in the leg. I had to pry him off."

"Good boy!" Wendy reached down and scratched the dog's head. Then, when she thought I wasn't looking, she snuck him half a yeast roll.

"See what happens when you wander the streets of Old Louisville in the middle of the night?" said Ramon from the side of the pool.

"Ah, middle of the night?" said Skippy, pushing his glasses up on his nose. "You see that stuff down here any time of the day, especially in this part of the neighborhood."

"Yes," I said, "you've got a point there." I took a drink of wine and sat back in my chair. "By the way, did I tell you I saw a wild turkey running down the street as well? The very same night."

"I'm surprised someone over at Fourth and Crazy hasn't captured it yet and roasted it over a barrel fire for a Thanksgiving dinner," said Skippy.

Beth laughed and took a bite of roll. "You've got some funny people at that corner, but it's hardly bad enough that you find bums warming their hands over barrel fires," she said. "They make the neighborhood all the more interesting."

"Not that you need to go in search of interesting things," said Laura. "Weird stuff happens to you all the time anyway," she said, spearing a bit of food with her fork. "Like your voodoo day today."

"I guess," I said, thinking back to the day's events. "It sure was a strange one today."

I had known it was going to be a weird day as I lay in bed that morning, dreamily looking out the window. I was mentally preparing myself to get up and go to the gym when I saw something scuttle along the windowsill. I lifted my head and saw a little salamander warming itself in the early morning sun. At least I thought it was a salamander, with its large head and all. There are little lizards and such in Louisville, but you rarely see salamanders. Up to that point, I had only heard about them, though. I certainly had never seen one crawl up to the second floor in any case.

Just then, an owl swooped down out of nowhere, in broad daylight, snatched up the salamander and flew away. There are owls in Old Louisville, but I had never seen one up to that point, either. I thought they only came out at night. Just then the three bats fluttered by. A voodoo day had begun.

Feeling sorry for the salamander, I put on my gym clothes and jogged to the YMCA down at the corner of Second and Chestnut. After my workout I walked home down Third Street, and as I passed the Spalding University Library, I felt drawn to one of the shrubs next to the sidewalk. Don't ask me why, but I felt the need to look behind one of the bushes. What was waiting behind that particular shrub? A huge duck-kind of bird, the likes of which I had never seen before, nor have seen since. It was that ducky kind of brownish gray that most ducks in this part of the country tend to be, but it had an eerie silver sheen to it. It also had a beautiful metallic green ring around its neck. And, not only that, it had a large metallic red ring outlined in black around its left eye only. It was scarily exotic-looking and reminded me in shape of dodo birds I had seen in old textbooks at school. When it saw me, it serenely looked up and said "Wuck" in a very nonchalant manner. *Wuck?* I returned the greeting and went home.

By the time I reached the front door, I was convinced that I had accidentally discovered a previously extinct species of bird, so I grabbed my camera and decided to return to the scene to document my find. Before I grabbed Fritz and jumped in the car, I succumbed to my desire for something sweet and got one of the huge 4-pound bags of Peanut M&Ms I had given Ramon for Christmas out of the cupboard. I opened a new bag, reached in, and pulled out a handful of Peanut M&Ms, all twenty-two of which turned out to be green. I know there's a math project there somewhere, but I figure the probability of a person reaching into a brand-new bag of Peanut M&Ms and pulling out twenty-two of the same color M&M, peanut or plain, has got to be astronomically high. For a minute, I wondered if those particular M&Ms might be cursed in some way or other, but in the end, my sweet tooth won out and I ate all twenty-two of them on the way to the car.

I parked down by Spalding University and Fritz and I went to find the bird, but when I looked for it behind the same bush, it was gone. It wasn't behind any of the other bushes I checked, either, and to my recollection, Fritz and I checked behind and under every single shrub at Spalding University.

Since I was out and about, and feeling dejected for losing the bird, I grabbed a venti decaf ice latte from Starbuck's and decided to drive around a bit and go to the West End and check out the old Ouerbacker Mansion, one of my favorite spooky old homes ever, at the corner of 17th and Jefferson. I really needed to go home and start baking and cooking for the reception scheduled for the dedication of the historical marker they were erecting in front of Widmer House the next day, but I soon found myself at a stoplight on Ninth Street. With the window down on the driver's side of my black Sable, I was enjoying the warm day while Fritz perched in my lap and stuck his head outside.

But, when I turned my head to the right, I almost had a heart attack.

There, in the other lane, was a tall blond man in a black Sable with a silver schnauzer in his lap. Like me, he wore a white tank top. Oblivious to the one-in-a-million chance encounter at his side, he stared straight ahead while petting the dog. I eventually couldn't stand it any longer, so I tapped the horn and watched the guy's face as he turned and beheld the mirror image to his left. I scrunched down so he could see me through the passenger side window and spread out both my hands, palms turned up, as if to say *What are the chances of this, huh?* At first the other guy smiled, but then it looked like he got a bit creeped out. He raised his window and sped off as soon as the light changed, but not before I saw him reach down and lift the straw from a plastic Starbuck's cup to his lips. Since it was a voodoo day, I knew it had to be a latte, but I wasn't sure if it was decaf or not.

Since Beth had arrived late, I gave her a quick recap of the strange things that happened during the day. "Of course it was a decaf!" she said, laughing, as I finished the story about my doppelganger in the black car. We finished the main course and I stacked the dirty plates and carried them inside to the kitchen, where dessert was waiting. However, when I opened the back door and entered the sun-washed room, a ghastly sight met my eyes.

Squirrels

I felt a wave of nausea sweep up from my stomach and wash over my face. "Oh, no!" Undulations of dizziness pulsed down from my temples and threatened to topple me, so terrible was the scene before me. I made for the nearest chair and sat.

"What is it?" asked Ramon. He had picked up the dirty serving dishes and followed me into the kitchen.

"Oh, no." I moaned and leaned back to calm myself.

"What's wrong? You look like you're having a heart attack. Stop being such a hobo."

My extended finger pointed in the direction of the disaster, toward the beautiful tray of desserts I had come in to retrieve. But the ornately decorated cakes and pastries I had baked earlier that afternoon—some were for the reception the following day, some I had set aside for dessert for the Tuesday Night Dinner Club—were gone. My shoulders sagged and I gave my most valiant effort to remain conscious. When Ramon looked over, it was obvious he was having a hard time comprehending the scene of devastation in his field of vision. Nothing but scattered random crumbs and bits of violated strawberry lay strewn about the silver platters I had so carefully assembled earlier that day. On the floor nearest the counter lay upside-down lemon tartlets and miniature carrot cakes.

"What happened?"

Limply, I raised my hand again and pointed to the counter under the cupboard where we kept wine glasses and crystal stemware. There, in the same spot the rat had pilfered my Sugar Babies from the silver bowl, stood a fat-cheeked squirrel greedily nibbling on a chocolate petit four. It was so engrossed in its gluttony that it hadn't even noticed us come into the kitchen.

"Hey, get out of here!" Ramon quickly grabbed a rag mop and shooed the critter off the counter and started chasing it around the house. Instead of running out the open back door, the squirrel chattered its displeasure and scampered off to the dining room. "I told you not to be a hobo and leave those windows open!" Ramon looked back and gave me a dirty look.

I got up from the chair and went to grab a whiskbroom and dust pan. Underfoot, I smashed sticky crumbs and half-eaten cakes that had been scattered about. Slowly, I swept up the pieces and formed a little pile near the trashcan. I gathered up the empty trays and stacked them on the table in the middle of the kitchen. I'd be up all night baking replacements.

"Hey, what's all the fuss about?" Laura had entered and surveyed the damage. "Oh my. What happened here?" Her eyes widened as she spotted the mess on the floor. "Did you drop something?"

I shook my head. "A squirrel got in and destroyed all my sweets for the neighborhood reception tomorrow," I said, reaching out for the broom behind the door. "Looks like we won't be having dessert tonight."

"The reception for the historical marker they're putting in front of the house? That's a shame."

"Here," said Skippy, walking through the back door. He handed me a folded piece of paper and scowled at the mess on the floor. "What's all this? Please tell me that wasn't our dessert."

"It was." I swept the pile of refuse into a dustpan and emptied it in the trash.

"Did you drop something?"

"No, the squirrel did it." I put the broom away and opened the paper he had given me. "What's this?"

"I don't know. What the heck do you mean *the squirrel* did it?"

I examined the sheet of paper in my hand and saw a drawing in pencil. "The squirrel on the counter ate all the cakes I made. No dessert for the Tuesday Night Dinner Club."

"What squirrel on the counter are you talking about?" Skippy opened the refrigerator door and rummaged around for another bottle of wine.

The sounds of a scuffle ensued from the back stairs and Ramon emerged in hot pursuit, the mop cleaving the air in front of him. Chattering noisily, the rodent bounded past us and out the back door, followed by the dogs who chased it over the back fence. Ramon put the mop away behind the door and angrily shook his finger at me. "I told you not to leave open the windows on the third floor!"

I rolled my eyes and looked at Skippy. "That squirrel," I said.

"Oh."

The week before I had left the three small windows in my office open, and the results were equally disastrous. Leaving the third floor to air out, I had gone out in the back yard and started nailing up extra fencing around the deck to prevent kids from the adjacent day care center from getting into the pool. It was exceptionally hot that day and I was sweating profusely. I was about to pound in the last nail when the doorbell rang at the most inopportune moment and caused me to smash my thumb. Cursing under my breath, I took my throbbing thumb to the front door and opened it. It was Uli, a neighbor down the road who had asked me to dog sit her Westie for two weeks while she went back to visit her family in Germany, and she was dropping off Pumpkin. Ramon's sister and her husband were out of town, so we were sitting their two dogs as well. Six dogs in one house had the potential for pandemonium, the chances of which increased exponentially when an energetic bushy-tailed rodent was added to the mix.

I told Uli to have a good time, closed the door and ushered Pumpkin into the back part of the house, where canine acquaintances would be made. I was surprised that the other dogs hadn't accompanied me to the front of the house when the loud buzz sounded and as I walked into the butler's pantry, I saw why: all five of them had crowded around a small wine cooler that stood in the corner, their gazes intent on something I couldn't see, something they had been chasing, something which now sought refuge in the small space along the baseboards. I pushed my way through the herd of dogs and peered down into the void behind the wine cooler. Two beady little eyes looked up at me and the squirrel issued a shrill rebuke at me, perhaps for having enticed it through the open windows upstairs.

I turned around and beheld six sets of eyes ready for a chase. Spurred on by some act of doggy telepathy, Pumpkin had scented the squirrel and raised her front paw as her tail boinged out straight behind her. Uli obviously had forgotten to tell her she was not a pointer. With Rocky, Bess and Fritz quivering in their spots, and Melvin and Mia inching ever closer, I decided to first corral the dogs and then help the squirrel find its way out. But as I reached for the first of the pups, the squirrel emerged from its hiding spot and took a perch on the little television set atop the wine cooler. After another chattering reproach, the animal surveyed the opposition and bounded over the pack, landing at the threshold to the dining room. It scuttled across the hardwood floors, its tiny rodent nails clawing and clattering wildly, and the dogs were off and running.

Up the front stairs, down the hall to the small room at the back of the house, then back out and down the second set of stairs to the butler's pantry, the squirrel managed to stay ahead of the dogs. Then it ran through the dining room again and followed the stairs all the way to the third floor, where it bounded through the guest suite and into my office, right past the window that had afforded it egress. It scrambled up the curtains and took up a position on top of my bookcase and then leaped through the air and landed in the bowl of the large stained-glass light fixture suspended from the middle of the ceiling, where it swirled around several times before nails clicked up the sides and an angry head popped over the rim.

As I caught up to the dogs, who had all remained silent to that point, they began barking and the squirrel hurled itself from the light shade to the landing outside my office and bounced up into the drapes on the nearest window. The curtain rod came crashing to the ground with the drapes, and the squirrel emerged from the mound of fabric, shot up, and rode the railing down to the next landing. Thanks to the mound of drapery that slowed down the dogs in the middle of the stairs, I made it to the bottom floor ahead of them and was able to lock the squirrel in the front parlor while I rounded up the dogs and secured them in a bedroom with the door tightly closed.

When I returned to the parlor and opened the doors, the squirrel was nowhere to be seen. Had it escaped through the fireplace and out the chimney? Hopeful, I approached the mantel for further inspection. The squirrel, however, was still in the room and had sought refuge under a slight wrinkle in the Persian rug, a fact I discovered while walking to the fireplace; I inadvertently stepped on the animal's tail and sent it shooting out from under the carpet.

It then embarked upon a whirlwind course of the room, knocking over end tables and lamps in its frenzied laps along the baseboard. After the third circuit, it clawed its way up into the drapes at the front window and scurried along the curtain rod before it dislodged and fell to the floor. The squirrel jumped to the top edge of the mantelpiece and scurried along, knocking off a large framed picture, which then landed on top of my favorite American Belleek vase and smashed it.

Finally, I flung open the parlor doors and let the squirrel have free reign of the house. An hour later—and after several downed curtain rods, three broken lamps, two smashed pictures and sundry pieces of bric-a-brac in varying degrees of disrepair—it finally found its way out the back door and scampered across the back yard. The next time I left the windows open on the third floor, I did so with the confidence that the chances of something that crazy happening again were next to zero.

Remembering the piece of paper Skippy had given me. I looked down and saw a rough pencil sketch of a gypsy woman scrying a crystal ball. Somehow, the rendering looked vaguely familiar. Where had I seen it before? Underneath the drawing, something was written.

"So, what's this all about?" I asked.

"I don't know." He opened the door and headed outside with the wine.

I rummaged around in the refrigerator and put together a plate with cheese and fresh fruit. Then I followed him out and sat at the table while the others jumped into the pool. "You're the one who gave it to me, so why don't you know what this is?"

"I don't know what it is. It was folded into a paper airplane and came sailing over the fence."

"Did you see who threw it?" I sat up straight and tried to see over the fence into the next lot.

"Nope," he said. "I heard someone say I was supposed to give it to you and then they scampered away."

"Me? I wonder if it was Lewis or Frederick. They always seem to be hanging around, looking for some extra work."

"I don't think so," said Skippy. "Those two know your name, but this person said 'Give it to the tall blond guy' like they didn't know your name. From the voice I couldn't tell if it was a man or a woman."

I turned the piece of paper over in my hand. I smoothed the creased paper out on the table and studied it again. "That's weird." Studying the figure drawn there, I immediately thought about the woman named Neptuna and wondered if she had delivered the undecipherable message. Quickly I ruled out that possibility since she couldn't have known where I lived, not to mention I had told her my name. Not only that, she had said they were leaving town earlier that morning.

"It was probably another random oddball in Old Louisville," said Wendy.

"Or maybe it was Josephine," said Beth.

I couldn't rule out either of those options, so I shrugged my shoulders and poured another glass of wine. "First it's a voodoo woman. Then I find out there were witches here. Now it's gypsies. What's next? Werewolves and vampires?"

"Is that what's in the drawing there? A werewolf or a vampire?" Skippy pointed at the paper I had smoothed out on the table and twisted his neck to get a better view.

"No, that's the thing," I said. "It's a picture of a gypsy, I think." I pointed to the script under the picture. "And there's something written here in some kind of foreign language. I can't make it out, though." I studied the writing and squinted. "Well, I'll snoop around and see what I find, but it's not like anything I've seen before." I grabbed another large strawberry and bit into it. "I wanted to go to the library tomorrow anyway and see what I can dig up about gypsies in this area. Maybe I'll uncover something interesting."

The sun slowly disappeared behind the canopy of a large tree and darkness soon enveloped the backyard. Across the pool, I watched as two shadowy forms scampered along the top of the fence. Eying me suspiciously, they jumped up into the nearest tree, found a low-hanging utility wire and then tight-roped their way over the table and onto the back roof of the house. Without looking back, they chittered their excitement to each other and bounded over the steep peaks of La Casa Fabulosa.

Jack and the Gypsy Wedding

After very little sleep, I got up the next morning around six and took the dogs for a walk. Several loud booms had woken me up in the middle of the night, but instead of getting up to inspect, I lay in bed and worried about the things I had to do to get ready for the day. Although groggy, I was happy that I managed to recreate all the items the squirrel had violated. Fortunately, all the canapés and savories had been safely stashed in the refrigerator, so I only had to worry about baking a new batch of cakes and tarts. As we strolled the quiet neighborhood, I mentally went over the preparations still needed to get the house in shape for the dedication ceremony and reception later that day.

Patches of fog clung to the dewy grass in Central Park as we crossed into St. James Court and passed the fountain splashing at its center. On the green, a net had been set up and two couples were playing an early morning round of badminton. It was only after strolling by them I recalled that they were all dressed in white—and in what appeared to be casual wear from the early 1900s. The guys wore pleated trousers and sweater vests, and the women had on long skirts, blouses, and beribboned hats. Why were people up so early playing badminton? I thought to myself. And why were they dressed like that? I shook my head and let the dogs lead me on.

At the Pink Palace, we turned left and followed one of the walkways through Belgravia Court, which glowed softly in the early morning flicker of the gas lamps. On Fourth Street, I tied the dogs up outside the Old Louisville Coffee House and went inside for a latte. When I came outside, I found an elderly gentleman stooping down to pet the dogs. He said his name was Jack and we soon got to talking about the neighborhood; as it turned out, as a young man he had lived in one of the houses I had been researching on Sixth Street and he proved to be a wealth of information.

"Those were the days, back when I was a kid in the 20s and 30s." A faraway look settled in his bright eyes. "The neighborhood was still hoppin' then, that's for sure."

"I heard there were gangsters and everything back in the day," I said.

"There certainly was. Capone used to come to town to meet with his bootleg associates, and a number of these big old places were converted into speakeasies." He raised a hand and pointed a finger toward a large mansion down the street.

"You know," I said, "I heard there were gypsies and voodoo queens and witches back then. You remember anything about them?"

"We did hear stories about witches and the voodoo doctors, but I didn't have any firsthand experience with them," he said. "There were lots of wealthy merchants moved up from New Orleans who used to live down by the river in big mansions on Frenchman's Row in the Point, so it'd hardly be surprising that voodoo made its way up here now, would it?" He scratched his head slowly and looked off into the distance at something unseen.

"What about gypsies?"

"Now gypsies, those I recall seeing." His eyes squinted and his head moved up and down. "When I was a young kid, you'd see them passing through town on occasion, looking for tinkering work or reading fortunes and things like that. They used to drive those big covered wagons like you see in the movies."

"That must have been a sight."

"Oh, yes, it was." A slight frown creased his face. "But you know, people didn't trust gypsies back then—or now, for that matter—because they thought they were all pickpockets and thieves. They dressed exactly like you saw in the movies, too. The women had long dark skirts, and the men wore those embroidered vests, and leather boots up to the knee sometimes."

A squirrel skittered along a branch overhead and the dogs tersed their leads. I wondered if it was a relative of the one that had raided the house the day before.

"You used to see their encampments down along the river at the Point when they were passing through town. There'd be big bonfires and celebrations with lots of dancing and music."

"No kidding?" I pulled the dogs closer to me and made ready to leave. "That's fascinating. It's amazing, how much of the past has been forgotten."

"Right you are!" He patted the dogs and as he turned to go, he gave me one last piece of advice: "Watch out for those voodoo queens!"

Smiling to myself, I let the dogs tug me along and followed them home. Once they were fed and watered, I grabbed my things and headed to the library. I was determined to learn about gypsies in Kentucky. This time I hoped to finally get some research done.

Given that the main branch of the Louisville Free Public Library has been known to attract its fair share of weirdoes, I should not have been surprised when Cookie jumped out at me from behind the microfiche files as I headed to the clippings collection.

"Gimmedatsommadatcookie?" He gave me a big grin and a wink.

"Hello," I said. "Still not sure what you're saying, but there aren't any cookies at the library."

"Notgonnasommadatgimmedatsommadatcookies?" An indignant look turned his grin upside down.

I tried to push past him, but he wouldn't budge, so I backed up and pointed to the cookbook section. "Why don't check out a book on baking? Then you can make your own cookies."

"Donwandemcookies!" he said. *"Wandemcookies!"*

"Gotta run!" I faked a movement to the left and dodged around to the right. At the end of the stack, I picked up my pace and retreated to the relative safety of the audio book section. Keeping watch from a distance, I returned to the newspaper clippings when the coast was clear.

The newspaper clippings section of the library consisted of an entire row of stacks with hundreds of old green cardboard box files full of newspaper articles that had been cut and pasted onto sheets of construction paper, and, from the looks of it, was a project undertaken in the 1940s or thereabouts. Files from Kentucky and Louisville that cover a wide variety of topics line the shelves, and I still tend to go there as a first line of defense when starting a local research project. That day I slowly worked my way through the titles on the yellowed labels along the spine of each box, and sure enough, after several minutes, I located one with "gypsies" as a category. I pulled it from the shelf and sat down at the nearest carrel.

Although there was only a single article about gypsies in the files, the one I found was extremely revealing. It ran in the *Courier-Journal* on July 10, 1938, and in the title author Oressa Teagarden described "Gypsy Headquarters Without Any Gypsies." Below the headline, a teaser read, "Never before this year did they fail to show up in Louisville, where they still have their money and lawyers." Intrigued, I read on:

"Once the favorite camping ground for the nomads, Louisville was the scene of every Gypsy ceremonial. Conventions, weddings, births, divorces, burials, feast days brought the clans together on the Point each summer. Families huddled together in cramped winter lodgings, eking out an existence while they longed for spring and the open road again."

So, it was true: Louisville had at one time been a hub of gypsy activity in this country. The reason for this was explained thusly: "Conveniently located between the North and the South, Louisville offered ideal camping grounds, and the bands were found here annually. They remained several weeks in summer; many, on their way to the North from Mexico or the Southern States, came together for Easter ceremonies. Leaving the cold Northern climate after Thanksgiving, they were again in Louisville two or three weeks before continuing their journey to the South."

In addition, "Gypsy history was made here in years past. In its making the Gypsies became involved in court actions; the time had come when they were, for some unaccountable reason, unable to agree within their organization. Attorneys who pleaded their cases before the courts, and guardians who helped them make their customs conform in some measure to law, became their friends." However, "[a]s they gradually gave up the city as a temporary dwelling place, they at the same time retained contacts with those who had aided them. Thus Louisville remained Gypsy headquarters in legal and business affairs." Those who had aided them were Clem Huggins, an attorney and Ben Johnson, their administrator and guardian. The grounds for their giving up the city as a dwelling place was attributed to increased police "pressure," which apparently left a bad taste in the gypsies' mouths. Although the lengthy piece went on to describe local gypsy customs and appearance—as well as make a number of observations that would today be regarded as politically incorrect at best ("Detesting most necessary contacts with Gentiles, except to pick their pockets, they have clung desperately to the two men in Louisville who have been their friends...")—the gist of the article expressed a sense of wonderment that the gypsies had quit Louisville. As far as nomads were concerned, it appeared that a number of American gypsies had significant ties to Louisville.

Rummaging through microfilmed editions of the local papers from the late 1800s and early 1900s, I found various references to gypsy bands when they passed through town, but not much more than that. After getting online and doing some sleuthing, I then discovered that gypsies had actually resided in Louisville as well. Much of this came from articles that ran in papers across the country in late April 1929, in which it was reported that hundreds of gypsies were en route to Louisville for a gypsy royal wedding. In addition to those traveling to Kentucky, some 200 gypsies of the same tribe who lived in town planned on attending the festivities as well. As it turned out, the bride to be hailed from the Derby City.

The *Atlanta Constitution* reported that Rosie Stanley, 16, the daughter of William Stanley of Louisville, would marry 17-year-old Frank John, the son of Chief Gregory John of Philadelphia. "Both are members of the John tribe, and the tribe is expected to congregate en masse for the ceremonies," it said. Then: "The wedding will take place in a three-acre field near the Ohio River," and "[p]igs, turkeys and chickens were being roasted all over town for the feasts. An orchestra from Cincinnati has been engaged to play continuously for the first 24 hours of celebration."

There followed a breakdown of the festivities, with a feast starting at 4 in the afternoon and dancing from 8 "until everyone is too tired to continue." The next morning there would be dancing from 9 until 4 in the afternoon, at which time another feast would take place. At this feast, Prince John, with much ceremony would pay Stanley an agreed-upon fee of $2,700 for his daughter, and "[a] marriage by magistrate [would] complete the wedding the next day."

However, whether the wedding actually took place remains unclear, because two days later, on April 28, national papers such as *The New York Times* wrote: "GYPSY WEDDING OFF; LOUISVILLE PUZZLED; Some Say Bride's Father Insisted on $300 More for His Daughter's Hand. OTHERS HINT AT

POLICE. Anyhow, Prince Hendrik John Fails to Win Rosetta and Bands Start for Chicago."

The discrepancy in the names most likely attributable to the fact that gypsies used two sets of names, the first line of the article read: "A band of gypsies, led by Chief John and his son, Prince Hendrik John, went trekking out of Louisville in high dudgeon today, and the city will not witness a royal wedding of Romany." However, instead of the "caravan of old," most of them left in "high-powered cars." The author went on to say that the father of the bride had said the ceremony would take place in Chicago instead, "where the people are more hospitable and where more gypsies can gather to engage in festivities worthy of the wedding of one of royal blood." It was also rumored that the police "had not welcomed the chief and his followers with open arms" and "pestering by sightseers and curiosity seekers had caused the gypsies to depart."

Sources close to the bridal party, however, appeared to corroborate the claim that the bride's father had upped the price at the last minute. When asked whether $3,000 wasn't a lot to pay for a wife, Ruby, the would-be bridegroom's sister replied: "Not for a good woman. My husband's father, he pay $4,000 for me. For my wedding they rent a hall in New York. There was maybe 400 people there. Everybody get drunk and the police arrest forty-three. The next day they fine everybody $1, whether they just drunk or kill somebody." But, as the reporter pointed out, "the price for gypsy wives must vary widely." Tessa, another sister, "brought only $4 and a collar button in the marriage mart."

I glanced at the clock on the wall and realized I had been in the library for most of the morning. I had to get home and get ready for the reception. I quickly gathered up my belongings and ran to return the box of dusty clippings to its place on the shelf. However, as I turned around to head for the exit, an angry figure stood in my way. It was Josephine.

Kentucky Voodoo

Wearing a tightly wound green turban on her head, Josephine seemed taller than the last time I had seen her. Her yellow blouse had a wide, lacy collar, and her cream-colored skirt seemed to have an iridescent pattern stamped over the fabric. At her throat, a large gold medallion dangled from a necklace of turquoise beads. A nerve in my left shoulder started to twitch as I met the gaze of her coal black eyes, and I prepared myself for the worst.

Then, with a hint of impatience, she arched an eyebrow at me. Slowly, I nodded my head, a silent signal to let her know that I would not offer any resistance. Again, her eyebrow lifted and her head jerked to the side in an impatient shrug. What was she trying to communicate to me? Should I say something?

Finally, she rolled her eyes in exasperation and threw up her hands. "Do you mind to let me pass?" she demanded.

Suddenly, I found my voice and moved out of the way. "Oh," I said. "Sorry."

She breezed past and went down the space between the bookshelves to the far end. Apparently, she didn't recognize me from our previous encounters, or else she had forgiven my transgressions, whatever they were. Emboldened by an unexpected sense of curiosity, I went after her. I followed her up the stairs, carefully trying to stay out of sight, and she eventually made her way to the botany section. Was she in search of strange plants to use in her voodoo rituals? Soundlessly, I took a position in the aisle next to hers and peered through the gap over the row of books in front of me.

From a pocket on the front of her skirt, Josephine pulled out a creased piece of brown paper, unfolded it and held it out at arm's length to read. After returning it to her pocket, she walked her fingers over the vertical titles before her and stopped at a spine with a colorful pattern. As she pulled it from its tight space, I craned my neck to make out the name, but before the words came into focus, something grabbed me from behind.

"Gonnagetsommadatcookie!" Cookie grinned at me as I spun around and instinctively lifted a fist.

"Leave me alone. I told you already that I don't have any cookies!" I returned my attention to the crack from which I had been spying on Josephine, but she had put the book under her arm and was preparing to exit the aisle.

"Hey!" Stepping up on his toes, Cookie noticed the object of my curiosity and knit his brow in an angry furrow. *"Staywayfromdatdeviltrickwoman!"* He raised a finger at me and shook it in irritation. *"Hexmomma!"*

"Gotta run." I scooted around him and out the other end of the aisle.

"Datwomangonndeviltrickyou!" he said. *"Gonnagetchabad."*

By the time I escaped, so had Josephine, and after several minutes of looking for her, I gave up and returned to the row where she had stood. I studied the gap the book had occupied and from the Dewey Decimal numbers on either side I was able to piece together an approximate catalogue number for the book Josephine had taken. I rushed to a computer and after several minutes I came up with the title I was looking for: *Magic and Medicine of Plants.*

A minute later, I was out on the street, headed back home. As I walked down Third Street, one thought kept running through my mind: Was Josephine really a voodoo queen?

By the time I arrived at my front door, all thoughts of the gypsies had fled and I was obsessed with voodoo. But I had other things to do first. I got things ready for the reception and soon the house was full of neighborhood people. There was a small dedication ceremony followed by champagne and hors d'oeuvres.

After everybody left, I ran upstairs and fired up the computer, and several hours later, random, surprising bits of information had surfaced, information that substantiated a voodoo presence in Kentucky. An on-line site dedicated to the topic explained that "[m]any carried the Laveau-inspired Voodoo faith from New Orleans, first up the Mississippi and Ohio to river towns such as Natchez, Memphis, St. Louis, Old Vincennes, Louisville and Cincinnati, then to places as diverse as New York, Chicago, Charleston, Savannah, St. Augustine and San Francisco."

In addition, I discovered that one of Louisiana's most famous voodoo personalities had hailed from the Bluegrass. Robert Tallant in his book *Voodoo in New Orleans* wrote that "Doctor Beauregard came to New Orleans from Kentucky in the year 1869. He was one of the only foreign Voodoos that came to the city. He was the most amazing in appearance of all the witch doctors because he had long hair that went all the way down to his knees. He also put the hair into a number of strange knots. In the knots, he carried all of his gris gris, bottles of oil, dried reptiles, small bones, and a hoot owl's head. After scaring some ladies on the street one night, he was arrested for throwing the hoot owl's head at the police and putting curses upon them. When he was released from prison he disappeared. Most people believe that he went back to Kentucky and went looking for new fields."

Although several other accounts contradicted the actual year of his arrival and arrest, the fact that a celebrated voodoo priest had lived and practiced in Kentucky seemed to be very well documented.

The most surprising tidbit of all, however, turned out to be this: apparently, the only official organization dealing with voodoo, The Voodoo Society, had its headquarters in Louisville.

I sat back in my chair, complacent in the discoveries I had unearthed, when something odd happened, something that made me jump. A small stone, jade green with flecks of brown and beautifully polished, landed in my lap.

Goats

I picked the stone up and turned it over. Flat and almost perfectly round, it measured an inch or so in diameter and would have been a perfect stone for skipping across the water. I had no idea of the geology that had led to its creation, but I could tell that someone had put it in a rock polisher. Where it came from was a mystery, but it appeared to be the same stone I had seen the previous night at the Witches' Tree.

I looked at the ceiling, but there was no sign of a crack in the plaster or anything else that might have accounted for its appearance, so my mind immediately turned to the paranormal. I had read about documented cases of weirdness where strange things, including coal, frogs and strips of meat—such as during the famous "Kentucky Meat Shower" of March 3, 1876—had fallen from the sky, and I now wondered if Widmer House was spitting things at me to get my attention. Since I had been making a concerted effort to ignore the ever-increasing frequency and volume of the odd crashes and unusual groans that plagued our day-to-day existence in the large old home, it was not entirely out of the realm of possibility. However, as had been the case in all the peculiar events happening at La Casa Fabulosa, I forced myself to look for a rational explanation before giving in to flights of fancy.

I told myself it had to come from somewhere, so I looked for points of ingress in my immediate surroundings. Right away, I trained my eyes on the only plausible source of an airborne rock in the room, the bank of open windows next to my desk, where lightly fluttering curtains hinted at a soft breeze outside. I got up and walked to the window seat under the three open windows. I kneeled, pushed aside the flimsy curtain that partially covered the window nearest the desk and stuck my head out.

Below, on the walkway leading to the front door, a tall figure stood and gazed up at me. Because of the large size, I took it to be a male, and he seemed to be wearing a long, dark coat. It also looked like he had very, very long dark hair.

"I must be going insane," I muttered, falling back into a sitting position on the cushions. If down there was Doctor Beauregard, the voodoo guy I had just read about, it was time to pack up and check into the loony bin. I pressed my eyes shut and willed the mysterious form away. Then, I poked my head back outside and hoped for the best.

But he was still there, and this time he raised a hand in greeting.

This is going to be good, I thought as I righted myself and started for the stairs. Ramon was working late again and wouldn't be back for several hours, but I wished he were there to witness the weirdness, and, by default, lend some credibility to the stories I would tell afterward. Slowly, my feet followed the treads down to the foyer, where I crossed to the front door and opened it.

When he saw me emerge onto the front steps, the man lifted his chin in acknowledgement and came to meet me. Although he stood one step below me, his eyes were almost level with mine, so I assumed he had to be close to six foot six. Immediately, I breathed a sigh of relief. Doctor Beauregard was described as an older black man, and this guy was definitely white and young. And although this guy did have very long dark hair, I was happy to see no signs of magic pouches or bones tucked away in its depths, much less dried reptiles or heads of hoot owls.

"Hey, you mind giving me my rock back?" He held out a hand.

"Why would you think I have your rock?" I asked. But of course he knew I had his rock because he had pitched it through my open window and it had obviously gotten my attention, which, I assumed, was his intent.

He lifted a hand and pointed at the smooth stone that I had been worrying subconsciously between my fingers. "Because you're holding it in your hand right there."

His tone irked me and I suspected that we were not going to get along. Nonetheless, I handed over the stone.

"Thanks."

Studying his size and appearance more closely, I began second-guessing my decision to come out and talk to this person, and I suddenly wished I had brought out my cell phone in case I needed to call for help. I looked up at the patchwork arrangement of lit windows in the Hillebrand House and wondered if Loretty sat up at her window, keeping watch with her father's binoculars. As if someone had read my mind, the light in her window came on and flashed off three times in a row. Smiling, I let out an inaudible sigh of relief.

"What's so funny?" He followed my gaze to the upper floor of the apartment building on the other side of the street.

"Nothing," I said. "Can I ask why you're throwing rocks through my window? You could have broken something." I crossed my arms and waited for an answer.

"Could have, but didn't." He crossed his arms and mustered a faint smile.

"So you're a good aim. What do you want?"

"I wanted to get your attention." A breeze skimmed across the front yard and rustled the ends of his hair.

"Ever heard of a doorbell?" I uncrossed my arms and jammed a hand into my front pants pocket.

He uncrossed his arms and did the same. "Yes, but I don't believe in using them."

"You don't believe in using *doorbells*?" I said. Overhead a roaring UPS plane

148

seemed to skim the top of the Hillebrand House as it came in low for a landing at the airport.

"Nope. Never have, never will." He looked up and studied the lights flashing on the wings of the aircraft. With the sound receding, it sunk behind a treetop and disappeared.

"I take it you don't believe in knocking, either." I noticed a small pile of sticks that had been left in the patch of grass to the left of the walkway. I stepped over to it for a better look. It didn't appear as carefully constructed as the last mound I had found and I wondered if Ramon had accumulated the small pile earlier that day when he was out front doing yard work.

"Knocking's fine, but you were up on the third floor. Might not have heard me knock." He followed me to the sticks and waited.

"How'd you know I was up on the third floor?" I picked up the small pile and carried it over to a small receptacle at the side of the house.

He followed me. "Saw the lights on," he said. "And you're always up there late at night."

"Are you a stalker?" I was getting creeped out. Overhead, as if on cue, the light to Loretty's apartment flashed on and off, on and off, on and off.

"No." His brow wrinkled, and an indignant look spread across his face. "I'm just observant. I walk up and down Third Street all the time."

"I don't know who you are or what you want, but this is sort of freaky. I gave you your stone back, so now you can be on your way." I turned to go.

"Hey, sorry, man," he said. "I had this story I wanted to tell you. And I know you like stories. Didn't mean to freak you out or anything."

Reluctantly, I turned around and faced him. "A story?" The bulb in the nearest street lamp flickered once and dimmed its light. A soft yellowish glare was caught in the waxy leaves of the pitifully small hedge bushes surrounding the yard. Once again, I was reminded that it would take years for it to fill out and grow into the lush border that I wanted.

"Yeah, I wanted to share a story with you." He reached out a hand to shake mine. "My name's Beau, and I live over on Fourth Street."

"*Beau?*" A weak tremor creaked my voice.

"Yeah, Beau." He nodded his head. "Short for Beauregard."

"*Beauregard?* No way."

"Yes, I was born and raised in New Orleans." He opened his dark trench coat and pointed to a Bourbon Street logo across the front of his shirt.

My temples had started to throb, and I squeezed my eyes shut to block out the creepy images of the Kentucky voodoo doctor of the same name. The budding coincidence at hand had all the hallmarks of the beginning of a voodoo day, however, my voodoo days always started in the morning. Either I was experiencing a voodoo day that was getting off to a late start or else we were getting a jumpstart on the next morning. Or, I thought to myself with trepidation, perhaps I would experience my first *voodoo night*.

"You are not from New Orleans."

"Yeah, I am," he said. "Why would I make something like that up? That'd be weird."

"The circumstances of this little encounter might be considered weird, so it would be par for the course." I studied him up and down. "Who goes around throwing rocks through people's windows to get their attention when there's a perfectly fine doorbell?"

"I heard you were collecting ghost stories from the neighborhood so I wanted to come over and see if you heard about that one-armed woman they see floating down Fourth Street. I've seen her myself."

"One-armed woman?" I crossed my arms and raised my eyebrows.

"Yeah, it's real freaky." He narrowed his eyes and continued in a conspiratorial whisper. "It's this old black woman with a bandana around her head. She doesn't have a left arm and she floats along the sidewalk like she doesn't know where she's going. I figured, maybe you knew something about it already."

"No, that's the first time I've heard about that one," I said. "So, what's her story?"

"Story?" Beau flicked a strand of hair behind his ears and paused as if he'd never considered that question before. "Hmmm. Not really sure what her story is, that's why I came to you. All I've heard is that she was an old voodoo woman or something like that."

"Voodoo?" My eyebrows shot up and I stared at him.

"Yeah, voodoo," he said. "Like in 'I like the voodoo that you do.'"

"Oh, come on!" My voice went up a notch. "She was not a voodoo woman, and you know it." I paused to look around, hoping to find the person responsible for this prank. "Who put you up to this?"

"No one put me up to anything," he said, a crestfallen look descending over his face. "I swear."

"Really?" I studied his features for any sign of deception. I didn't notice any, so I softened a little. "Well, I find it a little odd that the very minute I'm reading about Louisville's voodoo past someone with a voodoo ghost story should toss a stone through my window. Not only that, the guy who does the tossing is a Beauregard and I happen to be reading about a Dr. Beauregard."

"Doc Beauregard? The voodoo doctor from New Orleans?" He sounded impressed.

"Well, he was from Kentucky actually, but yes. You've heard of him then?"

"Sure thing," he said. "My mom's a tour guide down there and she knows all that stuff." A moment's hesitation followed, and his brows knitted together in concentration. "I sure hope she didn't name me after him."

"It would be a hoot if she had," I said.

"She wouldn't have done that," he said, not entirely convinced of the certainty of his claim. "Not after a voodoo doctor."

"Maybe you should ask her."

He thought for a minute and furrowed his brow. "Yeah, I think I will," he said finally. His head turned at the sound of a shopping cart being pushed along the sidewalk and then he went back to the original topic of conversation. "Hey, you want me to show you where I saw the ghost of the one-armed woman?"

At first, I planned on politely refusing his offer, but since it was time to take the dogs for a walk anyway, I agreed. They had been patiently standing at the front entrance, looking out through the iron security doors during the entire exchange. "Might as well," I said. "Let me get the dogs, and I'll be right out."

Five minutes later we were headed south on Third Street.

Even though summer had arrived, some of the leaves on the trees in the neighborhood had already started to tinge with rust, and the light from the streetlamps glowed softly below the maple canopy overhead. As we walked, every now and then, a leaf would loosen itself and waft down to dance at our feet before settling in among other random leaves on the sidewalk. Off in the distance, the rusty wheels of the shopping cart bumped their way over an uneven surface.

"Hey, have you seen that old woman who pushes around that cart full of sticks?" Beau pointed down the road, presumably at the source of the noise. "They say she's a witch."

"So I've heard." I followed the dogs to the next street, where we turned right. An imposing chateau-style mansion that had seen better days loomed on the corner and the light at the front door flicked off and on three times before we lost it from our field of vision.

"You see that?" asked Beau. "That was weird."

"Probably a short in the wiring or something."

"Or probably some freak standing there at the front door, trying to mess with us. That's more likely." He reached up, gathered a hank of his long hair and threw it back over a shoulder.

Along a section of Park, the lights on the street had apparently burnt out, and we walked over the bumpy bricks in darkness until we reached Fourth Street. Spreading out to the left, Central Park was a dark expanse of towering trees that stood sentinel-like and silent; before us a large brick mansion—the old Russell Houston House, which had been converted into the Inn at the Park bed and breakfast—basked in the shine of floodlights in the front yard. Here and there, bits of red stone trim added detail to an interesting assortment of arches, gables, and hidden balconies. On the top floor, a dark shadow blocked out the light as it seemed to approach a lone dormer window and peer down at us. I wondered if it was Annie Whipple, a former tutor for the children of the house, whose ghost was rumored to haunt the mansion.

We crossed the street and turned right at the sidewalk, Beau running ahead of me. "It was right here," he said as he approached a spot on the walkway in front of the Woman's Club of Louisville. "I was walking down the way we just came, and all of a sudden I looked up and saw this form floating down the sidewalk right at me." His arms dropped to his sides and he assumed a vacant, zombie-like stare before slowly float-simulating toward me. "That's how she moved," he said. "Except she was missing this arm." He pointed to his left and smiled. "Creepy, huh?"

"Yes, that sounds creepy all right. How long did you see her?" I turned around and studied the rest of the structures, all of them stone and brick that lined the street.

Beau flicked another long strand of hair behind his ear and thought for a moment. "Oh, it seemed like a really long time while it was happening, but it was probably five or ten seconds, somewhere around there." He flicked a strand behind his other ear and pretended to float down the sidewalk again.

"Do you know of anyone else who's seen this apparition?" I asked, moving out of the way so he could float past me. "It helps when there's more than one witness to talk to."

"Yeah, my roommate's mother has seen her," he said. "I'll give you his email so you can talk to him if you like."

I watched as Beau fake-floated down to the end of the block, turned and floated back to where I was standing.

He handed me a scrap of paper with some ink scratches on it. "You can reach him there."

Suddenly, a strange bleating noise reverberated in the darkness.

"Hey, man, what was that?" Beau stopped and gave me a quizzical look.

"Beats me," I said. "It sounded suspiciously like a sheep or goat, though."

Blehhhh. Bleh. Ble-ehhhhh. This time the bleat sounded nearer. I turned my ear toward the noise, which seemed to come from between the two houses nearest us.

"Man, we don't got livestock in Old Louisville, do we?" asked Beau, wide-eyed.

"It wouldn't surprise me," I said dryly. "I've seen goofier things down here. Saw a wild turkey not too long ago."

Bleh. Bleh. Bleh. Ble-ehhhhh. The swift clip of small hooves on cement echoed between the houses and a small dark form emerged, driven forward by a vague figure in white that materialized in the driveway of the Frazier House.

Bleh. Bleh. Bleh. It was a young goat, its coat a silvery black that glistened in the moonlight, and it ran to the end of the drive and turned toward us. Behind it followed the figure clad in white, a long staff clunking hollowly on the sidewalk as they made their way in our direction.

Fritz and Rocky had spotted the goat and began barking, so I pulled them back and quieted them. Without so much as a glance in our direction, the goat passed by Beau and me and bee-lined it to the next corner; several seconds after that, the figure in white reached us and walked by without a word. She wore an enormous, snowy white turban that concealed much of her face in shadows. Even before the light of the moon filtered through the leafy canopy overhead and washed over the woman's features, I had a suspicion that it was Josephine.

"Whoa!" Beau watched as she caught up to the goat at the corner with Ormsby Avenue and then turned left. "She looks like one of them Haitian voodoo women, wearing that white turban and that white dress like that. And holding that staff out in front of her like she's a shepherdess or something." He shook his head and looked at me.

"Like I said, you see it all down here in Old Louisville." We watched as Josephine and the goat rounded the corner and disappeared from sight. Silently, I prayed that the unsuspecting creature would not end up the star attraction at some gruesome full-moon voodoo ritual later that night. Or in some spicy curry on an Old Louisville table.

"You know her or something?" asked Beau. He had taken his stone from a pocket and was tossing it back and forth from one palm to the other. "You didn't seem all that surprised to see her."

"Wouldn't say I really know her, but I've seen her around before, if that was her. I couldn't really see her face, though." Off in the distance, I could hear a faint bleating. "They say she's some sort of voodoo doctor. Her name's supposed to be Josephine."

Beau stopped tossing his stone and it fell and clattered on the sidewalk and bounced into the grass. "Did you say her name was Josephine?"

"I don't know for sure, but that's what a lot of people call her," I said. "This neighborhood is full of so many oddballs, though; you never know who's real and who's the figment of somebody's imagination." Beau continued to stare at me with a wide-eyed expression. The dogs stared at me as well, wondering what our next destination was.

"That is so freaky, man," he said. "Because you made me remember something about the ghost with the one arm I was telling you about."

"What's that?" My ears strained as the distant bleating noise increased in volume.

"I remembered something my roommate's mom told me about that ghost: she said her name was Josephine. And that she was a witch doctor or something like that."

But before there was time for the coincidence to sink in and make me shudder, something struck me from behind and knocked me to the pavement.

Swans

Bleh. Bleh. Bleeeehh! The goat looked down at me, the dark, rectangular irises in its eerie yellow-green eyes blazing. Two nubby little horns jutted from its forehead and a tuft of beard hung from its chin. It looked disconcertingly Satanlike. After a perfunctory sniff, the little devil reared back slightly and raised its head and upper body in preparation for another butt; apparently, it wasn't satisfied with the job it had done and wanted to deliver the coup de grâce. The dogs were barking frantically and tried to get at the animal, but Beau had wedged himself between the two parties.

"Hey, man!" Beau yelled at the goat. "Get out of here!" He kicked it away from my prone form and shooed it off.

"Thanks," I said, the fingers of one hand gingerly feeling the back of my head where I had bumped into the sidewalk. Fortunately, I was able to break the fall with my arms, so my head didn't strike very hard; nonetheless, I could discern the faint swelling of a small goose egg. The dogs' leashes were tightly clutched in the other hand.

"That crazy goat came out of nowhere and got you in the back of the legs," said Beau. He reached down and helped pull me to my feet.

"You better be careful," I warned, looking around as I dusted off the seat of my pants, "because–"

There was the clicking sound of rapidly approaching hooves, and Beau suddenly lurched forward and tumbled to the ground. The dogs erupted in another pandemonium of baying and it was now my turn to give Beau a hand up.

He quickly jumped to his feet and turned on the goat, which in turn lowered its head and emitted a mulish *bleeehhhh!* Beau ran toward it to scare it off and yelled. "Get out of here right now!" The goat twirled around with a clatter of hooves and retreated down the sidewalk before disappearing in the driveway between the Frazier House and the Woman's Club.

I looked back in the direction the goat had returned from, waiting to see if Josephine would be chasing after, but it soon became apparent that no one was in pursuit. All was silent, and then a forlorn bleat echoed off the brick walls on either side of the driveway that had swallowed the goat. I looked at Beau.

"You think we should go after it?" he asked.

"Well, it can't be running the streets of Old Louisville," I said. "It might get hit by a car or something."

"Let's go find it then." He led the way to the goat's hiding spot. "Dumbass goat," he mumbled.

Large, inky shadows sliced through the darkness and lay across the thin strip of asphalt that was the driveway. To the rear, the light from a wrought iron lamppost softly illuminated a manicured courtyard and spilled out over a section of the drive. Carefully, we guided ourselves to the back of the mansion known as the Frazier House, where the dim light afforded more visibility, mindful of the clack of cloven hooves that would herald the advent of another caprine assault.

"I don't see that crazy thing anywhere." Beau inched slowly forward as his eyes scanned the gloom. "Where'd that dumbass goat go?"

I pointed at an expanse of wrought iron fence that sealed off the garden and connected the back of the mansion to the Woman's Club. "That's the only place it could have gone," I said, "so it must have squeezed through the bars on the fence and be hiding in the garden behind the house."

Beau drew near the gate, grasped the railing, and leaned forward. "Hey, goat! Where are you?" He paused for several seconds and listened, but no response came.

I joined him at the metal railing and peered over. After several yards another section of wrought iron fencing cordoned off a small memorial garden with a sculpture in the center. "He's got to be in there somewhere."

"How do you know it's a he?" Beau looked alarmed. He obviously didn't like to be left out of the loop.

"I'm assuming, with the horns and all," I said. "Maybe it's a she. Call it whatever you want."

"'He' is fine by me," he said. "I only thought you knew something I didn't know."

I scanned the backyard for a sign of movement, but all was still. A brick carriage house flanked the rear of the property and with the light that spilled over the fence from the house to the south, I squinted to make out the details of the façade. On one side of a set of double barn doors painted black, a shape caught my attention and I pointed it out for Beau. "Hey, see that?" I said. "It looks like a dog's head carved out of stone."

His eyes searched a bit and then he nodded his head. "Oh, yeah, I see it now." Then he cocked his head to the left and pointed. "And look right next to it. There's another head of some sort. I can't tell what it is, but I don't think it's a dog, is it?"

"Wouldn't it be a hoot if it was a goat's head?" I smiled, despite the weirdness of it all.

"Oh, man, that *would* be creepy," he said. "What if there's not even a real goat? Maybe it's a sculpture that comes alive during the light of a full moon. And that's why we can't find it. It changed back to stone and disappeared."

"Maybe," I said, diplomatically. "But chances are it just found a good hiding spot."

"Well, let's go find it then." Beau pulled himself up on the fence and straddled the top.

"Uh, I don't know if that's such a good idea," I said.

"Why?" Balancing on the fence, he looked down at me with a curious grin.

"Uh, because it's trespassing," I whispered.

"So you're going to tell me you've never trespassed before?" With a minimal amount of effort, he swung a leg over the top of the fence and slowly lowered himself down on the other side and stood to face me, the bars in between us. "I heard you on the radio the other day when they interviewed you about chasing down these ghost stories, and it sounds like all you do down here is trespass. So, come on."

I started to stammer a protest, but then I realized he had me. "Oh, I suppose." I tied the dogs' lead around the base of a spearhead and commenced the arduous task of heaving my bulk over the fence. On the other side, I sidled up next to Beau and we had to top another fence before we could enter the garden. Gradually, we moved out of the soft glow of the lamppost and into the shadows on the periphery of the courtyard.

"Goat!" he whispered. "Where are you?" He poked his head over a hedge and raised his voice slightly. "Where are you, goat?"

I followed behind, peering now and then into potential dark hiding places, and soon we stood in front of the door to the carriage house.

"Look," I said, pointing above the entry at the carved image next to the dog. "It's not a goat after all."

Beau leaned back and shifted his position to make better use of the light and studied the sculpted head. "Huh. What do you know?" he said. "A horse. That's almost as good as a goat," he said. "Most people don't have any heads at all carved on their carriage houses now, do they?"

"You've got a point there."

"They're both farm animals and all," he said.

"No disputing that." I moved away from the doorway and its graven animal heads. Nodding his head sagely, Beau followed and we searched out the rest of the courtyard. To the south was a fence that separated it from the neighbors' back yard. The neighbors were Susan and Jeff, and they lived in the huge old house with their daughter, Drew. Suddenly there was a click and the pump for their in-ground pool came on, filling the evening breeze with a soft buzzing noise. I stuck my face up to the slats in the fence and peered through. No sign of the goat in their backyard, or in the swimming pool. After making a second round of the garden behind the Frazier House, I went and stood at the gate with Beau.

"I don't see any goats back here. Do you?" His eyes darted over the trimmed hedges and flower beds.

"Not a one," I replied. "I wonder what happened to it."

"I'm telling you, man," said Beau, "it probably turned back to stone and jumped back up on the wall somewhere."

"We only saw a horse and a dog."

"I know, I know. It's probably up in some other spot." He turned and pointed. "Maybe over that window there. Let's go look some more."

"No, sorry," I replied. "It's late and I've had enough weirdness for tonight. It's time to go home." I jumped up on the fence and pulled myself over to the other side.

"Man!" Beau shook his head and scuffed at the brick underfoot. "This was starting to get fun." Reluctantly, he followed my lead and joined me in the driveway.

I freed the dogs from their imprisonment on the fence and ran with them to the end of the drive. We waited for Beau to catch up. "Beau, it's been fun," I said. "I'll let you know if I dig up anything on your one-armed ghost."

"Well, thanks for looking into it," he said. "I'm going to roam the neighborhood and see if I can find that dumbass goat. Take it easy." He turned around and walked to the end of the block; a half minute later he had disappeared into the darkness of Central Park. I heard a faint bleating noise, and I was relatively certain it was Beau, trying a different strategy by attempting to lure the animal with sounds of its own kind.

"Okay, time to go home," I said to the dogs, who started prancing about. We turned right at the corner with Ormsby and went down half a block to Amici, the neighborhood Italian restaurant, which sat opposite the mouth of our back alley, and then crossed the road to the alley. Suddenly, Bess let out an uncharacteristic bark, and I turned to see what the matter was. With the arrival of Beau's rock in my lap, the evening had taken a decided turn for weird—and it had only become weirder when we got out on the streets of Old Louisville. However, I wasn't prepared for the sight that awaited me when I followed Bess's line of vision to a small carriage house painted a bluish gray. There, under a striped awning over the entry that faced the street, stood a dazzlingly white swan. It somewhat regally stretched its neck, shook itself out, and leisurely dropped into a nesting position. Languorously, it began to preen itself, apparently unperturbed by our presence only several yards away.

I had never seen a swan in Old Louisville, and I began to ponder the circumstances that led to its arrival at the end of my alley; however, the dogs had started to quiver in anticipation of a good chase, so I pulled them over to the nearest fence and tied them up. Then I returned to the swan. An embarrassing run-in with a swan in Germany that left me with a painful, beak-shaped welt on my backside had taught me that these birds weren't particularly amiable. This one appeared to be non-threatening, though, so I cautiously approached and came to stand right next to it. It stopped its preening for a moment and looked up at me, a placid expression on its face. Slightly hesitant, I reached down and patted the top of its head, something that the swan seemed to enjoy. It stretched out its long neck and its head pushed back against my fingers for a more vigorous scratch. I squatted down and spent several minutes petting it.

Then the swan suddenly stood and swiveled its head in the direction of Third Street. It gazed intently, its stare transfixed on the massive First Church of Christ, Scientist that sat on the corner. Suddenly, several white forms appeared at the top of the steps, descended, and began running in our direction. The swan spread its wings, honked once and ran to the corner to meet three fellow swans that flapped their wings and honked a greeting in return. Then, they all turned and began running down Third Street to Oak, their jauntily outstretched wings providing added momentum as they flapped. With a series of nasal honks, they disappeared from sight, leaving a solitary white feather tumbling on the air current in their wake. I shook my head in disbelief and returned to the dogs, all of whom had started whining furiously.

When I grabbed their leads, they immediately ran to the spot where the swan had sat and they eagerly nosed the ground. They tried to pull me after them to Third Street, however, after several tugs they gave up and reluctantly started to follow me to the alley. But as I turned to go, something under the black and white striped awning caught my attention, and I stopped to look.

A long, arched panel of carved wood covered a space of six or seven feet over the door and window. Since it was tucked up under the awning of the carriage house, it was completely invisible to passersby; however, from my position I could see it clearly, despite the lack of light. Covered in a weathered coat of grayish blue paint was a scene that made me shiver: at the top was a partial sun with rays shining down on a large sunflower that had bent over at the stem; opposite that was what appeared to be a swan, its wings outstretched in the very same manner as the swans I had seen running down Third Street several seconds before.

How many times had I passed by this building and never noticed the unique frieze hidden under the awning? It had to have been thousands of times, I estimated, but I had no way to calculate the chances of finding a live swan sitting under the image of a carved swan in a neighborhood that didn't have a single resident swan as far as I knew. It was mind-boggling.

Back at La Casa Fabulosa, I pushed open the back gate and let the dogs run around loose. Before calling them inside, I peeked behind the hydrangeas growing along the side of the house to make sure there were no goats or swans lying in ambush. I somehow had a feeling there was more to come that night.

But then I felt something hard poke me in the back, and a gruff voice said: "Hands up or I'll shoot! Turn around slowly."

Voodoo Night

I almost wet my pants, but I didn't. When I turned around, Ramon was pointing the end of a wooden spoon at me. His grin quickly disappeared when the furious look on my face registered. "You didn't think I was serious, did you?" he said. "I thought you heard me in the kitchen. I just got back from work."

I slapped the wooden spoon out of his hand and chased him through the kitchen and butler's pantry, up the back steps and into the hallway on the second floor. After he found refuge behind a locked bedroom door, I returned to the kitchen and put a pot of water on the stove.

Overhead, the door opened once the coast had cleared and Ramon leaned over the railing of the back stairs. "I'm going to bed," he said. "It's late and I have to get up early in the morning."

"Hey, did you see any swans running down Third Street when you got home?"

Although I couldn't see his face, his expression was visible in the inflection of his voice: *"Swans?"*

"Yeah, four of them, running down toward Oak. They were white." I listened to the silence.

"Running toward Oak?" He laughed. "Have you been drinking?"

"No," I said. "There were four swans on Third Street. I think they were having a birdy convention at the First Church of Christ, Scientist, or something."

From above there was more silence. "Me no see no swans tonight," he said, finally.

"Okay, just checking." I grumbled a bit and then said good-night.

"You're such a hobo."

"Whatever."

After hearing his door close, I pulled out a tin of green tea from the cupboard. As I spooned the leaves into the pot, a low whine filled the air and I turned around to find Rocky, Bess, and Fritz patiently sitting in a line on the floor, all with expectant looks on their faces. Fritz was speaking for them all. I had forgotten to dole out the customary treats after their walk, and they were still waiting. I dug out a box of Milkbones, gave them each a biscuit and a scratch on the back, and then watched as they trotted into the old butler's pantry and jumped up onto the couch to watch television. After several turnarounds, they plopped themselves down and settled in.

I looked at the clock above the stove and saw that it was almost midnight. The teakettle started to whistle and I turned off the flame underneath, poured the boiling water into the pot, and replaced the lid. I put a tea cozy over the pot while the tea steeped, and in the next room I noticed that the dogs were all standing on the sofa, looking anxiously to the front of the house. At that moment, a series of loud taps could be heard as someone knocked at the main door. I stayed the dogs to prevent any barking, walked through the dining room, and opened the door.

The front stoop was empty, though, and there was no sign of anyone in the immediate vicinity. A light wind surged and sent an empty plastic bag sailing across the front yard, scrambling dead leaves before it and setting the hanging light fixture over the door to swaying. Pale yellow reflections jumped about on the white and blue mosaic inlay on the porch floor as a soft rustle tumbled the branches of the trees.

I shook my head, turned to enter the house, and walked through the entrance. The door closed behind me, I started for the kitchen when the grandmother clock in the foyer struck midnight. I had recently reset it, so I stopped to count the chimes and make sure there were twelve to correspond with midnight. On the twelfth gong, I started to walk away, but then came another set of chimes. *Ding dong.*

The grandmother clock in the foyer had struck thirteen o'clock.

The hair on the back of my neck stood up in an uncomfortable prickle but I convinced myself that I had miscounted. Nonetheless, I kept my eyes on the clock as I backed away and returned to the kitchen to check on the pot of tea.

I picked up the pot, poured a cup, and sat down with the dogs and flipped through the channels on the TV. As I sipped the hot tea, a nagging thought in the back of my mind kept telling me something wasn't quite right, but I couldn't put my finger on it. I was only able to identify the quandary when I drained the last bit of tea from the cup and returned to the kitchen for a refill: the quilted tea cozy I had put over the pot to keep it warm was gone. When I had poured that first cup it was gone already, but it hadn't registered until I went back into the kitchen and saw that it was missing. I searched for ten minutes and never found it.

Several dirty plates were stacked in the sink, so I decided to wash them by hand before I returned to the dogs and the TV in the butler's pantry. I picked up the drain basket and fidgeted with the thing on the bottom so it would prevent the water from draining away when I filled up the sink with soapy water, however when I pushed it down into the drain and opened the tap, the water filtered through to the pipes below. I wasn't terribly surprised at this turn of events, however, because drain baskets are—to my mind, at least—one of the great mysteries in life. When you want them to plug up the sink so you can wash a couple of dirty dishes at a quarter past midnight, they invariably stay open; when you want them to stay open so you can rinse off a bunch of grapes without all the water collecting in the basin, they will close, of that you can be sure. For me, it's always been a crapshoot. So, after the first time, I tossed it in again and ran the water. It still wasn't closed. So I picked it up again, jiggled it a bit and threw it back into the drain. For the third time, it was still open.

Normally, I get the opened or closed position I am waiting for by the second or third try, but on this night I had a hunch where it all was going. I picked up the drain basket, twisted the thing on the bottom and tossed it back into the sink before turning on the water. It was open. I tried it nine more times, and each time the drain basket remained unclosed. A total of thirteen tries. When I repeated the process for the fourteenth time, I was already positive of the outcome long before the metal basket settled securely into place and produced an effective seal that allowed me to finally fill up the sink and wash the dishes.

I looked at the clock and it was going on half past when several loud knocks sounded at the front door. "Not again." I darted through the dining room and across the foyer and yanked open the door. Once again, not a soul was in sight. I ran down the steps and looked down both sides of the house, but the shadows revealed nothing. A fat drop of rain splashed against the front window with a *splat* and several more followed, pelting me as I took cover under the porch. Soon, the pavement of Third Street glistened with a silvery coat of wet and the sidewalks were slick and blackened with rainfall.

As I closed the door behind me, the grandmother clock struck the half hour, a melodious *dong dong* echoing softly off the walls in the foyer, and my hands went up to cover my ears and shield them in the event the clock should decide to emit another series of thirteen chimes. "La la la la la," I sang out loud as I scurried by, "I can't hear you. I can't hear you." I rushed into the kitchen and poured myself another cup of tea.

As I returned the teapot to the counter, through the back window I noticed a vague form standing in the alley. I leaned closer to the window and peered outside. I couldn't be positive, but it looked like a male, and there was a dark hood over his head. The back gate stood wide open, and the curious individual had positioned himself in the opening. Quickly, I yanked open the back door and stared through the bars on the security door, but the form was gone.

Not more than a split second had passed since I had spotted the voyeur, so he couldn't have gotten very far. I ran to the back gate and looked both ways in the alley, but again, there was nobody around. I pulled the gate to, locked it, and then scoured the back yard, in case the intruder had decided to hide in the bushes; however, I found no one.

As I trudged up the steps on the back stairs, I once again had the niggling sensation that something wasn't quite right. Once I was inside again, behind locked doors, it finally dawned on me what had not seemed right: last I knew, it was pouring outside, but there wasn't so much as a single drop of rain in the back yard.

I quickly opened the back door and looked out. Everything was dry. When I ran to the front of the house and gazed through the window in the door, however, I was witness to a virtual downpour. Out on the porch, rain pattered the roof and splashed the edges of the steps as I stood and watched Third Street take a good soaking. When I ran through the house and exited the back door, everything was high and dry.

This cannot be happening, I thought to myself. Raining in the front yard, not raining in the back yard: that was crazy. Once again, I went to the front door and looked outside. Rain still came down in a steady stream, and it even seemed to be gaining in intensity. I turned around and when I walked out of the back door, there wasn't a drop of moisture in sight. I went down the steps and followed the walkway around the side of the house to see where the rain began. About half-way there, where the dining room jutted out at an angle from the rest of the house, I could see where the light gray concrete of the sidewalk suddenly changed to a slick black. When I looked up into the glare of a streetlight on Third Street, I could clearly make out individual droplets as they plummeted to the earth; when I turned around and stared at the light flooding in from the alley, I could see none. I stepped over the rain-soaked line and entered the downpour, listening to the faint rumble of thunder in the distance. Before my clothes could get wet, I smiled and crossed back over into the fairer weather. Despite the improbability, it was evident that one half of Widmer House was in a rain shower and the other half wasn't.

Remembering my conversation about the yellow monkeys with Frederick, in that very same spot, I felt a wave of gratitude surge up inside me. How many people could say they had stood directly under the edge of a storm cloud and had walked into and out of the rain at will?

I thought about calling someone and sharing the details of this weather-related phenomenon, but decided against it when I looked at the clock and saw how late it was. They probably wouldn't have believed me anyway. Instead, I walked back over into the rainy half and checked the hydrangeas for goats or swans. Finding none, I returned to the house and had another cup of tea.

When I returned to the third floor to putz around on the computer, I checked the windows over the cushioned bench in my office; it was still raining in the front yard. I closed the windows. When I walked to the door that led to the rooftop deck at the back of the house, I could see that the rear half was still clear. However, when I looked down to the alley, I was startled to see the strange hooded figure looking up at me. He was farther down the alley than before, but I could tell it was the same person. From my vantage point, it appeared that the figure was wearing a dark cassock as well. When he saw that I had spotted him, he turned and disappeared in the shadows between two houses.

Despite the creepy hood that prevented any look at the figure's face, I told myself that it was a homeless person looking for a place to sleep that night and returned to my desk. Rain splashed against the window behind my chair while I surfed the Internet and snooped for more information about voodoo in Louisville. I wasn't able to find anything; however, I did make a startling discovery: the most celebrated holiday on the voodoo calendar was the 24th of June, St. Jean's Day.

I looked at the calendar; it was the 24th of June.

Out of the Woodwork

The rest of the summer was largely uneventful, and by the time classes started for the fall semester, word had gotten out that abnormal things were afoot at Widmer House and that I was writing a book about neighborhood haunts. The *Courier-Journal* ran an article about it, and soon the phone began ringing off the hook. Although I had made no such claims, I had suddenly become an expert in the paranormal. I also received a steady stream of emails offering advice and informing me of other purported hauntings in the area. Some shared their stories of the supernatural and asked me for advice. So I was not terribly surprised when I received an email late one night from two university students who were convinced that their dorm room was haunted. I agreed to meet them in my office the next morning and hear their story.

The following day, they showed up at the appointed time and eagerly pulled up chairs next to my desk. Within several minutes, I had an overview of their paranormal experiences: strange reflections on the wall, orbs showing up on film, a ghost who liked to take the socks off of one person in the middle of the night and put them back on another.

"We've got tons of pictures to prove it, too," said one of the bouncy co-eds.

"Yeah, show him the one with all the orbs," said the other.

"Pictures are always good." I nodded my head, eager to see what anomalies they had captured on film. "Let me see what you have."

"Well, like, we took this picture on the weekend, and there's a bazillion orbs all over the place." The bouncier of the two reached across the desk and handed me a photograph.

I examined it briefly, taking note of the many white specks that the camera had captured floating around the small dorm room. I considered the picture for another second or two and then came to my conclusion. "You know, I am not a parapsychologist. I write ghost stories," I said. "So I'm not an expert. But I will tell you what I think is going on here and you can go on from there." They looked at me and nervously nodded their assent. "What people think are orbs oftentimes turn out to be dust particles and nothing more. That's what it looks like here. Especially since there are so many of them."

"No, those are orbs for sure," said the less bouncy co-ed. "I can feel it."

"Like I said, that's only my opinion, and I'm not an expert. I'll be happy to give you a few numbers you can call and maybe they can help you a little more." I scratched a couple of telephone numbers down on a notepad and handed the paper across the desk. "Out of curiosity," I said. "What were you doing prior to these pictures? Were you cleaning or anything like that? That could stir up quite a bit of dust."

"Naw," said the bouncier of the two. "Our neighbors and us was having a pillow fight. No cleaning or anything like that."

I paused for a moment and looked them in the eyes, wishing I had on a pair of reading glasses that I could push down the bridge of my nose to convey a sense of gravity. "You do understand that four girls banging each other over the head with pillows might cause a bit of dust to fly, don't you?"

"Yeah," said the less bouncy one, "but these were real orbs. I can tell."

The other one moved her head up and down in agreement. "Real orbs, yeah, for sure."

I tried my hardest to sound pleasant. "Now, what else do you have by way of pictures? What about these strange reflections?"

"Oh, yeah! Look at this," said the bouncier one. "There's this mysterious reflection on the wall that only shows up when we take pictures."

"Yeah," said the other one. "It's super creepy. I know it's a ghost."

I reached across the desk and accepted the photo she handed to me. The grainy picture showed the same dorm room, but from a different angle. To the left stood a wooden bunk bed, and two desks had been pushed up against the opposite wall. The walls were covered in a variety of large, shiny posters and smaller framed photographs.

"See?" said the really bouncy one, pointing to a small rectangle of light on the wall next to the bed. "It's a phantom or something hovering on the wall." Her expression conveyed a look of grave concern.

"Did you ever consider the possibility that this could be a reflection from one of the"—I paused to count—"thirty-two framed pictures on the wall? The glass looks awfully shiny to me."

"Naw," said the lesser of the bouncy girls. "It only shows up when we take pictures at night. Here, look at this one. You see almost the same thing." She handed me another photograph.

"You mean it only appears when the bright and shiny flash goes off?" I reached behind my ear and scratched my head.

"Uh-huh!" She had obviously missed the sarcasm.

"Well, like I said, I'm not an expert, but it looks like a reflection to me." I shuffled some papers in the hopes that they would take the hint and leave. "But, call one of those numbers for paranormal groups in the area and see what they have to say."

"I'm pretty sure they'll tell us it's a real ghost," said the non-bouncy girl with a frown. "Pictures don't just go around doing reflecty things and stuff like that."

"Hey!" said the more bouncy one, her eyes narrowing at the realization of my skepticism. "Do you really *believe* in ghosts or not?"

"Yeah," said the other one, lifting a strand of hair to her mouth and sucking on it. "If you write about ghosts and stuff like that, you better believe in them or else it's not fair."

I hate it when people ask me if I believe in ghosts. Not because it always puts me on the spot but because I get tired of having to come up with inventive answers. Sometimes I believe in ghosts, sometimes I don't. Like I sometimes believe in UFOs, Bigfoot and God, and then other times, not. On the rare occasion that I answer this question, I usually tell them that I don't believe in ghosts per se because I have never seen an actual apparition or any kind of physical entity that one might call a ghost. I usually qualify this answer by clarifying that I am a firm believer in the unexplained, however.

For me, the problem with ghosts is that nobody really knows what they are, if anything. Theories abound as to what constitutes them or the notion of hauntings, but are ghosts spirits that have been trapped in this realm and have not crossed over to the next, or are they souls that come back to visit us from the nether regions? Are they simply products of overly active imaginations, or could they arise out of mass hallucination or psychoses? Do the laws of physics support the notion of hauntings and could they be natural phenomena that science has yet to explain away?

I don't know if I believe in ghosts or not, and truth be told: I don't feel any particular compunction for the beliefs I have, nor do I feel a sense of obligation to make up my mind to believe one way or the other. For the time being, I am perfectly content to wonder what, if anything, awaits us out there after we die, delighting in the uncertainty of it all. For that reason, I decided to avoid the question and change the subject.

"Did you say something about a ghost changing your socks or something like that?"

"Yeah!" exclaimed the really bouncy girl. "That's the creepiest part of all. It's like someone is coming in at night and playing tricks on us."

Mildly intrigued, I crossed my hands in my lap and sat back in the chair. "What exactly happened?"

"Well, like," said the non-bouncy girl, "Saturday night me and my boyfriend went to bed. And like when we woke up the next morning, he had *my socks* on and I had *his* on! It was so creepy!"

"Yeah, I saw it with my own eyes!" exclaimed the bouncier one.

"Are you sure you didn't put on each other's socks by mistake?" I hoped the expectant look on my face would help her draw the most rational conclusion.

"Nuh-uh! No way," she said. "I would have remembered that!"

"I see. How many times has this happened then?" I picked up my pencil and prepared to take some notes.

"Just that one time." She nodded gravely and looked to her friend for support.

"What exactly were you doing that night before you went to bed, if you don't mind my asking?"

The non-bouncy girl blushed a bit and smiled before answering. "Ah, well," she said. "We were out at a party and—"

"Yeah," said her friend. "They got so wasted they could hardly walk. It was hysterical!" She started laughing and bounced with each intake of air. "Like *totally* wasted."

"I think most people would say you probably put on each other's socks and forgot about it."

"Nooo," said the other one. "I would remember something like that. And so would my boyfriend. He's real smart."

"I see." I shuffled the papers again and opened a file drawer. "Like I said, I'm not an expert, but please call the numbers I gave you. And let me know what they say. I'd be really anxious to get their take on it."

"Yeah," said the bouncier one as she finally rose from her seat and pulled her friend to the door. "I'm sure they'll tell us our room is haunted. Gotta be. No other logical explanation."

The least bouncy of the two turned and looked at her roommate. "Like maybe the girl who lived there before us was murdered in the room or something!"

"Yeah!" The other one's eyes widened with glee. "Wouldn't that be way cool? I bet that's why our room is haunted."

Bumping into each other as they squeezed themselves through the door, they disappeared into the hallway without saying good-bye.

When I returned that afternoon, the front bell was ringing as I walked in the back door. After quickly patting the dogs on the head, I ran to see who it was. A tall man, perhaps in his thirties, stood there and shuffled through a file he held out in front of him. When he saw me approach, he lowered the file and straightened out his shoulders.

"Hi, can I help you?" I said.

"Are you the guy writing the ghost book?" He looked expectantly at me and smiled.

"Yes." He didn't look very threatening, so I invited him inside.

"Thanks," he said. "My friend said he wanted to come too, but he's running a little late. He might show up. He lives over on Second Street."

"So, what can I do for you?" I led him to a sofa and asked him to sit down.

"I read about you in the paper and I was wondering if you could help me with a situation I'm having." He opened the file and cast a glance at its contents. "The house down the block where I live is haunted. Really strange stuff going on there."

"Really?" I scooted forward to the edge of my settee. "What's been happening there?"

He took a deep breath and sighed, as if preparing himself for a very long story. "Well, all kinds of things," he said. "When I moved in last year, there was a creepy feeling all over the house, especially in the basement. I have two cats, and they started going crazy. They hated it when I took them down to the basement." He paused and turned to look out the window. "They'd jump up in the air like they were fighting with something and then they'd end up hiding under the sofa."

"Hmm, that's odd," I said. "What other kinds of things happened?

"At first it was a bunch of weird feelings," he said, "but then I started hearing strange noises. Creaks and groans on the stairs when nobody was there—things like that."

"Well, they do say that houses can make peculiar noises all by themselves." I looked around the room and raised a hand for emphasis. "Especially old ones. They settle and things like that. Wood expands and contracts with the change of the seasons."

"Yeah, that's what I was thinking at first. But then I started seeing things." He leaned his upper body toward me and lowered his voice. "They started *tormenting* me."

"What did you actually see?" I said. "And what did they do to you?"

"At the beginning, I'd see white shadows out of the corner of my eye. Like they were following me or something. But then one day I turned around and actually saw one. Ever since then, they've been after me." He gave a paranoid glance over his shoulder and looked at me.

"Yes, but what did you actually see?"

"I'm not sure what they are," he said. "Most of the time you can't see them. But the few times I saw them, they looked like they're made of clouds or something. Sort of white and vaporous." He shifted uneasily in his seat before continuing. "I'm not sure if they're ghosts or aliens."

"Aliens?"

"Yes." His eyes grew wide. "They've got those big, almond-shaped eyes, and they're really short. But it's like they're not real, made of the stuff ghosts are made of. Ectoplasm or whatever you call it."

At the mention of aliens, my attention started to drift and I caught myself staring out the front window, until I realized the visitor was waiting for me to say something. "Oh, so what about this torment you've been experiencing?"

"They don't let me sleep." He lifted a hand to his face and rubbed it across his eyes. "They're always running around the house and messing things up. They're fighting with the cats all the time and bothering them. They won't let me keep a job and I'm going to lose my house."

I narrowed my eyes a bit. "How are they keeping you from your job? And losing your house?"

"I'm always so tired I'm oversleeping and missing work all the time. My boss has given me my last warning," he said. "I'm earning less than half of what I used to, so I can't make the house payments." He fell back against the rest and exhaled a long stream of air. "It's driving me crazy."

Although I had grown skeptical of the man's claims as soon as the word alien entered the conversation, I nonetheless found myself sympathizing with him and wracked my brain for suggestions that might help his current situation. I was leaning in the direction of recommending a visit to the psychologist, but that seemed such a heartless idea so I resolved to at least talk him through his current anxiety.

"Have you thought about ignoring them?" I said.

Unfazed, he said he had tried that already. "If I ignore them, then they get mean."

"Well, what exactly do they do?" I reached down and scratched Fritz, who had jumped up on the sofa beside me.

"They come down to the basement where my bedroom is, and they carve things on my teeth, for one." He rose quickly from his chair and started toward me.

I flinched and wrinkled up my nose. "What did you say?"

He knelt in front of me. Slowly, I inched back in my seat, and he opened his mouth and used an index figure to lift his upper lip above the gum line. With his other finger, he pointed at the top row of teeth. "See?"

Hesitantly, I leaned forward and studied the two central incisors in front of me. Once I was close enough, I was able to discern a smallish pentagram etched into the enamel of each tooth.

"Whoah!" I exclaimed, quickly pushing myself away from him. "Are they devil-worshipping aliens?" I asked.

"I don't know." He returned to his spot on the sofa. "Sometimes they carve triangles and circles, too. Last night was pentagrams for the first time."

"But I didn't see any triangles or circles."

"There's none there now," he said. "They usually go away in a couple of days."

"Are you serious?"

"Yes," he replied innocently. "These here will be gone in a day or two."

"I think you need to go see a dentist! Maybe he can tell you what's going on." I leaned back and pulled Fritz close for assurance.

"I don't need a dentist to tell me what is going on," he said. "Martian ghosts are carving up my snags at night, that's what's happening. I want to know why!" Exasperation had turned his face red. "And besides, I don't have insurance."

Desperately in need of something to change the subject, I got up from my chair and walked to the console with the decanters on it. "I'm sorry," I said. "I completely forget to ask if you'd like something to drink." Immediately, I wondered at the practicality of offering alcohol to a man who was receiving regular visits from pentagram-carving aliens.

But the clock had just struck five, so—despite my reservations—I put several ice cubes in a glass and poured some bourbon over them. "Tea? Coffee? Cocktail? Bourbon?" I held up my glass as an example. "We've got juice and soft drinks, too."

He hesitated a brief moment and then shrugged his shoulders. "Sure, thanks," he said. "I'll have what you're having."

"Okay. Bourbon on the rocks." I prepared his drink and dropped it off before I sat down in my spot.

After the first swallow, his shoulders relaxed a bit and he smiled.

"So, what's in there?" I waved my glass in the direction of the file in his lap. "Anything to do with this story?"

He placed his drink on an end table and eagerly opened the file. "That's the thing," he said. "I have a couple of pictures of them."

"Of the aliens?" My voice rose a decibel.

"Yes." He eagerly nodded his head. "Aliens, ghosts, whatever they are."

"How did you manage to get pictures of them?" I said.

"My friend Nate—Nate's the one who said he might meet me here today—knows all about this stuff and he told me to have a couple of cameras lying around, in case, you know." He reached down and lifted a large photograph from the stack in his file. "He said when I sensed they were nearby I should start shooting shots all over the place and hope I caught something. So I did."

"And you actually got something on film?"

"Oh, yes." He handed me the picture in his grasp. "A couple of days ago I was down in the basement and I could tell that *they* were there because the cats were going crazy. My pets kept hissing and jumping up in the air like they were attacking something. I was trying to sleep on the couch and had left a disposable camera on the coffee table. When the cats started acting up, I jumped up and started taking pictures all over the place."

I studied the enlarged photo and flinched when the main image came into view. In the background, an armchair in a corner of a paneled room took up one

173

half of picture; the other side of the picture was covered with a milky shape that was unmistakably part of a face. I clearly made out a small mouth, openings for nostrils where the nose was, and a huge, almond-shaped eye.

"It looks like I got half of his face as he was looking in my direction," the man said. "Right?"

"Yes," I said. "It's a face all right. But of what?"

"Yeah. Just like I said. Ghost or alien?"

"I'm not sure, but I'd probably say alien." I couldn't believe my own ears. "It looks exactly like the drawings of aliens you see on TV or in the magazines."

"Cool. Here's the other one," he said, handing over another enlarged photograph. "I've got more, but these are the best two."

The picture showed the same basement but from a different angle. In the center of the shot, an orange tabby cat hovered in the air, fangs bared in an apparent hiss as it splayed out its limbs at an attacker. The attacker was a wispy, white shape that bent over the cat in taunt. Although the lower part of the body tapered off into nothingness, the upper portion had a distinct human form and a head with two enormous, almond-shaped eyes seemingly focused on the cat.

"Creepy, huh?" A large grin had spread over his face.

"Very creepy indeed," I said. "If these are real things you're capturing on film, you need to show them to a real parapsychologist or a photographic expert, someone who might be able to help you better."

Suddenly the doorbell rang.

"That could be Nate," he said from the parlor as I went to open the door.

"Hi, I'm Nate." An individual stood on the other side of the door. He held up a palm with splayed fingers in the familiar Klingon greeting.

Ah, a trekkie, I thought to myself. Or trekker, whatever they're called. "Come on inside," I said. "Your friend's in here."

After another Klingon salute, he sat down on the sofa next to his friend. "So, what do you think about those pictures?" he asked. "Far out, huh?"

"Oh, yes. That they are." Seeing the wistful glance he gave his friend's glass of bourbon, I offered him a drink and got up to serve him. For several minutes the conversation drifted from ghosts to aliens to cats, then Nate started asking questions about the book I had started.

"That's a cool idea to write a book about the ghosts in Old Louisville," he said. "You should write one about Lexington, too. They've got tons of ghost stories there."

"Yes, that would make a great book," I said, "but I think I'll leave it to someone who lives in Lexington. I'm not from there, so I don't know that I'd have the expertise to write something like that."

"I know what you mean. I'm not from here, either."

"Oh? Where are you from then?" I grabbed a dish of mixed nuts and passed them around.

"No, I'm not from *here*," he said with a raise of his eyebrows, placing an inordinate amount of emphasis on the last word.

"You're not from Louisville? Are you from somewhere else in Kentucky?"

"No, I'm not from *here*," he said. "I'm not even from this *planet*."

"Oh, I see." I shifted nervously in my chair, making sure to keep a smile painted on my face. I had absolutely no desire to carry on the conversation in the same vein; however, good manners compelled me to make a further inquiry or two. "What planet would you be from then?"

The location and coordinates he gave me sounded suspiciously reminiscent of something William Shatner might have said in his slimmer days. "How nice," I said. "Was it hard adjusting to life in this galaxy?"

"Not really," he said. "And now I've been here so long it feels like home. But," he whispered in a conspiratorial tone, "I think these things fighting with the cats in the picture here might be my people. They're coming back for me."

"The space spooks?" I said, looking at his friend. "Well, then they must be aliens, right?"

"I'm not sure, either," said Nate. "They look more like ghosts to me."

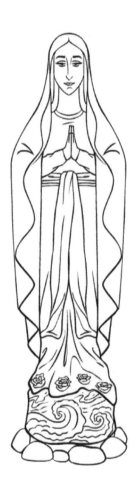

Big Momma Cheese

Several nights later, the doorbell rang. I sat up in bed. The dogs started barking, but I calmed them down and made them settle back in. A quick glance at the cell phone revealed that it was half past three. Who'd be stopping by at such a late hour? Hopefully, it wasn't one of the neighborhood drunks looking for a handout. Since Nate and his friend with the etched teeth had shown up for bourbon in the front parlor, it seemed that more and more oddballs were making it a habit to ring the front doorbell at La Casa Fabulosa. I snuck downstairs and pressed myself up against the wall in the foyer so as to keep out of sight of whoever stood at the door. It had worked before, so it couldn't hurt to try again: if it appeared to be an unsavory character or a weirdo, I could ignore the annoying doorbell and hope they went away; if it was someone I knew or someone in distress, I would let them in. Usually, it was an unsavory character.

From my post against the wall, I stuck my head out a bit and saw the shape of a woman on the front porch. With the glare from the streetlight behind, I couldn't make out much more than that, but I could tell that she had a frizzy mane of long, black hair that provided an unruly frame for a face I could not see. Although I felt a slight pang of hesitancy, I emerged from the shadows and turned on the light in the entry hall. Then, I carefully opened the front door.

Before me stood a woman who could have been anywhere from forty to seventy years of age, and deep creases worked their way across a large, round face. She appeared to have something of a natural scowl, an attribute that was only heightened by the jowly makeup of her jaws; her lowered dark eyes darted back and forth as I studied her.

"Yes?" I tried not to sound annoyed. "Can I help you with something?"

Her eyes rose and met mine, and I saw that she wore a type of black woolen cape over an old quilted housecoat. She wore pink fuzzy slippers as well, so I assumed she was from the neighborhood.

"You need to be careful," she said in a halting voice. "Some people don't like what you're doing, you know."

"Careful about what?"

"Careful about digging up the ghosts in the neighborhood. Lots of people don't like that shit. *She* told me to tell you." The woman turned her head and looked over her left shoulder and then turned to look over her right.

"She *who*?" I asked. "I'm not sure what you're talking about." I couldn't decide if I should be alarmed or amused. Since word had gotten out about me working on a book of ghost stories from the neighborhood, I found myself having more and more interesting conversations with the residents.

"Her, the Big Momma Cheese," she whispered, pointing to her left breast. She made a dramatic sweep with her eyes. Again, the woman turned and looked over one shoulder, and then the next.

"You call your boob the Big Momma Cheese?" I grabbed the door handle and got ready just in case I'd have to make a speedy exit and shut this nut job out.

"No, dummy. *She's* the Big Momma Cheese. She's hiding out there." She pointed at her breast again. Then she looked dramatically over her shoulders again.

"I don't think I know any Big Momma Cheeses. And I'm sure I don't know any who live under your coat."

Slowly—but only after two more dramatic over-the-shoulder ganders—the female visitor used one hand to slowly open the left side of her coat-cape. She extended an index finger and pointed again. "*Her.* The Big Momma Cheese."

"Where?" At first, I didn't see anything. "What in the devil are you talking about?" A patch of light blue suddenly caught my attention. Then, a form gradually came into view as I stooped and angled my face to better see. It was a large plaster statue of the Virgin Mary the woman had cradled in the crook of her arm.

"Oh," I said, "*that* Big Momma Cheese. How nice."

"Yes, *her.*" She did the look-around thing again and widened her eyes at me. "She told me to come over and check on you. Let you know that everything's going to be okay."

"Well, that's nice of you both," I said. "I appreciate it a lot." I slowly started to back away so I could close the door, trying my hardest not to give her the impression that I wanted to get rid of her. Somewhere in the back of my mind, I recalled a crazy woman talking to a statue of the Virgin Mary in a John Waters film. What was the name of that movie?

"But watch out for the people who don't understand." She lunged forward to wedge herself between the door and me. "Be careful."

"I will," I said. "Thanks for stopping by."

"Big Momma Cheese has got your back! Don't you forget it." The woman closed the front of her cape and smoothed her hair. Then it appeared she lowered her head so she could whisper something to the statuette.

"Thanks, I won't." I managed to close the door and keep her outside. "Thanks again." I turned to go upstairs and took a step, but then I decided to return to the door so I could watch her leave and see where she came from. The porch and the front walk were both empty, and she was nowhere in sight.

I hummed the melody of the theme from *The Twilight Zone* and slowly made my way across the foyer so I could go back up to bed. The next time I saw my friend Kelly, an ardent Catholic, I'd have to ask if he knew about this woman who was friends with the Big Momma Cheese. I grasped the railing and took the first step to go upstairs when the telephone rang.

After a moment's hesitation I picked up. "Hello?" I said, curious as to who would be calling at such a late hour.

"I see you finally got rid of that weirdo on your front porch, hon. I was going to call you and warn you, but you got to the door before the call went through."

Ah, Loretty. I should have known better.

"I bet she was lookin' for a handout, wasn't she?"

"She was telling me to watch my back." I sat down on the bottom step of the stairs and listened as Loretty coughed and cleared her throat. "Say," I said, "aren't you up awfully late?"

"Me?" she said, taking a noisy drink that caused ice cubes to clink together in her glass. "I don't sleep much, maybe a couple hours every night. And then all I do is hang upside down from the rafters a bit, like a bat."

I laughed and told her that must be quite a sight. Then I grabbed the cord and pulled the phone into the parlor. At the front parlor I flipped the light on and off three times.

"Yeah, I see you down there," she said. "Here, hang on a sec."

I looked up and saw a lone window on the top floor fill with light and then go on and off. "OK," I said. "I see you."

"So what was that dingbat telling you to watch out for?" said Loretty. Even though she said she didn't need much sleep, her voice had a tired edge to it.

"Oh, that some people didn't like the fact that I was writing about the neighborhood and the ghosts down here," I replied. "But she told me that the Virgin Mary was watching out for me."

"Oh, it was that nut bag with the little statue hidden under her coat, wasn't it?" said Loretty. "I thought it might have been her. If she isn't over on the corner of Fourth and Crazy selling her charms and hitting people up for handouts, she's over at St. Louis Bertrand on Sixth Street. I think that fatty young priest lets her camp out in one of the confessionals when nobody needs it."

"She seemed pretty harmless to me," I said. "But it's good to know you've been keeping an eye out."

"Yeah, good ol' Loretty keeps an eye on this neighborhood," she said with a yawn. "Well, hon, I better let you go. Time for Loretty to go and hang upside down from the rafters."

"Thanks for calling," I said. "Good night."

I put the phone back and went up to the second floor. But, at the top of the stairs I realized I was wide awake and full of energy, so I decided to go for a walk. Since Fritz had gotten out of bed with me when the woman who was friends with Big Momma Cheese came to the front door, and he hadn't gone back to bed, I got his leash and we headed over to Central Park. There were no clouds in the sky, just lots of stars, as we followed our usual route down Third Street and strolled through St. James Court. At the south end of the park I found a large Osage orange tree that was as gnarled and whorled as the Witches' Tree and we sat ourselves down underneath it.

Back across the street, the limestone of the massive Conrad-Caldwell House seemed to glow in the darkness and from my vantage point I studied the squat turrets and towers that jutted above the roofline. Scattered here and there about the rough-hewn surfaces, whimsical yet menacing faces looked down at us from their perches where they were sculpted in the 1890s. Some had the visages of owls or lions while others had the faces of distinctly mythological creatures. We sat there in the shadows for half an hour; and aside from the sounds of the night, we were alone.

Sitting under the tree and doing nothing except listening to the raccoons and squirrels in the branches made me hungry, which in turn made me think about recipes I had been working on over the previous few days. I had decided to develop a recipe for a fig cake with bourbon but I hadn't been able to find any fresh figs. My aunt Jane had sent some home-canned ones up from Louisiana for the last Christmas, so I started thinking about using them, but then all of a sudden I remembered the fig tree behind the Magnolia Bar and Grill, barely two blocks away. There were probably tons of figs on it at that time of year, so Fritz and I headed over that way.

Even though the orange-red letters of the old neon sign out front spelled out "Magnolia Bar and Grill," they stopped serving food years ago but never quite got around to removing the "Grill" part. It was always one of the better known dives in Old Louisville and on any given night you were sure to find a good mix of crusty locals, college students, and devotees from other parts of the city. That night as Fritz and I came around the block to the Mag Bar, as most referred to it, there was still plenty of time before the four o'clock closing hour rolled around, and lively music dulled by the overpowering din of conversation spilled out onto the street.

Rounding the corner, I passed an old hitching post made of incised stone at the edge of someone's front yard and went to the side of the bar. Through the front door and windows it was easy to see the place was packed. Throngs of people bounced and gyrated to the music and Justin, the bartender, looked on and smiled as several women got up to dance on the bar. Behind the building, Fritz and I slipped through a hole in the fence and we found oodles of ripe figs dangling from the branches. In the corner of an adjacent yard, a large bathtub Mary gazed somberly across the grass in our direction. Fortunately, I happened to spy two clean-looking plastic bags on the ground near the trash cans at the back door and I seized them and quickly filled them. When I turned to sneak back through the fence I noticed a possum hidden among the fig leaves, its beady eyes watching me as it slowly nibbled at a large fig.

As I made my way along the sidewalk, I almost collided with a passing figure and stepped aside to let him pass. When I looked up, I saw that it was Micah, the violin case swinging at his side as he walked toward Third Street. But instead of following him that way, we turned and went back to Second Street. For some reason, I still wasn't tired and early morning hunger pangs niggled at my stomach so we crossed the intersection, walked over to First Street and down a couple of blocks to Juanita's Burger Boy. Juanita's, as most people called it, was one of the few restaurants in the city that stayed open 24 hours a day and it was a notorious dive. For breakfast it couldn't be beat. A row of white lights twinkled along the low roof as we approached, passing a front yard where an enormous rose of Sharon bush seemed to collapse beneath its own weight. Streaked with red, a multitude of lavender blooms caught the glow of a nearby coach lamp and when we arrived at the door to the restaurant, there didn't appear to be much activity inside. Aside from an older gentleman nursing a cup of coffee at one end of the counter, there was only a young couple sitting at a two top near the door. But I knew that would change when the bars closed and hundreds of hungry college kids turned out onto the streets of Old Louisville.

I tied Fritz up outside, near a window so I could keep an eye on him. He sadly wagged his stub of a tail and lowered his head when I assured him I wouldn't take too long. I found a stool at the counter and let the woman at the grill pour me a cup of coffee. When she removed the pen from behind her ear and pulled her pad out of an apron pocket, I ordered a platter of scrambled eggs with hash browns and whole wheat toast. For Fritz I got a side of bacon. When the food came and I took the bacon out to him, he gobbled it up in two bites and let out a long howl of appreciation.

Back at the counter, I had almost finished my food when someone sat down next to me at the counter. I looked over and saw that it was Kim Bob, a man from our neighborhood association who sometimes liked to dress as a woman. When he was dressed as a male, he had told us, he preferred it when people called him "Bob" and when he was dressed as a female he wanted to be called "Kim." Since nobody really knew if he was going to be dressed as a woman or a man on any given day, most of the neighbors I knew called him Kim Bob.

In all the time I had ever seen him, however, he was always dressed as Kim and that night was no different. He wore a brown wig with straight hair to the shoulders and he had on a gold lamé party dress trimmed with black velvet. If I wasn't mistaken, it was the same dress he had been wearing the first time we met, a half year before.

I had joined the neighborhood association and was attending my first meeting, which was at Clark and Polly Wood's house, when Kim Bob walked in that night and sat down next to me and Ramon on a large sofa. He introduced himself as Kim, and I complimented him on the nice duds, and we chatted a bit before the meeting started. A couple of minutes later, when Clark Wood walked in and sat down next to his wife, he spied what he assumed to be a new member perched on his couch, so he leaned over and loudly whispered "Who's that over there in the gold dress?" in Polly's ear. "Is she new to the neighborhood?"

Polly, in turn, slapped her husband playfully on the arm. "Clark, that's Bob," she said in a low voice. "You already know him." Polly had a head of snowy white hair and brushed a strand back behind an ear.

"Who?" said Clark, who was a bit hard of hearing. "I don't think I know her."

"Of course, you do," Polly replied. "That's Bob, from down the street." A look of confusion caused Clark's brows to wrinkle. "Who?" he had insisted.

"THAT'S BOB FROM DOWN THE STREET!" Polly replied, raising her voice and leaning in closer to her husband.

There was a momentary pause while the words sank in and then Clark's eyes opened wide with the realization. "No shit?" he had said in a tone of slow wonderment, and the meeting was soon called to order.

That night at Juanita's Burger Boy I finished my scrambled eggs in near silence because Kim Bob didn't appear to be in a chatty mood. Before I knew it, the stool next to me was empty and the hungry after-hours bar crowd started filling up the place. I went out front, where several people had gathered around Fritz to say hello, and he offered eager tail wags in exchange for them scratching the top of his head. When I approached the little cluster, I saw that one of them looked familiar. It was Beau. He had on the same dark trench coat, but this time his long brown hair had been pulled back in a ponytail.

A smile spread across his face when he saw me. "I thought this here dog looked like someone I knew." He turned to his companions and told them to go inside and get a table, where he would join them shortly. "Dude," he said, coming closer. "I've been meaning to come by and see you."

"If you do come by, feel free to use the doorbell."

"Man, don't say that word." He scrunched up his nose and shook his head as if a shudder had run down his spine. "I hate those things and you know it."

"So, what were you going to tell me this time?"

"Remember the other night when we saw that goat on Fourth Street?" He jammed his hands into the coat pockets and hunched his shoulders.

"Yes," I said. "I saw you go off after it. Did you follow it over to Central Park?"

"Damn straight," he said. "That crazy old goat ran into the park and then back out again and then started running all over the whole neighborhood. I followed it for half an hour before it made its fool way back to the park."

I suppressed a grin at the thought of Beau chasing the goat around Old Louisville and untied Fritz from the bike rack in front of the diner. "And what happened when you finally caught up with it?"

"That's the thing I wanted to tell you about," he said. "Remember that woman we saw, the one all dressed in white and with the bandana on her head?"

I nodded my head and stepped to the side so several rowdy people could enter the restaurant. "Yeah, what about her?"

Beau motioned for me to follow him to a small wrought iron table and chairs on the sidewalk. "Well, she was there, and the goat just walked up to her like he knew what he was supposed to do. Not only that, she wasn't alone. She had several people there and it was sort of like they were doing a ritual or something."

"Really?" I said. "What were they doing?"

"I'm not sure," said Beau. "They stood around in a circle under one of those big oak trees and were speaking some kind of gibberish in a weird language I couldn't understand. But the goat waited there in the middle, not saying a thing."

"They didn't hurt the goat or anything, did they?"

"I don't think so," he said. "They ended up putting it on a rope and taking it away when they saw me. I was hiding behind a tree, trying to stay out of sight, but then one of them saw me and decided to break things up."

"How many of them were there?" I said. "What else were they doing?"

"Not really sure," he said. "Five or six? They had a little fire going and were passing around a bottle of something. The one we saw wasn't in charge, though. I think she delivered the goat and then beat it."

"Josephine wasn't in charge? I thought she would have been the leader."

Beau shook his head. "The leader was a really short little woman with dark frizzy hair. She had a weird little friend in a black cape at her side who kept pulling out this statue of the Virgin Mary and pretended like she was talking and listening to it."

"The Big Momma Cheese!"

"Huh?"

"That's what the odd little one calls her Virgin Mary statue."

"Whatever. You know the life story of every last weirdo in this neighborhood, don't you?"

"No comment."

"Well you should have seen the *other* women assisting them. They were each like seven feet tall." He held a hand above his head to illustrate.

"That's awfully tall," I said. "Maybe they had on high heels or something."

"I don't know, but they were some tall bitches, that's for sure." Beau leaned over and patted Fritz on the head. "Well, I need to get inside and get me some food soon," he said. "Just wanted to let you know what I saw. I guess it was kind of like a voodoo ceremony or something like that." He stopped and scratched his chin for a moment. "Or wait, man, maybe they were like druids or something.

Maybe it was like some type of full moon ritual." He cupped his chin with his hand and squinted. "Trippy."

"Speaking of trippy, I did some research and have an old newspaper article you'll want to see."

"Yeah? About what?"

"Your one-armed ghost."

"No way. You mean you found something?"

"Yes, an article in *The Atlanta Constitution* from March 17, 1903. That morning somebody found the decaying arm of an unknown black woman hanging from the front door of a Fourth Street mansion. It looks like it was one of those houses where we were creeping around looking for the goat."

"No way! You think that was Josephine's arm?"

"I have no idea what to think. This neighborhood is something else. Stop by sometime and I'll give you a copy of the article."

"Sure thing."

"Well, I don't want to keep you," I said, pointing to the crowded interior of the diner, where his friends waited at a table against the dark paneled wall. "Nice seeing you again, and thanks for the information."

"Yeah, man," he said. "Good seeing you, too. I'll probably run into you in the park or on the sidewalk sometime soon." Beau left and joined his friends.

But when I turned to go, there was the terrible screeching of tires as a black Cadillac swerved at the intersection and came barreling toward me and Fritz.

Stormin' Norman and the Galt House Ghost

It was Tuesday evening of the next day, and instead of anyone cooking, the gang had decided to meet at Bearno's by the Bridge for beer and pizza. Located on the bottom floor of a massive building originally built as offices for the Louisville and Nashville Railroad, the well-known pizzeria sat in the shadows of the Second Street Bridge. The waitress was about to bring our order and I had resumed my recap of the previous night's events.

"So I was getting ready to cross the intersection with Fritz and go back home when this car ran a red light and had to swerve to miss another car. It missed us before it ran up on the curb and hit a stone retaining wall." I took a sip from my beer and passed around the basket of bread sticks. "The car lost its two front hubcaps and they came rolling back across the street and missed us by a few feet."

"Wow, you guys were really lucky," said Laura.

Beth nodded her head and made room for the arriving pizza at the center of the crowded table. "It's a good thing nobody got hurt."

I helped myself to a slice and doused it with parmesan cheese and red pepper flakes. "The front end of the one car was messed up, but other than that, it wasn't too bad. It sure added a bit of excitement to the evening, that's for sure. Everyone from Juanita's ran out to the street to see what was going on."

"You better watch out," laughed Wendy. "One of these days your luck is going to run out and the mean streets of Old Louisville are going to get you."

"We'll see." I deposited another piece of pizza on the plate Skippy held across the table in my direction. "But so far, so good."

"Oh, look!" Wendy shifted slightly in her seat and pointed to the stairs at the front of the restaurant. "It's Micah." Sure enough, the tall figure with the violin case entered and passed near our table. "I wonder where he's going," she said as he drifted from sight.

"Funny," I said. "I saw him right before I walked over to Juanita's last night. Almost ran into him on the sidewalk outside the Mag Bar."

Beth chuckled and wiped her mouth. "You should ask him if he knows Josephine or the Stick Witch or any of these other people that are supposed to be haunting the neighborhood."

Suddenly my mind raced back to the night before. "Speaking of hauntings," I said, "I think someone might have given me a lead on a new story."

"A ghost story?" Skippy grabbed the pitcher of beer and refilled his glass. "Or maybe a story about one of the neighborhood weirdoes?"

"A ghost story," I said. "When we were out on the street after the accident last night, this older guy started talking to me and said the place attached to Juanita's is haunted." I described the tall frame house sharing a wall with the diner and everyone seemed to understand the building I was talking about. "Supposedly two ex-cons or something like that broke into the place when the woman renting the apartment on the top floor was working her shift waiting tables at Juanita's. It was back in the 70s and the woman left her daughter up there by herself. She was seven or eight, I think."

"Oh, no. What happened?" Laura stopped chewing and seized a napkin as a look of dread came over her.

"This old guy claims they killed the little girl and left her body in the closet. The mother found it when she came back from her shift that night, and the closet's been haunted ever since, he said." I popped a naked bit of crust into my mouth and chewed. "People who've lived in that apartment say they always hear crying coming from that little closet."

"Oh, that's really awful." Beth laid a crumpled napkin on her plate and then pushed it away.

"Yes, it is, if it really happened like the guy said. I'll have to snoop around and see if I can find any record of the murder." I drained the last bit of beer from my glass and sat back in my chair.

The waitress brought us the check and we chatted for a while longer. When it came time to leave, I boxed up some of the leftover pizza to take to Ramon, who had to work late that night, and we made our way up to the sidewalk and said our good-byes.

In front of the old ashlar building was a historical marker about the famous Galt House, and I stopped to read it. Although the building housing the basement pizzeria had been built in 1877 as office headquarters for the Louisville and Nashville Railroad, the original Galt House Hotel had occupied the site before that, from 1835 until 1865, when a fire destroyed it. Charles Dickens had stayed there once and so had a host of other notables, including General Ulysses S. Grant, who met there in March 1864 with General Sherman to plan his infamous "March to the Sea." I had always heard rumors that the place was haunted and that the basement was riddled with a maze of underground tunnels that led to the river, but somehow I had never managed to penetrate the secret parts of the old building.

Once I was done reading, I prepared to round the corner and return to the car, which I had parked down on the street behind the old building, when something caught my eye. It was a large vertical sign painted in a recess on the façade and there, staring down at me, was a gypsy woman scrying a crystal ball. When I saw the turban on her head and the hoops dangling from her ears, I remembered the paper airplane message Skippy had handed over to me not too long before—

and all at once I knew why the sketch I had seen looked so familiar. It was a hand-drawn reproduction of the sign that loomed over me—complete with the Great Dane that stood on its hind legs and a comical rendering of a stereotypical ghost. The only thing missing on the drawn version I had received were the words such as "Madame Zelda" over the gypsy woman and the entertainment "featuring Stormin' Norman & the Galt House Ghost every Saturday at 9:15"—and, of course, the words at the top of the sign, which advertised something known as "Squirrelly's Magic Tea Room."

I had seen the figures on the drawing before and now I was standing in front of their inspiration. Squirrelly's Magic Tea Room was something of a local legend, a bit of quirk that all Louisvillians knew about because of its proximity to the heavily trafficked bridge that crossed over to Indiana from Second Street. How many times had I driven past and read the colorful sign without really knowing what it was all about?

Coincidentally, I had run into my friend Kelly a few days before and when Squirrelly's Magic Tea Room somehow came up in conversation, he was a wealth of information. It seems a man by the name of Larry Jones was the brains behind the operation and he first became interested in magic as a teenager living in New York in the early 1940s. After getting a law degree from the University of Virginia he moved to Louisville to join a law firm in the 1950s. Under the stage name of Baron LaValle, he achieved a certain degree of national recognition and even appeared on the *Ed Sullivan Show* and on the *Captain Kangaroo Show*. When he was in his 60s, and still practicing law, he opened the Squirrelly's Tea Room in downtown Louisville, where he designed a 75-seat magic theater upstairs in the old Louisville and Nashville Railroad building. People started calling him Captain Squirrelly and ever since he had been delighting weekly audiences with his burlesque magic show.

Even though it wasn't Saturday, the night of his regular performances, it appeared that a lot of people were entering the building and going upstairs to the magic tea room area, so I made my way back into the building and up the stairs. On the way I bumped into the one of the waiters, someone who used to work with me at the Seelbach Hotel, and when I asked him what was going on, he said there was a private party that evening and that Captain Squirrelly himself was on hand for the entertainment. It didn't take much before he motioned for me to follow him through a door to an area off-limits to all but the employees, and he told me to feel free to hide out there as long as I wanted while I eavesdropped and took in visual tidbits of the show.

Colorful, oversized posters of old-time magicians hung on the walls and on the stage stood an older gentleman I assumed to be the selfsame Squirrelly. He wore a brown plaid suit and had pulled a pigeon from a hat. To the side was a wooden table draped with a red cloth where he had laid out some of the tools of the trade: several silver rings, a vase of flowers, a saw, and a number of smaller unidentifiable items.

After several card tricks, I grew a bit antsy and decided to explore a bit on my own. I found my friend and asked him to point me in the direction of the basement, which he was reluctant to do until I lied and promised that I would not get into trouble or do anything stupid.

"If you get caught," he said, "I'm saying I've never seen you before in my entire life." Then he gave me a detailed set of instructions on how to access the secret parts of the building. As I left the magical tea room there was a roar of applause and laughter as Squirrelly delighted the crowd with another trick.

Pretending that I knew where I was going, I made my way to the stairs. On a mid-point landing, I discovered a recessed area in the brick wall that might have doubled as a closet, had it not been for the colorful bit of painted archway framing the entryway. Painted to simulate an intricate and multi-hued mosaic pattern, the sculpted piece of wood looked like it might have been inspired by a palace from the Middle East.

I had discovered Madam Zelda's lair. And there sat the enigmatic woman herself, at a small table in front of an exotically tapestried wall hanging. On the other side of the table, where the flame of a solitary candle flickered in the semidarkness, an attentive customer leaned in and listened as Zelda told her fortune. But instead of using the crystal ball depicted on the sign outside, the fortune teller appeared to be reading her client's palm. There was no sign at all of a crystal ball in the immediate vicinity.

Not only that, instead of the turban-wearing gypsy woman with the fiery eyes and large hoop ear rings, this lady looked like a plain old—and decidedly non-clairvoyant—senior citizen in her black satin blouse and close-cropped white hair. I stood off to the side so I could eavesdrop.

"You will meet a man who will bring you lots of happiness and wealth," she told the eager listener. "And prunes. He will come bearing prunes," she said with a bit of a twang and no small degree of solemnity. What? This palm reader didn't even have the slightest eastern European accent. And what kind of fortune teller saw prunes in somebody's future? Muttering to myself, I returned to the stairs.

Mentally following my friend's directions I made my way to the main area of the restaurant and eventually stumbled across the employee lounge he had described. Uncomfortable-looking black chairs were scattered about and a tired man hunched over a newspaper and a cup of coffee at a corner table, but other than that, the room was empty.

As instructed, I strode to the back and pushed through an inconspicuous door, beyond which lay an entirely different world, a realm of murky shadows and cavernous spaces that couldn't be reached by the stark florescent lights of the break room. Letting my eyes adjust to the dimness—the only light seeped through a multitude of dirt-streaked windows that faced the bridge and the street lamps that lined it—I was amazed to find myself in what appeared to be an entirely different building than the one I had entered.

Apparently vacant and unused, the entire back part of the old structure looked like an eerie time capsule that went back to the 1920s and 30s. Here and there, intruders had left footprints in the thick layer of dust covering the floor in most of the rooms, and random cardboard boxes and crates rested against the wall in the main corridor. Steps away beckoned the grand staircase, which led to more prohibited floors and vacant rooms above, and I went over to it and let my hand glide up the railing as I made my ascent. Curiously, the railing had a cool gleam and was free of dust as if people were still traipsing up and down it all the time.

I followed the steps to the top, looked around, and then made my way back down. On the walls around the stairwell hung an assortment of old pictures and framed newspaper articles about the original Galt House Hotel and other local landmarks. Some of them reported on infamous murders and well-known hauntings in the area.

In one yellowing article, a reporter claimed that the building constructed on the site of the former hotel was supposedly haunted by a man known as Captain Jack. Along with a woman named Elizabeth and her young daughter, he was trapped and burned to death in the fire. Not too far away I found a framed poster with a woman's face emerging from a wisp of cloud or smoke. The caption written across the front of the poster asked: "Is this the woman whose spirit many have claimed to see in this building?" The fading orange of the poster background seemed to match the leatherette upholstery of an Art Deco circular sofa that rested nearby, the pillowed backrest column rising from its center dulled by a thin layer of grime.

After trespassing in the dark crevices of the upper levels, I stopped at the top of the stairway leading to the basement. Reputedly, the subterranean area was huge and stretched all the way to the river, where bootleggers unloaded moonshine deliveries during Prohibition and engaged in all types of illicit activities. If I listened hard enough I could almost hear their coarse language and the shouts of river rats echoing off the walls beneath my feet. I tried an antique push-button light switch in the wall, but to no avail: the light sconce down on the next landing remained dark.

I looked over my shoulder and saw a number of shadows thrown across the wall. Probably people walking by on the bridge, I told myself. I leaned forward and tried to see to the bottom of the steps, but the weak light streaming through the windows failed to reach the lowest portion of the basement stairs.

Even though I knew it was better to leave, my feet wouldn't cooperate, and before I knew it, my hand was gliding down the smooth railing to the next landing.

Grit and sand seemed to punctuate every step I took with abrasion, and soon I found myself standing in total darkness. Cursing under my breath, I grabbed the railing and lowered myself into the void. In the back of my mind I had convinced myself that I would find a working light switch at the bottom, but when I stepped off the last tread and started feeling around on the wall, I only found another push-button set that turned nothing on when depressed. After feeling around and coming up empty-handed I finally decided to leave and was making my sluggish way back to the steps when I bumped into something.

It felt like a small bedside table or something that had been pushed up against the wall, and upon further examination my hands discovered something that brought a smile to my face. After a bit of fumbling, I found the button, pressed, and hoped for the best.

Sure enough, it worked; and a sudden beam of yellow light sliced the darkness. It was a large industrial flashlight, the square kind with a top handle, and it must have been left on the wooden stand for people wanting to go on further into the basement. I shone it around to get my bearings, and in a far wall I saw a door.

Hobos

After pausing a moment to listen and make sure nobody else was skulking about, I went to the door and pushed it open. A loud scrape echoed across the floor as the warped wood at the bottom caught the concrete and stuck—until I forced my way through to the other side.

It appeared to be an enormous underground room that went on for a hundred yards or more, but how far it really extended I couldn't be sure because the flashlight only illuminated the first 10 or 20 yards. From somewhere in the darkness came the faint trickle of water.

It also seemed that the odor of cigarettes hung in the air. I swung the flashlight beam to my right and then to my left, where a rivulet of water ran down a seam in the nearest wall. Although the area seemed largely empty, clusters of boxes or old pieces of furniture had been deposited here and there. In a recessed area of the wall to my right several enormous casks rested on their sides, and several yards away rotting staves had been swept into a mound. Against the wall stood three rusty circular bands that had probably held the barrels together at one time. From the generous circumference of the iron hoops, I assumed the casks to be the typical hogsheads that at one time rolled through the streets of downtown Louisville by the hundreds. Back then, if they weren't packed full with a thousand pounds of tobacco, chances were they contained pork, whiskey, or any number of other items processed in the city.

I stopped to listen again, and as I stood there a distant roar seemed to rise above the trickling water. Could the basement really extend all the way to the river? It sounded like the far-off rushing of water, but then again it could have been nothing more than an acoustical phenomenon triggered by the unusual surroundings. Letting the yellow beam of light guide me, I moved forward into the shadows. Farther on, several more barrels stood on their ends, and an enormous and empty picture frame leaned up against the wall.

Next to that waited a man wearing a gray trench coat and a baseball cap.

I gasped. Was this a real person, or was I hallucinating?

"Do not worry," the man said, in a gravelly voice. "I will not hurt you." He shifted his feet and moved his face to avoid the immediate glare of the light.

My heart pounding in my throat, I jumped and almost stumbled backward. I was too startled to speak and my feet were telling me to back away from this stranger.

"Sorry, I did not mean to scare you." He took a drag on a bit of cigarette held between his thumb and forefinger and then cast it to the ground, where he mashed it out with the heel of a worn-out boot. "I was not expecting anybody to find me down here. Usually, I am here all by myself."

Finally, my heartbeat slowed a bit and I was able to regain my speech. "Sorry if I'm bothering you," I said. "I thought the place was empty."

"Yes, so did I," he said. "But every once in a while someone finds his way to the underground."

A niggling in the pit of my stomach told me to make a hasty exit, but curiosity got the better of me and I stood my ground. "I guess that means you're in this basement a lot then?"

"More often than most." He took a step in my direction. "I know my way around down here as well. It goes on and on." Squinting, he stopped and studied me for a moment. "Now you don't look like you come to the underbelly of the city very often."

It was at that moment the formality of the man's speech hit me. He didn't sound like he was from the area. Despite the haggard voice, there was a precision to his words and a certain clipped elegance to his accent.

"No," I said. "I don't come below much at all."

"Not many people do," he said, "but sometimes young people find their way to these dark passages in the middle of the night. Or else the employees from the restaurant get bored and creep down here on a dare. It does not happen very often but I usually stay out of sight when they do."

He took another step in my direction and reached into his pocket. "I watch." After taking out a cigarette, he lit it and examined the glowing end. "Sometimes I just watch."

I observed the gray stubble on his chin as he took a long drag on his cigarette and then exhaled a long stream of smoke through his nostrils. "I guess I should be going. Sorry if I disturbed you." I started to back away.

"Do not let me scare you off," he said, taking another slow step. "On rare occasions I do like to talk to the people who come below."

"Well, I really should leave." I took another step backward and that was when an overpowering odor reached my nose. It seemed to be the intense mix of body reek and alcohol that I had smelled on severe alcoholics before, the result of years of cheap booze saturating the perspiration that oozed through their pores.

"My name is Norman," he said, catching me off guard. "What is yours?"

I hesitated for a minute. "My name's Jim," I lied.

I wanted to turn and hightail it out of there, but suddenly a thought struck me. "Say, you're not Stormin' Norman of *Stormin' Norman and the Galt House Ghost*, are you?"

"Who?" He inhaled a lungful of smoke and held it in for several seconds before releasing it with a slight groan. "Did you say something about a ghost?"

"Stormin' Norman and the Galt House Ghost," I repeated. "You know, the ones advertised on the big hand-painted sign on the front of the building."

"No, I do not know Stormin' Norman or the Galt House Ghost," he said. "And I do not believe I have seen this sign you describe."

I raised a finger and pointed above us. "It's up there, on Second Street, on the front of the building," I said. "You can't miss it. It's right there when you come in the main door."

Norman shook his head slowly and took another drag on his cigarette. "I have never come through that door," he said. "Or any other door up above for that matter." Eyes narrowing ever so slightly, he studied me for a moment and scratched the stubble on his left cheek.

"Then how do you—?" I stopped short when I realized he must have gained access through the creepy basement. Did this guy have knowledge of the supposed system of secret tunnels that ran under the city?

Almost as if he had read my mind, Norman nodded his head and smiled. "When you are a hobo such as I you learn about the hidden places in a town."

"What?" I laughed nervously. "You didn't say you were a hobo, did you?"

For a few seconds there was silence between us, a lack of conversation that was punctuated by the sharp sound of trickling water.

Then he sucked on his cigarette and released the smoke with another slight groan. "Yes, I did say that I am a hobo," he said. "I've been riding the rails most of my life. Almost as long as I care to remember."

I studied Norman and my brows furrowed together as images of hobos flooded my mind. Hobos really came into their own during the Great Depression and they tended to hang out near the railroad tracks, where they roasted weenies around campfires and ate pork and beans straight from the can. And they dressed a certain way. True, Norman did have a nice hobo coat, but the baseball cap looked out of place. I was doubtful about his assertion.

"I know what you are thinking," he said, like he had read my mind again. "That hobos are a thing of the past. But they are not. We are amongst you today." He flicked a bit of ash from the tip of his cigarette and crossed his arms. "We do not carry bindles anymore, just so you know."

For the first time, I noticed the chill in the dank room, and a light shudder ran across my back. "What's a bindle?"

"You know," he said, "it is the pack hobos carry at the end of a stick in all the cartoons. Hobos always carry a bindle in the cartoons."

"I didn't know there was an actual name for those things." Maybe Norman was a real hobo, I told myself.

"Yes," said Norman. "Such a contraption is called a bindle and nobody uses them nowadays." His arms still crossed, he raised the cigarette to his lips, took one last puff that caused the end to flare, and ground out the butt with his heel.

"You learn something new every day," I said. There came a slight scurrying sound from a distant wall and I directed the flashlight beam in that direction. Whatever it was remained hidden in the shadows, however.

Norman didn't appear bothered by the intrusion and continued his didactics. "There are those of us who still use some of the old things, though," he said. "For example the old carvings and symbols left on fence posts and the sides of buildings. If you know how to read these signs you will know if a town welcomes you or despises you, where food and medicine can be had, and so forth."

Although the topic really was starting to interest me, I could feel a tightness behind the eyes that signaled the late hour and reminded me that I needed to get home. In addition, I had slowly come to realize that it probably wasn't a wise move to be all alone in a dark and abandoned basement with a complete stranger, no matter how nicely he spoke. "I should really head back upstairs."

"Wait," he said. "Let me show you something." Without waiting for a response, Norman walked over to a section of wall where the hogshead barrels rested. Then he leaned down and shouldered one of them to the side. There, in the wall, were the outlines of a small door that was maybe five feet high. He extended one of his arms and pushed the door open. "There," he said, brushing dust from his coat sleeve. "This will take you to many secret places. Come with me." He motioned for me to follow and ducked inside.

I walked over to the doorway and shone the light inside. Caught in the glow of the flashlight beam, Norman stood there and waited. The sound of rushing water seemed to be much more intense now. The ceilings in this space were very low and had to be less than six feet. If I went inside I would have to stay stooped over the whole time, but I told myself that would be a small price to pay to finally get into the famed secret tunnels below the city, if that's where I was indeed headed. From the looks of it, the room Norman had entered was very long and extremely narrow and had the appearance of a tunnel.

"Come." A gleam filled his eyes and he motioned with an arm.

That's when I got creeped out and knew that I couldn't follow Norman the Hobo into the depths of underground Louisville.

"Thanks, Norman," I said. "But I really have to go. It's been nice talking to you." I turned and quickly found my way out of the basement and up the stairs to the main part of the old Louisville and Nashville Railroad building. On the sidewalk in front of the sign for Squirrelly's Magic Tea Room I took a deep breath of warm air and went down to the next street and found the car.

194

Iron Hoops

A glorious Indian summer still nipping at its heels, fall soon arrived in Old Louisville and set about to cooling the evenings and fading the leaves on the oaks and cottonwoods to a palette of mellow orange, pink, and gold. Darkness arrived earlier and earlier, and soon St. James Court and the surrounding areas buzzed with activity.

With the first days of October came the St. James Court Art Show, a neighborhood celebration started in the 1950s that faithfully brought in hundreds of thousands of visitors to admire the work of oodles of artists and craftsmen against the backdrop of wonderful Victorian architecture. Our neighborhood association always hosted a number of participants in booths along Third Street and Magnolia and it fell to volunteers to check on the artists and see if they needed anything, and occasionally, watch the booth for them when they left to take a break.

I was in front of Mike and Judy Seale's house on the first day of the fair, watching a booth while the potter selling her wares there ran off to get something for lunch, when a turbaned figure on the sidewalk caught my attention. Her upper body emerged from the passing throng and she glanced briefly into the booth where I perched on a foldable director's chair. Then a stream of shoppers washed her away. I jumped down and tried to locate her in the crowd, but she was gone by the time I made it to the sidewalk.

I hadn't gotten a good look at her face, but I was relatively certain it was Josephine.

Pausing for a moment to gawk at the large Italianate house before me, I studied the façade. My eyes wandered to a long piece of architectural detail under the roofline. It was a strip embellished with stylized tobacco leaves, the source of the first homeowner's wealth. To the south stood a whimsical turreted residence built in 1892 for the owner of Azra, that year's winner of the Kentucky Derby. After gazing at its beautiful arched entryway and sculpted stone trimming, I retreated to the less crowded confines of the booth. Suddenly I felt something hit me in the back of the legs before I could jump back onto my perch. It wasn't another errant goat, was it? Perplexed, I turned around and watched as a large metal hoop bounced back, rolled several feet and fell flat onto the ground, barely missing several expensive pieces of ceramic on the nearest shelf.

"Oh, I'm ever so sorry," said a pleasant voice, as a tall form rushed in, ducking his head and evidently in pursuit of the errant ring. "She got away from me there for a moment." Before bending down to retrieve the hoop, the tall man spread his hands, reached out his arms, and traced a circular shape in the air over the ground. Then he made an involved gesture that somewhat resembled the sign of the cross and stood up, raising the hoop perpendicular to the ground so it rested at his side.

"Not a problem." I moved aside so a prospective customer could get a better view of a large fruit bowl.

"Hello," said the man with the hoop. "My name is Godwynn Goodwynn." He reached out his hand and shook mine. He wore a black straw hat with an immense brim that reminded me of something the Amish might wear.

"Nice to meet you."

"Have you heard of the Church of the Iron Hoop?"

My eyes drifted from his face, clean-shaven and boyish, to the dark trench coat he wore. It had come open and revealed dark linen slacks and a black vest over a white shirt with a grandfather collar.

"We believe in the circular nature of life and worship the Sacred Circle." He picked up his hoop and held it out for illustration.

"Well, I can't say that's something I've heard of," I said. "Are you a priest?"

He laughed. "Oh, no, I'm not a priest. They wear white. I'm an adherent, that's all. But we are looking for new devotees today." Then he smiled. "That's how it goes: you start off as a devotee, then become an adherent, and finally a priest." A low chuckle ensued as he lowered his voice. "Church of the Iron Hoop, anyone?"

"Well, thanks," I said, "but I'm not one for organized religion."

"Oh, but we're only very *loosely* organized," he said. "We believe in most any viewpoint—we're almost Unitarian in that respect—as long as it recognizes the Sacred Circle and the cyclical nature of this existence." Then he turned serious and narrowed his eyes at me. "You do recognize the Sacred Circle and the cyclical nature of this existence, don't you?"

"Cyclical nature of this existence, yes; Sacred Circle, not so sure."

"But we are all part of the Sacred Circle," he said, shaking his iron hoop for emphasis, "and we must do what we must."

"Yes, we must do what we must." Repeating it half-heartedly, I was suddenly elated to see the pottery vendor headed in my direction. I breathed a sigh of relief.

She resumed her post and thanked me for the break. I, in turn, said good-bye and quickly exited the tent; Godwynn Goodwynn followed.

"We must respect all religions as part of the Sacred Circle." He quickly rolled the hoop along at his side as he struggled to keep up.

"I quite agree," I said, trying to look like I had someplace important to go. I had half an hour before I had to go to the next booth, so I decided to walk down

Third Street.

"Christians, Muslims, Jews," he said. "Buddhists, Taoists, Hindus. We're all one. Why, shamanism, spiritualism, and voodooism even have something to offer."

I stopped dead in my tracks and looked at him. "Voodooism?"

"Oh, yes," he said in all earnestness. "I went to a lovely voodoo gathering not too long ago. Nice people, those voodooists."

"Here in Old Louisville?" Despite evidence to the contrary, I was still having a hard time coming to terms with a real voodoo presence in Kentucky."

"Oh, yes indeed!" He leaned in and smiled. "Back in June it was, to celebrate St. Jean's Day."

Immediately, my mind drifted back to the night Beau had summoned me to the front door by means of his polished green rock. Then I remembered his story about the gathering in Central Park. "Say, did you all have a problem finding your star attraction of the evening by any chance?"

"Star attraction?" Godwynn's face went blank.

I leaned in for a conspiratorial whisper. "Yeah, you know, a sacrificial *goat* or anything like that?"

"Sacrificial goat?" He wrinkled up his nose as if he'd gotten a whiff of something extremely unpleasant. "No, no, no, no, no," he said, moving his head back and forth. "There were no animals involved whatsoever. Modern voodooists do nothing of the kind, I tell you. Voodoo today is all about root work and spirit worship, things like that. No blood involved." He stopped and appeared to think for a minute. "At least, from what I've seen."

"Just asking." Seizing on his momentary distraction from proselytizing, I decided to continue with the changed subject. "So, anyway, where exactly did you say you attended this voodoo meeting in Old Louisville?"

"Well, it was over by the–" He stopped abruptly and reconsidered his answer. "Ooooh," he said, drawing out the word as he shook his head and mustered a pitying look. "Ever so sorry, but I was sworn to secrecy and promised not to divulge the location. But, don't fret: the voodooists are indeed amongst us, if that's what you need to find your way to the Sacred Circle and the Church of the Iron Hoop."

With that, he broke away from me and joined another similarly clad man rolling a hoop down the sidewalk. But before they had moved out of earshot, I heard Godwynn Goodwynn say, "Goodness! I almost slipped up and told him about the voodoo ceremony at Fort George." Then the crowd swallowed them up and nothing could be seen except their black, wide-brimmed hats bobbing on a sea of heads.

Fort George? It seemed to ring a bell somehow, but when I tried to match the name with a location in Old Louisville, I came up empty-handed. Wracking my brain, I wandered from booth to booth before stopping to admire a collection of hand-woven baskets in front of the old Samuel Culbertson residence. Built in 1897, it was an enormous house in the renaissance revival style, built for the son of Indiana's wealthiest man, William Stewart Culbertson. Suddenly, a snippet of conversation caught my attention and I turned to see two elderly women pointing at the huge orange glazed-brick mansion in front of us.

"Iron hoops!" said one lady. "Old-fashioned iron rolling hoops, that's what they had."

"You don't say!" said the other. "I heard that, too."

"Yes, indeed." Her friend bobbed her head up and down. "I know several people who have seen them. The ghosts of two young boys who run around laughing and playing with those old rolling hoops—and right up there, in their former bedroom." She jabbed her finger at an arched insert enclosing two windows on the second floor of the Culbertson house.

Strange. I had been researching stories of two ghostly apparitions at the mansion, and I desperately wanted to talk to the two ladies to find out what else they knew. Clumsily, I tried to navigate upstream and catch them, but they disappeared in the steadily moving river of passers-by. I hadn't progressed more than a few yards when I came face to face with Godwynn Goodwynn and his hoop-wielding, wide-brimmed accomplice.

Upon seeing me, Godwynn smiled and raised the hoop so it framed his face. "Don't forget the Sacred Circle and the Church of the Iron Hoop!" he said in passing. "We'll be watching for you." That was when the iron hoop coincidence hit me, and I began to wonder if I wasn't in for another voodoo day.

I was passing in front of the Bishop's Hat House, named for the large parapet in the shape of a bishop's miter on the façade, when Ron Harris, the owner, came out the door and walked down the front walk. "Hey, Ron," I said. "Do you happen to know anything about Fort George? It's supposed to be here in Old Louisville somewhere." Behind him, his wife, Jane, stood in the doorway and waved.

Ron scratched his chin and thought for a few seconds. Then his eyes lit up with a bit of recognition. "Hey, isn't that the little cemetery over there where the Toonerville neighborhood is? On Brook or Floyd, I believe."

"That's Fort George?" I had passed the tiny little park with its stone marker numerous times, but never thought of it as a cemetery. "And it's a cemetery? I don't remember seeing any graves or anything."

"Well, there might only be one or two small headstones, but I believe it is a graveyard of sorts." Ron scanned the crowd, obviously in a hurry to get some place. He was booth sitting as well, while Jane stayed inside and from the foyer sold Happy Balls, the bourbon candy made up on the third floor of the Bishop's Hat House. "Sorry to run," he said, "but that woman selling artificial floral arrangements made from fish scales is expecting me to relieve her. Gotta go." He lowered his head and entered the moving throng.

I let the current of people sweep me along to my next booth sitting appointment. In my mind, I was already planning my evening.

Rocky and Bess had already had a long walk that afternoon and they were tuckered out; so Fritz—panting happily as we strolled—was my only companion when I left the house that night. But while closing the back gate behind us, I noticed something was different about the wooden door that opened onto the back alley. I leaned in for closer inspection and discovered that somebody had carved a series of crude symbols into the wood. They looked like they could have been part of the old hobo system of communication that Norman had told me about and I made a mental note to look up their possible significance when I had a chance. Then we headed over to Toonerville, the neighborhood with Old Louisville's only cemetery.

For some reason, all but one of the streetlamps along the 1200 block of Floyd Street had gone out, and I let the dim blue of a solitary light guide me past the rusty wrought iron fence and up to the small gate that gave onto the little plot of land known as Fort George. Before entering, I paused and looked around me. On one side of the grassy lot crouched a small bungalow-type house, the faded paint of its siding begrudgingly catching the dull glow of the lamplight; to the other side sat a simple frame house, upright and painted in a dark blue that allowed it to slip away into the night. Unblinking and solemn, dark windows stared out from the houses and questioned my presence in their midst. Ignoring any warning they might have been trying to impart, I opened the gate and stepped onto the walkway.

Several old-growth maples soared overhead, branches hanging heavy with golden leaves that swayed gently in the breeze. Broken twigs from a recent windstorm littered the ground. Wild grape vines and undulating ribbons of waxy English ivy wove themselves through the perforations in an old chain-link fence that enclosed the space on three of its four sides. Ahead and to the left, a squat stone marker, rounded at the top like a tombstone and with unruly tufts of weeds poking out at its base, hunched close to the ground.

I let Fritz snoop around a bit and then pulled him closer to me while I knelt and used the light from a small key-chain flashlight to examine the dedication on the face of the monument. The Daughters of the American Revolution had placed it there in 1947 to commemorate the burial ground of Kentucky pioneer Captain George Gray and his wife, Mildred, who had been friends and neighbors of George Washington. Farther down the walk stood two small rectangular gravestones—one presumably, was for George, and the other, for his wife. According to the one on the left, Mildred had died in 1828. I could see that George had preceded her by five years, dying in 1823. At my feet, Fritz stirred and drew the line taut. There was a rustling noise off in the blackness.

"You over here lookin' for ghosts?" asked a deep, raspy voice from a darkened corner of the lot. A low, roiling growl in his throat, Fritz lunged forward and strained the lead until I calmed him and made him heel. "Sorry, didn't mean to startle you," said the voice, which seemed to emanate from a small dot of orange light in the distance.

"No, not looking for ghosts." I cautiously inched toward the disembodied voice. "Out walking my dog."

As I approached, the red-orange glow flared and the smell of smoke wafted through the air. Soon a form took shape in the dim glare of the nearest light and I spied a sitting figure with a cigarette on a nearby bench. With the glowing end dancing around in the semi-darkness, the hand that held the cigarette motioned for me to come closer.

"Come on over and sit a spell," said the husky voice. "You're that guy I saw on the news, aren't you? The one with the weird stuff happening in your house, right?"

"I guess so." I watched as Fritz neared the hand offered him and sniffed. Deciding the figure presented no imminent threat, he trotted back to me and wagged his approval. Then I sat down next to the person and took a closer look.

"My name's Candy," said the unmistakably masculine voice. "You're David, right?" He held out a richly bejeweled hand, large and calloused, and shook mine in greeting; with the other he lifted a long-stemmed ivory cigarette holder and put it to his lips. Rhinestones of varying sizes formed an elaborate pattern along the duct down to the mouthpiece and they sparkled when a breeze picked up and pushed the branches clear of a solitary bulb illuminating the side entrance of the frame house. In the flickering light afforded by the jostling and swaying of the branches, Candy's features revealed themselves and I was able to see a good amount of dark stubble covering his chin. He wore what appeared to be a red wig that had been bobbed to the shoulders, and on top of that was a black beret that perched jauntily to one side.

Suddenly self-conscious, he raised a hand to his face and grimaced. "Sorry, I was too lazy to shave today," he said. "I didn't think anyone was going to see me tonight, and there you go waltzing into my own private little park when no one ever comes over here."

"Oh, don't worry about me," I said with a laugh. Then I took a seat on the bench while Fritz snuffled about in the dry grass. "I didn't shave today either." I smiled and reached up to rub my chin in a gesture of solidarity.

The branches swayed in another strong breeze, and I caught a glimpse of the rest of Candy's outfit: a red satin gown cinched at the waist with a shiny black belt, a mink stole and black pumps. Around Candy's neck was a string of pearls, and there were matching earrings as well. A small, handbag embroidered with an art deco pattern sat next on the bench to the side.

He took a long, luxurious drag on the cigarette and focused his eyes on me. "So, you come over this way often?" His eyes closed as he savored the intake and then exhaled a long stream of white smoke.

"No, not usually, but I heard this was actually a cemetery and wanted to come and see for myself." Much to my relief, the stirring wind changed direction and blew his next lungful of smoke away from me. "I don't know how many times I've passed by here," I said, "without ever noticing these tombstones."

"Yes, they've been here for a while," he said, the toe of the shoe crossed over his leg carving lazy circles in the air. "Some hoity toity housewives had them erected after World War II." He took another drag from his cigarette and cradled his elbow before breathing out. "Bitches."

I stifled a laugh and asked why he had said that.

"I'll tell you why: 'cuz they're all a bunch of East End snobs, that's why. Thinkin' they're better than everyone else all the time." He hunched down so the stole covered more of his neck and paused as someone pushed a squeaky shopping cart down the sidewalk. Once the person had passed, Candy straightened up again. "You ever see some of those houses out in the East End?" he asked. "Those *McMansions*? They're awful! And what they wear? Puttin' on their fancy shmancy dresses and goin' to their fancy shmancy parties and not inviting their brother because he's not good enough." He stopped abruptly and I could see that the hand holding the cigarette was shaking.

Fritz lifted his head and studied Candy for a moment; then he returned his attention to the grass and resumed exploring. He wandered over to a large mound of moonflowers and stuck his nose in among the huge white blossoms.

"Yes, they're an uppity bunch out there in the East End," said Candy. "Not nice and friendly like the people here in Old Louisville." His calm regained, he placed another cigarette in the holder, lit it, and puffed contentedly. "So, you were interested in this cemetery?"

"Do you know much about it?"

"I've heard some things, but I'm not sure how much is fact and how much is fiction." He waved his cigarette in the direction of the stone marker and blew a double stream of smoke out through his nose. "Now, there you've got the facts: that George and Mildred lived on this piece of land, when they died, etcetera, but I've heard some stories that I'm sure you'd find interesting—that is, if you haven't heard them yourself already."

"I don't know a thing about this place, other than what I've read on the marker," I replied. "What have you heard?"

A voice echoed somewhere off in the distance and Candy flinched slightly. "Hope that's not Susan," he said under his breath. Seeing the blank look on my face, he explained: "Susan's my wife. She doesn't like it when I raid her closet and go out for a stroll in her stuff."

"Ah, okay," I said. "I get it."

"She was sound asleep when I left, but she might have woken up." He flicked a bit of ash and looked around. "The old banshee."

A slight whirring could be heard, accompanied by the sound of running feet, and the silhouettes of two young boys appeared on the other side of the wrought iron. Rolling two large hula-hoops alongside them as they ran, they sped down the sidewalk and disappeared from sight.

"Hula hoops, now that's something you don't see every day," said Candy with a chuckle. "I guess they must be coming back in style." He started to toke on the cigarette but quickly reconsidered. "Oh, yeah," he said. "I was telling you about the old place that used to be here."

"Yes. Was it an old fort or something?"

"Well, my grandparents used to tell us stories, you know, and they said it was a big old house with a high fence around it. I guess for when the Indians used to attack and stuff like that. It was built in the 1700s and was a pretty impressive home for its day." A screen door slammed at one of the houses nearby, and Candy paused to listen. Satisfied that Susan wasn't coming after him, he continued.

"This was back in the olden days, you know, so they had slaves and all back then. Supposedly, some of them were caught doing some of the voodoo rituals they brought with them from Africa, and that didn't sit too well with the overseer. He punished them, and that's when the trouble really began." He gave a dramatic pause and studied me for my reaction.

"And what happened then?" I rested my elbows on my knees and leaned in a bit to hear better.

"One night when George and Mildred were away, the slaves set fire to the house and burned it to the ground. Some say George was actually inside the house and died, but I don't think that's true." He took a long drag on his cigarette and leaned back against the bench.

"What happened to the slaves then?" Off in the distance, a strip of cloud slid through the night sky and exposed a full moon. Overhead, the branches rattled and two long, hollow *hoots* echoed in the leaves.

Candy raised his head and waited for a few seconds before answering. "They supposedly ran off and intermarried with the Indians and started their own little clan. A voodoo clan, I guess." He smoked his cigarette down to the end and opened his handbag to retrieve another. "From what I hear, descendants of those slaves still live in this area."

I watched him fit the cigarette in the holder as I tried to visualize the details of his story in my mind.

He lit the cigarette with a gold-plated lighter and stowed it in his handbag.

"One of them is supposed to be a big voodoo woman in these parts."

Josephine. My heart skipped a beat. "You wouldn't happen to know her name, would you?"

"Can't say that I do. Like I said, I don't know what's true and what's not true. All I know is what was told to me."

In a nearby house the dry scrape of a window sash being raised broke the momentary silence, and all of a sudden, a jarringly female voice pierced the air. *"Ran-deeee!"*

"Ooops, time to go!" Candy jumped to his feet and smoothed down the front of his wife's dress.

"Ran-deeee!" screamed the banshee-like voice. *"Where are you? You better not have on my new shoes again!"*

"Well, nice talking to you," said Candy. "Maybe I can sneak through the back window without her noticing." He quickly ran to the gate, stumbling slightly as he pushed his way through, and then made a mad dash across the street. Several houses down, he crossed a front lawn and disappeared into the shadows between the homes.

Mama Wawa and Miss Maybelline

A canopy of golden maple leaves sifted the light, depositing yellow flecks on the sidewalks of Third Street. From random stoops leered cheeky jack-o'-lanterns, their insides eagerly awaiting the warmth of a candle, as residents inside the houses hurried about and prepared bowls of candy for the onslaught of trick-or-treaters. Oblivious to this all, the dogs steadily towed me along and plowed through the carpet of leaves, their noses close to the ground in search of new smells. Soon it would be Halloween.

Kelly laughed. "So, you're telling me that out of nowhere a goat shows up and knocks you over?"

"Yes, just like that," I said. "Ran up behind me and butted the back of my legs."

"That's some weird stuff." He shook his head and laughed.

"Oddball stuff has been happening since we moved into this place." Changing the subject back to the original topic of discussion, I stopped and turned to face him. "Are you sure this woman—this Mama Wawa or whatever they say she calls herself—is for real?"

"Yeah, man, exactly what you need for your new book," he said. "She's from the islands somewhere and grew up doing voodoo. She's the real deal, a high priestess or something like that. Sacrifices a cat every now and then, stuff like that." Kelly gestured with an imaginary cigar and moved to the side as a band of early trick-or-treaters raced down the sidewalk.

"She kills cats? I don't want anything to do with a cat killer."

"Oh, it's not that bad. Maybe it's all rumor," he said. "She lives out in the South End somewhere, where a lot of the immigrants are, see?"

"You think she'll really be there?"

"Can't hurt to find out," he said. "They say most afternoons if she's not at the Peppermint Bar out by Iroquois Park, then she's at the Tavern here in Old Louisville." He lifted his wrist and examined his watch. "It's still afternoon, and I was at the Peppermint Bar and she wasn't out there, so—"

"Okay, okay," I said, picking up my pace. "Let's hurry up and see if she's at the Tavern."

Several minutes later, after dropping off the schnauzers, we stood in front of an unassuming little red brick building at the corner of Fourth and Gaulbert. A large sign over the front door touted their "famous Knocker Burger" and its red lettering boasted that the bar stayed open "22 hours a day," proving itself a watering hole that took full advantage of state liquor laws. Not only that, "plate lunches daily" and "breakfast anytime" were served "since 1933." To top it off, red neon letters in tiny horizontal slits that doubled as windows cheerily flaunted the three main virtues of the Tavern: BEER. WHISKY. FOOD. Our kind of place.

A guy in jeans and a baseball hat was sweeping the pavement in front, but Kelly and I breezed past him into the dim interior. Before the door slammed shut behind us, I heard a strange putt-putt noise and turned around to see an odd little man on a miniature motorcycle speed by on the sidewalk. Another one of Old Louisville's colorful characters, no doubt. Undaunted, we entered the dimly lit interior of one of the Derby City's most famous dives. The place was clean, with wooden tables and shiny booths gleaming under the polish of a fresh scrubbing, and the aroma of fried food guided us to a row of booths to the left. We sat down, the faint smell of sauerkraut hanging in the air.

I looked around. Two burly biker types were sitting at the bar, their mugs of beer perilously close to empty, and three frat boys sat at the booth next to ours. A petite white-haired gent with over-sized sunglasses and a cigarette dangling from his lower lip had parked himself on one of four chairs at a table in the back. On the last stool at the bar perched a huge black transvestite with a Diana Ross afro and a skin-tight, blue leather suit that zipped up the front.

"Excuse me," I said to Kelly. "I don't see anyone on the premises who looks like a Mama Wawa." Then I let my eyes roam the dim interior yet another time. "Actually, I don't see anyone who looks like a Mama anything," I added. "That drag queen at the end of the bar is the closest thing we got."

"Be patient," said Kelly. "They say she usually comes in here." He accepted the menu offered by the barkeep and opened it. Then he twiddled his fingers at the side of his face again. "Since we're here, we might as well get something to eat."

"Something to drink, in any case." I gave the menu the once-over and ordered us each a double bourbon on the rocks. Kelly ordered a Knocker Burger with fries, and I went with an omelet. Cheese and tomato.

The food arrived rather quickly, and not too long thereafter the front door creaked open—and in walked a dark woman with an enormous tangle of frizzy curls bound atop her head with a bright yellow scarf. Clad in a pair of red clam diggers and a lacy white blouse, she headed listlessly for the bar, sandals slapping at her feet as she moved. A large straw handbag hung from her shoulder.

"Hey, Mama Wawa!" said the large transvestite, spinning around on her barstool. "How's it going?"

I was dumbstruck.

"Oh, everything's right as rain, right as rain," replied Mama Wawa. Her voice had a distinctly Caribbean lilt to it, perhaps Jamaican. She took a seat at the bar next to the drag queen and smiled as the bartender approached.

"Same as usual?" he asked, sliding a cocktail napkin down in front of her.

"Yes, same as usual," she sang, "same as usual."

Turning to the row of bottles behind him, the bartender grabbed a small water glass, filled it to the top with rum and set in down in front of Mama Wawa.

"Thank you, thank you," she said, raising the glass and clinking it against the bottle of beer in the transvestite's outstretched hand. "Cheers, honey."

Kelly raised his eyebrows and gave a smug grin. "I do believe there's a Mama Wawa in the house." He did that thing with his fingers at the side of his face again.

"I have to admit, she doesn't look quite like what I had anticipated."

"How so?" Kelly lifted the burger to his mouth and took a bite.

I cut off a piece of omelet and pushed it around on the plate a bit before spearing it with my fork. "Oh, I guess I was expecting white turbans and flimsy cotton blouses and skirts. That kind of stuff."

"Ah!" He popped a fry into his mouth and chewed quickly. "That's how it is in Haiti," Kelly said. "There are different forms of voodoo throughout the islands, *see*?" It finally dawned on me: he was doing his W.C. Fields voice.

I swilled the rest of the bourbon in my glass and raised it for the barkeep to see. He nodded his head and pointed to Kelly, who did the same. "So, what do we do now that we're all here?" I said.

"Well, you go over and talk to her, I guess."

"I can't just go over and talk to her." I leaned in and whispered. "I'm sure it's against voodoo protocol or something like that."

Kelly guffawed and took a healthy dram of bourbon. "What are you talking about, buddy? All you do is walk around this neighborhood at all hours of the day and night talking to people you don't know. I'm sure you've approached people more threatening than Mama Wawa." He raised his fork and jabbed it in her direction. "Look. She appears perfectly harmless."

At the bar, Mama Wawa and the large transvestite laughed at a private joke before lifting their respective beverages to their lips and drinking. It must have been a good one, because Mama Wawa cackled and shook her head while her palm slapped the counter. "Ooowie!" she said. "Too funny, that one! Too funny!" Still laughing, she hopped off her perch and headed to the bathroom at the rear of the bar.

"Now's the time. You can intercept her when she comes out of the john."

"Well, I don't know," I said. "Why don't you talk to her first?"

"Man, you're the one snoopin' out the voodoo in town, you go talk to her!" He finished the last bite of food and pushed his plate out of the way. "Look! Now's your chance." He nodded in the direction of the open door at the back.

"Here she comes."

Mama Wawa had exited the bathroom, the door swinging shut behind her, but instead of returning to the bar, she approached the dainty white-haired man at the back table. "I be back in a bit, Miss Mable," she said to the huge drag queen. "I need to talk to these nice people first." She leaned down to the old man and asked him something; after thinking for a few seconds he shook his head and mouthed the word *no*. Then she sauntered in the direction of the frat boys in the next booth.

"Oh my goodness," I said under my breath. "Is she going to come and talk to us?"

"Maybe she can read minds," Kelly chuckled. "Voodoo mind control or something like that." He reached out a hand and fluttered his fingers.

Mama Wawa approached the frat boys and whispered something unintelligible. They all shook their heads as if to answer her question in the negative, but one of them said: "Try over on Belgravia Court. There's always a ton of them over there." She smiled at them and then moved in our direction.

"She's coming this way! She's coming this way!"

"Good day, gentlemen." Her flip-flops scraped along the floor as she came to a stop at our table. "Sorry to bother, but I was wondering if you knew of anyone who had a cat they didn't want. Or where I could find a stray, maybe?"

"A *cat?*"

"Yes, a cat," she said. "Meow. Meow."

Automatically, I lifted several inches out of my seat and pointed a forceful finger at her. Trying to keep it to a whisper, I said: "You better not be looking for a cat to sacrifice!"

She gasped and took a step back. "But, but . . ." A hand rose to her bosom and clutched a string of onyx beads handing there. "But who, who . . ."

I wagged my finger at her again. "I mean it. If you're looking for cats to kill, I will report you!"

She gasped again. "I never . . ." Using her other hand, she smoothed a tangle of hair while fighting to regain composure. "I'm looking for a cat," she said. "For myself. I love the little creatures." She forced a smile. "Silly man."

"Oh, really?" I said. "How many cats have you had in your life?"

She thought for a minute. "Oh, many, many. Too many to count."

"Do you have any cats now?" My eyebrows rose as I waited for an answer.

"Oh, yes." She eagerly nodded her head, but I didn't believe her.

"Oh, really? How many then?" I said.

"Three?"

"What are their names?" I tapped out the syllables with my empty bourbon glass.

"Uh," she looked to the side in an effort to buy more time as she thought. "Well, there's Fluffy," she said, keeping a mental tally of the names. "Then there's, uh, uh, Miss Kitty, and, uh, there's, there's, Fido."

"You named your cat Fido?" I said.

"Fido not a good name for a cat?" She widened her eyes.

"It's a dog's name," said Kelly.

"Oh." Mama Wawa's smile faded as she thought for a moment. "She a mean kitty cat, almost like a dog."

"And, it's a name for male dogs," I said.

"Oh." She paused and considered a good response. "She sort of mean, like a man, too."

"Humph," I snorted. She had never possessed a cat as a pet in her life.

Sensing an opportune moment to slip from view, Mama Wawa started backing away, toward the bar. A big grin on his face, Kelly polished off his drink and motioned for another round when he caught the bartender's attention.

"Not so fast, Mama Wawa," I said, seized by a temporary bout of bravado. "Why don't you sit a spell and tell us a little more about this voodoo that you do."

Another loud gasp escaped her lips. "But how do you know my name?" She cautiously inched her way back to the table. "And who told you I can do the *obeah*?" Her eyes compressed to tiny slits. "It is *obeah*, not voodoo."

"I'm in the south part of Louisville a lot," said Kelly, "and I've heard people talk about you. I heard if you're not here, you're out at the Peppermint Bar."

"Oh, yes," she said, the tone of her voice warming slightly. "A wee sip of the rum everyday does a soul a world of good."

"Looks like you've been having a pretty good sip there," I mumbled, rolling my eyes at the bar and her glass of rum, almost empty by then.

"And what is that supposed to mean?" A chill had returned to her voice.

"Oh, he's joking." Kelly slid down the bench so there was room for her to sit. "Why don't you join us for a bit? We're curious, that's all."

"Tell us a little something about yourself," I said. "But leave out the parts about animal sacrifice, if you would."

Mama Wawa slapped the air in front of her face and scoffed. "Oh, all that," she explained. "We hardly ever do that. Only now and again for special occasions or to appease the evil spirits—the *baki*—and then it's usually a chicken." She tried to look indifferent. "Or a cat."

Before there was a chance for me to protest, Kelly jumped in and encouraged her to explain more. "So, where are you from? How did you learn to do this *obeah*?"

Mama Wawa swiveled her head to the bar. "Miss Mable! Why don't you come over and join me and these silly men? Bring my drink, if you would."

"Okay, I'll be right there." The large transvestite swung a muscled leg off the stool, grabbed the drinks and minced across to our table. "How y'all doin' today? My name's Maybelline." She plopped down and squished herself into my side of the booth. "Nice to see such handsome men in the establishment today!"

We exchanged pleasantries and then Mama Wawa leaned across the table and whispered in Maybelline's direction. "They know about the magic I do and want to know more."

"Ooh!" Maybelline's voice came out in a scratchy falsetto. "You told them about the *obeah*?"

"No, I didn't tell them a thing!" said Mama Wawa. "They found out from someone else."

"Who's been talking then?" said Maybelline. "We all agreed to keep quiet about your little ceremonies."

Kelly and I exchanged glances, caught up in the intrigue unfolding before us. "If it's any consolation," he said, "we don't plan on saying anything about what you tell us. Mum's the word."

I nodded my head in agreement. "Yes, I won't say a word," I lied.

"Oh, it's not such a big deal," said Mama Wawa, "but we do like to maintain a certain level of secrecy, that's all."

"Yes," Maybelline said. "Some people misunderstand what we do. Think it is devil worship and stuff like that."

"So, what exactly do you do?" I said. "Is it voodoo or not?"

"Well. Yes and no." Mama Wawa sipped on the last of her rum and took a breath. "I come from the hills of Jamaica, and there we call this magic *obeah*; my parents, on the other hand, were Haitian, so they practiced the *voudon*, or the voodoo as you call it."

"What Mama does is a little of both." Maybelline primly crossed her legs and smiled.

"You don't say," said Kelly. "Kind of like a voodoo hybrid?" The W.C. Fields voice again.

Mama Wawa swirled the last taste of rum and tipped it to her lips. "A little bit of this, a little bit of that."

"Any chance of someone like me tagging along and watching one of your ceremonies sometime?" I asked. "As long as there are no cats or other animals involved."

Maybelline froze, her lips pursed, and then slid a sideways glance in Mama's direction.

Mama looked up from her empty glass and stared at me before answering. "Such a thing might be possible," she said, "however, discretion is essential in these matters."

"Sure thing," I said. "When could we come to one of these shindigs?"

"As a matter of fact," said Mama Wawa, "we'll be performing a ritual this evening."

"Halloween?" I arched my eyebrows and looked at Kelly.

Mama Wawa smiled and nodded her head. "Yes, indeed. All Hallows Eve is one of the most sacred days on our calendar. It's a night for spirits and magic."

Kelly returned my gaze and shook his head. "Sorry. No can do. I've already got plans tonight and can't get out of them. You go by yourself."

"Well, maybe I could wait until the next time, so Kelly can come along," I said.

"Oh, now if you're afraid and would like to wait till your friend can join you, that is quite fine, but Halloween is a powerful time for the *obeah*," said Mama Wawa.

Taking the bait, I jumped right in. *"Afraid?* I'm not afraid," I said.

"Knock yourself out. Let me know what happened afterwards," said Kelly.

"Well, that settles it," I said. "I guess I'll be joining you tonight."

Maybelline clapped her hands together and bounced in her seat. "Oh, this gonna be fun. This gonna be *real* fun."

"So, where do we meet?"

"Do you know the Eastern Cemetery?" Mama Wawa took out a silver compact and checked her lipstick. "We shall meet there shortly before midnight."

"Eastern Cemetery?" Now I was getting a bit afraid. In 1989 Eastern Cemetery made the national news when the press discovered that since the 1920s employees there had been interring bodies in graves that already held coffins. In some places there were five or six cadavers stacked one atop the other, and in others, rotting caskets with remains had managed to work their ways to the surface, where they poked into the open air. Although several cemetery officials had gone to trial, they were eventually acquitted and Eastern Cemetery was abandoned and left to vandals and the destructive forces of nature. Most knew it as one of the scariest places in town, and not just for the marginalized spirits that supposedly haunted it: after dark it came alive with the homeless, drug addicts, and sundry shiftless characters. Maybe even a hobo or two.

"Yes, Eastern Cemetery," repeated Mama Wawa. "What? You afraid of that, too, Mr. Silly Man?" Across from her, Maybelline stifled a giggle and wriggled anxiously in her seat.

"No, I'm not afraid," I said, albeit not very convincingly. "But is it safe to be in there after dark?"

"Oh, most assuredly not," said Mama Wawa, "but we'll have our own little security system, so there's no reason to worry."

"What security system is that?" I said, somewhat warily.

"The best one ever," she said. "Her name is Miss Tabitha, and she will take care of things for us if we have any trouble."

"Miss Tabitha? Who's she?"

"Miss Tabitha is our security system, silly man," said Mama Wawa, getting up to leave.

"Yeah, and you don't want to mess with Miss Tabitha." Maybelline wrinkled up her nose and jabbed a coquettish finger into my chest. "Or she'll getcha good!" Then she dislodged herself from behind the table and joined Mama Wawa at the door.

"We'll see you tonight! And make sure you wear something pretty!" Maybelline waved at us and then turned to say good-bye to the bartender.

"Yes, right before midnight," said Mama Wawa. Followed by Maybelline, she breezed through the door and was gone.

"Wear something pretty?" I looked to Kelly for clarification. "What's that supposed to mean?" I looked down at my attire and frowned.

"Beats me," he said. "But, I bet you're in for a memorable evening, to say the least."

We exited our booth and found ourselves outside in the bright sunshine. The putt-putt noise crescendoed from the distance and soon the weird guy on the goofy miniature motorcycle veered into sight and shook his finger at me as he squealed his tires and spun around back to the street. "I got a picture of this place in the 1937 flood!" His voice croaked as he tried to raise it above the buzz of the motor. From the looks of it, he was probably around for the flood of 1937.

I was about to turn around and tell him I found his revelation very interesting when something suddenly crashed into me and I was sent flying. I landed in a heap on the sidewalk several feet away.

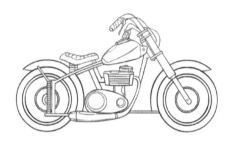

I parked the car on one of the side streets off Bardstown Road and softly closed the door. Approaching the gate to Eastern Cemetery, I crossed the street while I rubbed the bump on the back of my head.

A friend of the old man on the little motorcycle who had lost control and bowled me over in front of the Tavern, offered to drive me to the doctor's, but I had politely refused. Getting knocked down to the sidewalk in Old Louisville was turning out to be a pastime of mine, so I had brushed myself off and gone home. After handing out candy to several motley groups of trick-or-treaters I went upstairs and rummaged through the closets until I found a pair of brown woolen slacks from Banana Republic and a body-hugging sweater from DKNY. For my feet I picked out a pair of mousy brown buffed leather shoes I brought back from Italy the last time I was there. That was as pretty as it got for me.

Standing in front of the open gate to the cemetery, I could hear the steady, comforting whirr of traffic as cars and trucks sped by on Bardstown Road. Every now and then, the distant beam of a flashlight cut through the darkness and illuminated random headstones and crooked monuments at the rear of the graveyard; evidently someone was already there, and I hoped it was Mama Wawa and her entourage. I feared it was vandals or rowdy Halloween revelers in search of a paranormal thrill, however. Casting a last glance over my shoulder to the lights of Bardstown Road, I entered the cemetery and, my feet crunching as I went, followed the rutted gravel road that disappeared into the blackness.

Remembering the miniature flashlight I had stowed away earlier, I extracted it from my pocket and used the filmy beam to guide my way. Picking out faded inscriptions on mossy, weathered headstones, I slowly made my way to the back of the cemetery. Although no specific place to meet had been determined, I assumed we'd stumble across each other sooner or later and I kept following the gravel way. According to my watch, it was five minutes before midnight.

A hundred yards down the trail, a small limestone structure, Gothic-looking and elegantly eerie, loomed up over the hodgepodge of crowded tombstones that surrounded it. In the darkened sky beyond, the moon slipped out from a bank of steely gray clouds and shot a tendril of blue light into the blackness. Behind the stone funeral vault, the skeleton of a majestic oak tree caught the momentary light in the silhouette of its branches and reached bony limbs up into the night. Then, another bank of clouds drifted across the moon and, shrouded in gloom, it disappeared from sight.

Off to the left, a muffled whoop echoed and bushes rattled; I pointed my flashlight in that direction and picked my way over broken headstones and bare patches of earth until I arrived at a large brick structure tucked away in the far corner of the cemetery. The Columbarium. I had read about this building in the newspapers. Constructed in the 1950s in a Modernist style, it had served as the crematorium until the cemetery board's misdeeds were brought to light. For the last two decades, it had sat vacant and forlorn, a silent victim at the mercy of man and nature, and time had taken its toll. Hooligans had broken out windows and scrawled graffiti across the walls, and litter lay strewn around the entrance. At the front, a massive door with a broken hinge was ajar, held open by a tattered cardboard box holding jumbled files and manila envelopes.

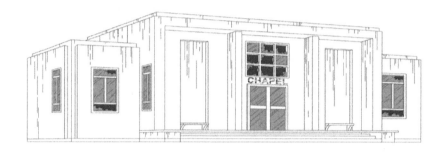

I looked at the time: it was one minute before midnight. Well, I guess this is as good a place as any, I thought to myself. I raised my hand to knock but put it back down, struck by the absurdity of knocking on the door to gain admittance to an abandoned building. A split second passed and the door suddenly pushed out with a scrape; Mama Wawa poked her head out at me.

"Ah! There you are, silly man!" She fairly cackled with glee. "Right on time you are. We're about to commence." She motioned with her arm that I should enter, so I squeezed through the opening and followed her inside.

Immediately I scanned the room for signs of a kidnapped feline—not that I would have seen any for all the mess and clutter. An overturned desk lay against a far wall and several cardboard boxes of papers sat near a set of stairs winding down to a lower level. A dirty sleeping bag had been laid out in a corner, and nearby the needles from at least a half dozen hypodermic syringes glimmered in the flickering glow. Flames from a small fire danced in a banged-up soup kettle in the middle of the floor.

"Come here, silly man, and join us." Mama Wawa stood at the fire with several other individuals. One of them was Maybelline—she was clad in a black leather unitard and a furry dark cape—who waved flirtatiously after catching my attention.

"Are you sure it's a good idea to be in here?" My eyes lingered uneasily on a broken urn behind her. A grayish scattering of an unknown material fanned out next to it and I was afraid I knew the identity of the former contents, if not the former occupant. Nearby were several more needles. "They say this place is full of crazy homeless people," I whispered.

"Tonight it's safe," she said, gesturing in the direction of the door to a tall figure in the shadows that I had walked by without noticing. "Miss Tabitha scared them away and if they know what's good for them, they won't be coming back tonight."

"Miss Tabitha, the security system?" I let my eyes adjust to the dancing silhouettes on the wall.

"You bet. That's me." A tall female form with an upturned pitchfork stepped forward and emerged from the shadows. Her voice was several octaves lower than mine and with her chunky high-heeled boots, she was a good two heads taller. Jet black hair—maybe it was a wig, I couldn't tell—hung down to her shoulders and her bangs had apparently suffered a severe work-over at the hands of a stylist with a Bettie Page fixation. Like Maybelline, she wore a dark unitard and a matching fur cape. She sneered and gave me the once over before retreating into the shadows. "That outfit is *so* last year."

Resisting the urge to comment on her own dubious sense of fashion, I ignored her—she had a pitchfork after all—and returned my attention to Mama Wawa and her helpers. Next to Maybelline stood two additional drag queens, both of them towering and similarly attired, who puffed on pungent cigars. One of them had a bottle of rum in the other hand, but as far as I could tell, Miss Tabitha was the only one wielding barnyard implements.

"This is Miss Claudette," said Mama, pointing to a heavy-set person with a blond ponytail. The other one, a seemingly anorexic brunette who stared at me with eerily milky blue eyes that I hoped were the result of funky contact lenses, she introduced as "Miss Giselle." After leisurely drags on their respective stogies, they both looked me over from top to bottom and graciously withheld any comment about my choice of attire for the evening.

"Hello," I said. "Nice to meet you."

"Likewise, I'm sure," said the blond ponytail in a husky voice.

"Nice to make your acquaintance," responded the skinny one, her voice a nasally warble. The fact that she was a white-eyed, cigar-smoking, cape-wearing drag queen in a unitard getting ready to participate in a voodooist ritual in an abandoned crematorium in a haunted cemetery on Halloween night hadn't seemed to faze her in the least. Her eyes lowered surreptitiously to study my feet and then, urges finally getting the best of her, she blurted out her dismay: "Those shoes really aren't right for the season."

I looked down at her scuffed dominatrix boots and bit my tongue.

"Oh, you shush your mouth," said Maybelline, who rushed to my side and draped a sinewy arm over my shoulder. "I think his shoes are cute, so you leave him alone!"

"Silly man, silly shoes! Who cares?" Mama Wawa nudged Giselle out of the way. "It is midnight, and we must commence with the *obeah*." She cozied up to the fire and extracted a small leather satchel from the folds of her skirt as the others circled in. With one hand she reached into the pouch and with a deft flick of the wrist she cast a pinch of some powdery substance into the fire. A plume of flame shot to the ceiling and rained down a shower of tiny copper sparks before dissipating to its original size.

Giselle lifted the bottle of rum to her lips and sprayed a mouthful of perfectly good alcohol into the fire, which erupted into another column of fire. After wiping her mouth with the back of her hand she uttered some sort of gibberish that sounded like "*oh-mah-boh-mah-let's-go-home-ah.*" Noticing how the corners of my mouth had started to curl up in a snicker, Giselle pointedly raised her eyebrows at me and directed a glare of aspersion at my feet. Mindful that Mama Wawa not see my gestures, I returned the favor and gave Giselle the stink-eye while slowly pointing to her boots.

She tried to ignore me and wasted another perfectly good mouthful of rum on the fire, but by the glare of the tiny bonfire I could see her looking at me out of the corner of her eyes.

Mama Wawa spread her hands over the fire and slowly intoned a breathy litany in a language that appeared to be a form of pidgin English interspersed with patois French-sounding words such as *joujou, bamboula* and *bambouche.* Then her body started moving back and forth, left and right, her voice crescendoing in another series of mostly unintelligible words that was repeated by the three drag queens in her consort. They, in turn, started to sway back and forth, then right and left. *"Mamabunga. Woongaboongaboonga,"* they chanted in unison, or something like that. Rocking to and fro, Giselle opened her eyes and scowled at me.

I tried to suppress a grin, but failed; the silliness of the whole situation was catching up with me and I finally gave over to a hearty laugh when I once again beheld the colossal drag queens mimicking Mama Wawa. *"Oombagoomba. Oombagoomba."* I joined in and found myself swaying on the balls of my feet in spite of myself.

Suddenly, a commotion erupted near the entrance and all heads turned, the chanting interrupted. Miss Tabitha fell into a lunging position, the rusty tines of her pitchfork pointed menacingly in the direction of the door. "Who goes there?" she called out in a husky baritone.

The soup-pot campfire flared up and sent shadows flickering across the walls around us. Mama Wawa raised a vertical finger to her lips and used the other hand to motion us away from the door.

"What the hell y'all doin' in our house?" demanded an angry voice from the other side. "Get on outa there before we cut you!" The murmur of accompanying voices outside hinted at a mob in its fledgling stages.

"*Your* house?" Mama Wawa heatedly jostled her way around Miss Giselle and stormed over to the door. "Who says this is *your* house?" She pressed a nose up to the crack and peered outside. "This place is *abandoned*, you dumbass! You scat on away from here right now before Miss Tabitha get after you with her pitchfork!"

Miss Tabitha squeezed up to the door. "Yeah, you run on home, or I'm gonna getcha!" Knuckles turning white, she clutched the farmer's tool to her ample bosom and called out her warning. "Run on home now!" She turned away from the door and grinned excitedly at the rest of us: she was enjoying her confrontation with the rabble on the other side of the door.

"This is our home, you dumb bitch!" said another voice from outside. "I'm tired and wanna go to sleep. If you messed up my bedroom, I'm gonna cut ya good!" Nearby, a set of my dusty footprints had been tracked across the rumpled old sleeping bag, which, I feared, was the bedroom in question.

"Y'all get on down to the Wayside Christian Mission where y'all belong," said Miss Tabitha in a smoky voice. "Have yourself a donut and some coffee and get one of them nice cots."

"We don't want no coffee and donuts, you tranny bitch!" yelled a third voice. "Get outa there right now or we're gonna cut ya!"

"Get out right this instant!" said another voice in impeccable English. "Or we will cut you!" Miss Tabitha and Mama Wawa looked at me, seemingly for an explanation as to why one of the hobos sounded more educated than the others. I shrugged my shoulders and widened my eyes to signal my shared sense of bafflement.

Miss Tabitha leaned an ear up to the door and listened for a second. "You got an awfully pretty way of talking for being a crack whore. You go to college or something?"

"Who are you calling a crack whore?" said the voice, furiously. "I am *not* a crack whore!"

"Ha!" One of the other voices started laughing on the other side of the door. "She called you a crack whore."

"Yeah, you a crack whore, Whistle Dick."

"Shut up!" said Whistle Dick. "I am not a crack whore. *You're* the crack whore."

Several of the other voices whooped and hollered. "Yeah, you a crack whore, Johnny!"

"I'm not a crack whore!" objected Johnny.

"You are so!" said Whistle Dick. "If you're not a crack whore, then why do you have that nickel bag in your pocket?"

"I don't have a nickel bag of nothin' in my pocket," he complained. "You're on crack."

Before he could continue, a different voice cut in. "You got a nickel bag of crack in your pocket and you know it! I saw you buy it from Swampy Pete out in front of Phoenix Hill Tavern not fifteen minutes ago."

While the horde outside squabbled over who was a crack whore and who wasn't, Mama Wawa turned away from the door and returned to the small fire, which had started to die out. "Silly crack whores!" she sighed, shaking her head. "Perhaps we should use this time to make our exit. We cannot complete the ceremony in any case."

Giselle threw her cigar to the ground and ground the life out of it. Mama Wawa gathered up her belongings and pointed to the steps that wound their way down into the darkness. "Let's go that way."

Glancing over my shoulder to make sure the door was still closed, I followed the others as they felt their way down the stairs and descended into the darkness. In the dying light of the fire, I caught a glimpse of a disconcerting message scrawled in paint on the wall of the stairwell: *You will die.*

Suddenly, a loud scrape reverberated through the concrete structure as the heavy metal door was pushed ajar. At the bottom of the steps, Mama Wawa spun around and I shone the weak beam of the flashlight in her direction as the last of the group got off the steps. "There must be a door to the outside around here somewhere," she whispered, pointing at the cluttered space. "Look for it!"

Overhead, the heavy door grated on the cement floor again as the angry horde pushed through. Everyone below froze and listened intently, eyes turned to the stairs as motes of dust swarmed about in the feeble light. Maybelline whispered in a tremulous voice. "Do you think they'll find us down here?" Trying to crouch behind me for security, she grabbed my shoulders with shaky hands and hid her head.

"Don't worry about them coming down here." Tabitha dashed to the foot of the stair and took up her position with the pitchfork. "See if you can find a way out of here!"

An indignant voice echoed from upstairs. "Someone's been in my bedroom!" It sounded like Whistle Dick. Maybelline dug her fingernails into my shoulders as we listened for more. "Damn it! Those tranny bitches were jumping on my bed!" Then it sounded like someone kicked a box across the room.

"Where'd they go?" asked another voice, perhaps Johnny. "Maybe down the stairs?" For several seconds there was silence, and then came the slight shuffle of shoes in the direction of the stairs.

Using the flashlight for guidance, I urged the others to follow as I sprinted to the end of a short hall, found a door and pushed it open. One the other side waited the cool night air of the cemetery.

"We will have to reschedule for another night of *obeah* in this location." Mama Wawa panted as we raced to a nearby headstone to gather our thoughts. "Silly man, you know where you can find me and Maybelline."

"Oh, yes," said Maybelline. "How's about we do lunch tomorrow?"

But before I had a chance to come up with a diplomatic turn down, the door to the Crematorium burst open with a crash, and out poured the irate mob.

"Hey! Where are those tranny bitches?" said an angry voice.

"They're gonna pay for messin' up my bedroom!" cried another.

Then they spotted us.

"Time to run!" said Tabitha, crouching into position with the pitchfork. "Y'all run to the gate and I'll meet you there."

Mama Wawa ran in one direction, followed by the rest of her coterie; I ran the other way.

I made for the Gothic wake house in the distance and soon found myself on the rutted gravel road leading to the front gate. But suddenly a terrifying screech filled the air and I was sent tumbling ass over teakettle into the dew-dampened grass at the base of a decaying old tombstone.

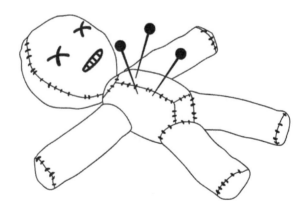

Zombies

More than a week later, when I picked up my clothes from the dry cleaners on the corner, Dot, the gray-haired woman at the counter, shook her head when I told her about the tumble in the cemetery that had caused all the stains.

"This is the hardest job we've seen in a long time," she said. "Dirt and grass stains all over the place." She shook her head again and punched some buttons on the cash register. "The girl in the back isn't very happy with you, I can tell you that for sure."

"Sorry." I mumbled and shrugged my shoulders. Keeping my eyes averted, I handed over my credit card. Outside, a solid stretch of white cloud seemed to cover the entire morning sky. A fine mist hung in the air, reminding residents that the chill of winter was right around the corner.

"And all this because you been hiding out in cemeteries in the middle of the night, getting yourself in trouble again." She clucked her tongue and processed the payment. "Better watch out," she said. "Zombies will get you if you're hanging out in the cemeteries all the time."

"We've got a lot of weird things in Louisville, but I don't think we have to worry about zombies."

The portly woman stopped and gave me a deadpan look. "I think you might have lots of things to worry about, if you ask me, and zombies would be the least of them. If out of the blue an owl swoops down from a tree and knocks you over like you said it did and you get your pretty clothes full of stains, then you got things to worry about." She shook her head as if I were a lost cause. "I don't want to see stains like that for a long, long time."

"Sorry," I said. "How was I to know a cemetery owl was going to mistake me for a rabbit or whatever else it was hunting for and knock me over?"

Dot looked up from the credit card machine and raised her eyebrows. "What were you doing? Hopping around and eating a carrot?"

Realizing I was in a no-win situation, I decided to shut up and quit while I still had a few shreds of dignity left. I signed the receipt and handed it back to her with a smile.

She removed my order from a nearby rack and handed it over. "In the future, please stay away from all wildlife and birds of prey," she said. "And don't go creeping around anymore cemeteries or other spooky spots in the middle of the night. Those places tend to have lots of dirt."

"I'll see what I can do," I said and left. I had no intention of staying away from the creepy places, but the woman behind the counter didn't need to know that.

After dropping off the dry cleaning at home and letting the dogs out, I walked down the alley to Ormsby. Before I left, however, I had to give Fritz a bath because when I came down to the kitchen after letting the dogs back in, I found him sitting in the middle of the floor with a large can on his head. He had rummaged through the garbage and discovered the empty container of Jif I had discarded while testing several recipes for peanut butter cookies earlier that morning, and, with Rocky and Bess looking on, he perched on his haunches and licked the dark insides of the can as it sat on his head. Chuckling to myself about the indignant look on his face when I deprived him of his peanut butter smearings and then had the nerve to shower him down in the kitchen sink, I walked over to Buck's and met my friend Jerry Rodgers for lunch.

Located on the ground floor of the old Mayflower Hotel, Buck's was by most estimations one of the fancier restaurants in Old Louisville, and with its Art Deco decor and hallmark mismatched china and silverware it was a popular spot for the lunch set, especially the ladies-who-lunch set. When I walked in, Jerry was nursing a cocktail at the bar, which, as usual, was lined with large crystal vases overflowing with an assortment of white blossoms. Clad in a knit sweater with a corduroy blazer, he smiled and waved when he saw me. The hostess showed us to a table in the middle of the room and after placing our orders we caught each other up on our writing projects. Soon, Jerry had finished his hot brown, and I my crispy fish with sweet chili sauce, and we said good-bye until the next time.

Out front, I was going to turn and return home when something at the other end of the block caught my eye. From the flouncy skirt and turban, I could tell right away that it was Josephine. To ward off the cold, she had draped a bright red shawl over her shoulders. Quickly making my way to the next street, and trying to be inconspicuous, I followed her up to the corner with the Witches' Tree. Instead of going into the brick apartment building as expected, however, she veered from the walkway and went straight to the gnarled and twisted trunk of the old tree. She dangled a small wicker basket from one hand and from it she extracted something and appeared to affix it to the tree. Then she skirted around the hedge and jaywalked into the park, the basket swinging jauntily at her side.

I strolled nonchalantly past the apartment building while trying to keep an eye on Josephine, but before I knew it she had disappeared beneath the leafy canopy that shaded the park. Glancing back over my shoulder, I could see something hanging from the tree, about five feet up from the ground. As I approached it, I saw that it was a small doll-like figure and it had been tacked to one of the big burls. Upon closer inspection, the body appeared to be made of stuffed fabric, and the head looked like someone had formed it by smoothly wrapping a piece of white cloth around a ping pong ball or something similar. It had no nose and the eyes, nothing more than simple x's, might have been drawn on by black magic marker. The mouth seemed to be ink as well, but the person who drew it had evidently put in a considerable amount of effort to make it look like the tight-lipped grimace of someone whose mouth had been sewn shut.

In addition, three stick pins had been sunk into the doll's chest.

Well, that's sort of spooky, I thought to myself. I had seen mysterious amulets and cute little charms left near or on the tree before, but nothing quite as creepy as this thing, whatever it was. Then, I noticed another figure tacked to the bark nearby. This one appeared to be constructed of sticks wrapped in rough fabric. What was it exactly, though? Another voodoo doll? But there were no pins stuck into its chest, and the arms on this figure had been pulled together and forward so they extended perpendicular from the chest. That was when I realized I was looking at a miniature representation of a zombie.

I shook my head back and forth, trying to erase the notion while calibrating my reality gauge. Hobos and gypsies were real people, I told myself, and so were witches, maybe, but only the kind that mixed potions and worshipped the earth, not the kind that flew around on brooms and turned people into toads. Voodoo priestesses were a fact, but zombies, their most legendary creations, I quickly reminded myself, did not really exist. Studying the figurine hanging on the tree, I thought back to the dry cleaner's and the cashier's warning about zombies in the cemetery, and I had to wonder if another voodoo day was in the making. Afraid that my even contemplating it would make it happen, I pulled myself away from the tree and walked home before running some errands.

After stopping at the bank and then picking up a country ham in preparation for Thanksgiving, I had to drop off our Halloween outfits at the costume shop. So I drove over to Floyd Street, where a large sign that read "Louise Cecil Costumes" hung from a tall pole with flaking white paint. On the sidewalk ambled a tall man in a heavy coat and a knit cap and from the violin case he carried, I could tell it was Micah. As he strolled out of sight I parked in an alley off Floyd Street and walked around the side of a large red brick warehouse till I found a small door tucked under a bit of awning. I rang the buzzer on the intercom and walked inside, to a cramped sort of foyer with marred quarter-sawn floors. After a bit of searching, I found a small hallway almost hidden behind a low-hanging bend in the narrow stairway winding overhead, and I ducked under and went to the elevator shaft. It was a large freight elevator and the opening was barred by a door of widely spaced planks. I pressed the UP button.

From above came a creaking and a shuddering as the elevator made its slow descent to the ground floor. After what seemed like an eternity, the cage rattled to a stop and the plank barrier slid up, revealing a metal floor and a dank interior large enough to accommodate at least a dozen people. At the control panel stood an imposing man who barely nodded his head in acknowledgment as I entered the space and stepped to the side so he could pull down the door. After a few buttons were pressed, there came a loud shudder and the cage lifted and started its tedious ascent to the costume shop. After ten or fifteen creaky seconds, we passed the next floor, an empty expanse whose barren walls and cold floors could be seen through the slats on the elevator door, and then all went dark before we emerged into the light of the third floor, another vacant space with dingy windows lining the brick walls. Finally we reached the top floor and the door slid up, revealing an explosion of color and noise.

Someone dressed as Marie Antoinette strolled by, her wide embroidered skirt brushing my legs in passing. Behind her trailed a bent-over figure with auburn blond hair, and apparently she was checking the hem of the dress as the other woman walked. When the stooped lady saw me, she smiled and removed several straight pins from her mouth so she could speak. "Well, hey, honey, how are you?" It was Louise, the owner of the shop and something of a local icon when it came to costumes. "You can hang your returns over, there," she told me, pointing to a rolling rack already crammed full with dozens of costumes on hangers. "Did you have a good Halloween?"

"Yes, thanks," I said. "Everybody loved our costumes. We even won first place at one of the parties."

"I knew you would," said Louise.

Nearby, several additional racks seemed to groan under the weight of just as many returned items, and throughout the large rooms that comprised the costume shop, there were dozens more racks and massive piles of clothing and fabric. There were rumored to be over 10,000 costumes in all, many of them hand-stitched by Louise herself, and she kept track of everything with a simple system of receipts and tickets, refusing to use a computer to track the inventory. Shelves along the wall seemed to burst with all types of accessories, including bowlers and top hats, rubber masks, jewel-encrusted crowns, angel wings, and turbans. After attending to Marie Antoinette, Louise breezed by with an armload of flapper dresses and deposited them onto a large velvet armchair next to me. "I heard you're going to help organize a Victorian ghost walk as a way of showcasing the haunted stories in the neighborhood," she said, heading over to an enormous mound of costumes by the entryway into the next room. "That's a lovely idea."

"Yes," I said, amazed by how quickly news spread in the neighborhood. Only the day before had I met with several neighborhood people to discuss ways of capitalizing on Old Louisville and its ghostly past. "We'll see if we can pull it off."

"Oh, you'll pull it off and I'll be happy to help with costumes. The neighborhood needs more things like that." Louise reached into the pile of clothing and, after a bit of rummaging around, she pulled out an enormous witch's hat with a crumpled peak and handed it to me. "Here, try this on and see how it fits," she said. "I can get you a big black tunic and an overlay and then you'll be the perfect Stick Witch next year."

I turned over the hat in my hand. "Me as the Stick Witch?" I moved my head back and forth and chuckled. "I don't think so."

"Oh, come on. It'll be a hoot," said Louise. "People love it when men dress up as witches." She walked over to another enormous pile of objects, reached an arm in up to her shoulder, rooted around, and then produced a large walking stick with a carved skull on one end. "Here, this will make you more convincing," she said with a laugh. "A stick witch needs a stick."

Although I smiled and accepted the carved walking stick, I didn't really have any intention of using it. Before I had a chance to change the subject to something other than me dressing up as a witch, someone on the other side of the room called out to Louise and she zoomed over to help him find a Dracula cape and a set of vampire fangs. "See you later," she called over her shoulder before disappearing into an aisle crammed full of costumes.

Stepping aside to let pass a teenager dressed as Little Bo Peep, I made my way back to the freight elevator and waited as the silent attendant slowly lowered me and three creepy-looking clowns to the bottom floor. One of them smirked slightly when he noticed me holding a witch's hat and walking stick, and I had to stop and wonder if it wasn't one of the voodoo acolytes from my Halloween night adventure in Eastern Cemetery. Definitely tall enough, I thought to myself, but it was too hard to ascertain with all the makeup and clownly accoutrements. Soon the elevator shuddered to a stop, the attendant rattled up the door, and we all got out.

I stowed the hat and the walking stick in the trunk of the car and drove over to Bardstown Road. As I passed the main campus of the University of Louisville and turned onto Eastern Parkway, I noticed another unfortunate semi had gotten itself hung up under the viaduct crossing spanning Third Street. A crowd of onlookers watching on as a squad car pulled up and turned on its lights, the driver stood there and scratched his head while studying the mangled mess of metal wedged under the overpass.

I almost laughed out loud when I spied Micah again, shuffling by on the sidewalk, but then a logo on the side of the truck caught my eye. It was for a costume shop and although the first part was illegible because of the damage to the side of the trailer, the word "zombie" was still clearly visible. Next to the logo was a large airbrushed figure of a person dressed up as a zombie. With his arms stretched out before him, the man seemed to wander across the side of the trailer in a trance.

Shaking my head in disbelief, I hit the gas and sped down Eastern Parkway to Bardstown Road, leaving the zombie truck and the crowd of onlookers behind. Given that zombies had already worked their way into my day twice already, I really shouldn't have been surprised to find zombies advertised on the side of a semi hung up under the Third Street overpass, but it caught me off guard nonetheless. The whole time at Louise Cecil's costume shop I had harbored the sneaking suspicion that I would run across someone disguised as a zombie, and when that didn't happen I somehow, and apparently erroneously, thought I was home free for the rest of the day.

By the time I reached the Highlands, fortunately, I had cleared my mind of all thoughts of zombies and I was looking forward to dinner out with the Tuesday night crowd. The group had decided on Ramsi's so we met out front and chatted while the hostess prepared our table. We got our usual round table in the front right-hand window and sat down and ordered a couple of bottles of wine, and chips with queso.

When it came to deciding on our meals, most of us got the same things we always did and I ordered the tortellini graciela. Soon after the crispy fish at Buck's earlier that day I had begun craving the combination of tri-colored pasta with broccoli and mushrooms in cream sauce and I had to restrain myself from wolfing down the whole bowl when it arrived. After a couple more bottles of wine and lively conversation, the gang disbanded and I boxed up most of the tortellini to take home, knowing how good it would taste for lunch the next day.

Outside, even though darkness had fallen, milky clouds covered the sky and their pallor cast a good deal of illumination over the busy streetscape. The car was two blocks away and I crossed the street and headed in that direction, but I stopped dead in my tracks when a strange sight unfolded before my eyes.

Walking trance-like down the sidewalk, from the opposite direction, were three people with their arms held out stiffly before them. Dragging their feet, they slowly shuffled toward me and I was able to get a better look at them. Blood seemed to ooze from the corners of their mouths and from a multitude of open sores on their hands and faces. Streaks of black and red rimmed their lifeless eyes and all three were groaning loudly.

"Onhhhhhhh. Onhhhhhhh. Onhhhhhhh."

They were zombies.

Frances

I was still chuckling about it the next day, as I cleaned up the kitchen after testing some recipes for an article for *Arts Across Kentucky* magazine. The three zombies I had encountered the night before on Bardstown Road were nothing more than people in costume, of course, but it had given me a real fright. One of them, as it turned out, was a student of mine and he stopped to say hello when he saw me. It was a good thing that he recognized me because I had no way of knowing who he was with all the gory makeup on his face. When I asked him what was up with the zombie getup and the trance-like walk, he told me that he and the other two were doing a photo shoot to promote an upcoming event in Louisville. It was to be a zombie walk, he said, a get-together that would attract hundreds of the living dead in August as they roamed Bardstown Road in search of fresh brains and other zombie delicacies. I was going to ask him precisely what these other delicacies entailed when I spied the photographer standing nearby and tapping his toe, evidently peeved that I was interrupting his artistic endeavors, so I told my student to keep up the good work and I took my leave.

As I stowed a cooling pumpkin pie in the fridge, the phone rang.

"You got a skunk in your back alley, right next to your car, you know that?" It was Loretty and she sounded especially cheerful. "Don't go out there, though," she said with a laugh. "You'll just get it mad and it will stink up the whole neighborhood and then you'll have to take a bath in tomato juice."

"If you say so." I had never come across a skunk in the neighborhood, and I really wanted to rush out back and see for myself, but the thought of having to take a bath in tomato juice made me reconsider. I didn't even have any tomato juice, come to think of it.

"Yeah, I know what's going through your head," said Loretty. "How is it that there are skunks in Old Louisville?" She paused and from the other end I could hear ice cubes tinkling together as she took a drink. "Well, I'm not sure," she said, "but every once in a while you do see a skunk down here. Even saw a groundhog rooting around someone's yard the other day."

Given the abundance of wildlife and other creatures I had already discovered in the neighborhood, I didn't have the heart to tell Loretty that I was not surprised in the least to hear that a skunk was sniffing around the back alley. Or that I had seen a groundhog the other day myself. "Well, it's a regular wild kingdom down here in Old Louisville, isn't it? I met somebody the other day who said she had a flock of pelicans in her back yard."

"Yeah," she cackled. "Wild kingdom, all right, just like Mutual of Omaha's

Wild Kingdom with Marlon Perkins. You weren't too young to see that program on the television, were you?"

"No," I assured her, "as little kids we used to watch that every Friday night."

"That's good," she laughed. "Television programs today are such crap. It's good you got to see some of the decent stuff before it all went downhill." I listened to the ice cubes shift in her glass as she took another drink. "By the way, you been having any more strange things going on in your house? You know, footsteps and stuff like you were hearing all the time before."

"Well, every now and then something weird will happen," I said, "but not too much over the last couple of months. I still get the strong smell of coffee in the morning and sometimes it smells like someone's been ironing in the back room on the second floor, but I haven't been hearing the footsteps and stuff like I used to." I debated telling her that I had bought a white noise machine for my bedside and that ever since I seemed to be sleeping more soundly at night. So who knew if there were still the odd creaks and groans in the house.

"It's getting cold out so maybe the oddballs out on the streets will be leaving you alone," she said. "It's not warm enough to be out all hours of the day being a worthless bum and panhandling passersby on Oak Street." She took a drink and coughed. "Don't worry, though, if they get too close to your house, I'll let you know. I'll let you know." She cleared her throat. "Loretty's up here with her kraut spy glasses and she sees the whole damn neighborhood, freaks and all."

"Well, that's good to know," I said, going to stand at the window in the front parlor so I could look up and wave at her.

"Yeah, I see you standing at the window," she said with a dry cackle. "The house looks real nice now that you got it all fixed up and painted. And that front parlor really sparkles since you put up that shiny wallpaper."

"Thanks." I plopped myself down in the chair nearest the window. The cloudy sky from the day before had cleared and now bright sun streamed through the glass and flooded the room. On the walls, the covering of gold anaglypta caught the light and dazzled my eyes. There was a soft padding sound in the foyer and Fritz suddenly poked his head into the parlor.

"Thanks yourself," she said. "Before I forget, I wanted to tell you that I have seen that one woman with the turban and the big skirt snooping around your dumpster a couple of times now."

I sat up straight in my chair. "Josephine? What was she doing back there?"

"Not sure who it was, but I did see a colorful turban or kerchief on top of her head," said Loretty. "She was rootin' through your garbage like those possums you got hanging out in your back yard."

I moved aside a basket of tools and other items I had been using to adhere brass studs and colored stones to the lincrusta and anaglypta walls. "Really?" I cradled the phone between my ear and shoulder so I could help Fritz jump up into my lap. "I wonder what she's looking for."

"Not sure what she's after, but whatever it is, it's not a lot," said Loretty. "I couldn't see what it was she took because it was too small, but she's found a couple of things that interested her and carried them away."

I relaxed my shoulders and gave Fritz a pat on the head. "Weird. I wonder what she found."

"I don't know but maybe it was some of your hair or something else she can use for her voodoo doll. All I know is she must be some kind of freak show." Loretty took a loud drink and started laughing. "Oh, hang on a sec—" she said, her voice suddenly serious. "I do believe you've got some company."

But before I could say another word Fritz raised his head and started barking. I turned around in time to see a small form move up the steps to the front porch. Several seconds later came the loud electric buzz of the doorbell.

"Better go and see who it is," said Loretty. "I'll call back later and find out who it was, but it doesn't look like a bum to me. Looks like a real person."

"Bye." I hung up and returned the phone to its table. Then I shut Fritz in the butler's pantry with Rocky and Bess before running to the front door.

Out on the street a nice Lexus had been parked with the front right wheel up on the curb. Standing there at the entryway was a short little woman in a tan suit. Her auburn hair had been stylishly coifed and there was a twinkle in her eye when I opened the door and greeted her. A blue-tailed skink darted across the sunny part of the front steps and disappeared down a crack in the concrete of the walkway.

"Well, hello, darlin'," said the lady, who brushed past me and pushed into the foyer. "Well, look at all these pretty walls in this house. I knew it was pretty from the outside but I had no idea how pretty it was in the inside." She paused for a moment and turned around to get a better view. "Heavens, this is pretty!" she said. "Such a pretty house. This will do nicely for my Antiques Club."

"Antiques Club?" I had no idea who this woman was, much less the slightest inkling as to what her 'antiques club' was.

"Oh, heavens, darlin', I haven't even introduced myself yet, have I?" she laughed and extended her hand. "I'm Frances, Frances Mengel. My late husband's family used to live in the big mansion down on the next block but I've lived out in the East End most of my life, but I still love coming down here to Old Louisville and I make it down her at least once or twice a month now. I've been a member of the Woman's Club right over there on Fourth for many years, but I got my own little group going now and we like to call ourselves the Antiques Club, and not only because we all love antiques but because we all *are* a bunch of antiques now." At this point she finally took a breath and erupted in a fit of pleasant laughter. "Me? I'm 84, but you'd never know it, would you, darlin'?" She paused and spun around so I could assess the situation for myself.

"No, I'd never have guessed," I agreed with a smile. "But what exactly—?"

"Yes, darlin', I like to keep moving and that's one of the secrets to not growing old. You can't just sit down in a rocking chair and give up like so many of these old people do." As if to prove that she wasn't going to stop moving, she waltzed into the dining room and pushed through the door to the butler's pantry and went into the kitchen, where the dogs swarmed around her. After petting each of them and telling me about the large French poodle she had at home, Frances turned around and zoomed back to the foyer, her heels clacking across the hardwood floors. "Yes, you've got a beautiful place here and the antique ladies will love it. You know, I've been driving by this house for months now and every time I passed I saw that you had done something else to the place. So when I got the news this morning that the venue for the next meeting of the Antiques Club had fallen through I thought of you right away and that's really why I'm stopping by." She walked to the oak desk where I had relegated the framed lithograph of the pig that had kept falling from the wall in the butler's pantry when we first moved in. She picked it up and smiled appreciatively.

"Venue fallen through—?" I said in the two seconds afforded me.

She put the lithograph back in its spot on the desk. "Yes, I told them in the first place I didn't think we could count on that other man and then sure enough this morning Lucie called me and told me he had backed out. You know Lucie, don't you? Lucie Blodgett? She writes for the social column for the *Voice Tribune* and we've been friends forever. Oh, good lord, we've been friends *forever*." Frances paused for a quick breath and let out an exclamation that was half sigh and half laugher. "Oh, lord, we've been friends a *long* time, Lucie and I," she said, leaning in for a conspiratorial whisper. "Bless her heart, she's a mess, but I still love her to death!" With that she erupted in another gale of laughter and pressed a hand to her heart while she used the other hand to dab a tear from the corner of her eye. "Yes, I tell you, that Lucie Blodgett is a character!"

"But—"

"Oh, what am I saying? You'll find out for yourself what kind of character that Lucie is when she comes over next week. That's when we need to use your house for our meeting, by the way." She stopped short when she saw the worried look on my face, but quickly resumed. "Oh, don't worry, we won't be here for very long. A bunch of East End housewives, about three dozen, that's all we are, looking to have a little fun and have our monthly meeting. It'll be for a few hours around lunch time and we'll have the food catered and you can join us, of course, but I suspect it will be entirely boring to you, but you'll be fine, you'll see, you might even have some fun and learn something new, but you need to be there because you will be our guest speaker and I want you, of course, to talk about this house and all the spooky stories you've uncovered about the neighborhood and to tell us about the book you're working on." She clasped her hands together over her bosom and sighed with contentment. "Goodness gracious! It will be so much fun, darlin', let me tell you."

"You didn't say you were all a bunch of East End housewives, did you?"

"Oh, well, not every single person is from the East End, darlin', but that's where most of us live. I've lived in the East End for ages, but did I tell you that my deceased husband's family used to own the big mansion down the block?"

"Well—" I was going to tell her that yes, she had mentioned that, but at that moment her train of thought chugged forward.

"Yes, that place was grand. So many bedrooms, at least a dozen, and at least that many fireplaces," she said. "And all that lovely woodwork! Hardwood floors in every room and such extravagant mantelpieces. You know the Mengels were big into lumber and millwork, didn't you? Oh, yes, they owned the companies that brought in a lot of the wood to these places." She raised a richly bejeweled finger and indicated the panels stenciled with the word "welcome" in different languages around my foyer. "Yes, they had lovely details in that big old house like you have here—now did I ever tell you about the time in the 1920s, or was it the 1930s, when the Mengels had two chimpanzees they kept as pets? What were their names? Ike and Mike or something like that. Or was it Ikah and Mikah? Yes, I believe that was it! Well, one day those monkeys got loose and they were scaring the entire neighborhood and they eventually ran all the way over to Eastern Parkway where the sheriff had to shoot them. Or did he have to shoot just one of them? I don't remember exactly, but it was in the newspapers and everything. Well, they never kept monkeys in the house after that." She interrupted her monologue and put her hands on her hips. "But who am I to be telling stories? You're the one with the good stories and I can't wait to hear them all next week at our meeting. It'll be a hoot, don't you think?"

I wanted to express my sympathy for the monkey or monkeys that had been shot but I was so surprised at having the floor that I didn't know what to say.

"Well, what's wrong, darlin'? Cat got your tongue?" Frances reached into her handbag and removed a compact mirror so she could check her makeup.

"But my dining room table only seats eight," I said. "And the one in the butler's pantry only has room for four, so there's no way I can accommodate the more than three dozen people you have in your club."

She returned the mirror to her purse and laughed. "Oh, don't worry about that, darlin', because we all don't have to sit at the table." She pointed to the staircase and then the French doors leading into the parlor. "Some of us can sit on the steps here, and then you've got all these sofas and settees in these two front rooms." She turned and walked into the dining room then, coming to stand in front of the table. "And we can squeeze another six around this table, if we have to." She clasped her hands and raised them to her heart. "Oh, darlin', we are

231

going to have such a wonderful time, you'll see. Thanks so much for opening your house to the Antiques Club!"

Any form of protest, I realized, would be futile, so I kept my mouth closed and nodded my head once.

"Say, what size are you, darlin'?" Frances took a step toward me and made me turn around once. "We need to get you a tuxedo, so you can be my date to the Phillies Ball in the spring. Oh, you'll have fun. The Phillies are another one of my little clubs."

"Phillies—?" I followed Frances, who had started for the door.

"Yes, the Phillies Ball," she said. "It's a wonderful event at Derby time and you'll love it, I swear. Lucie Blodgett will be there because she's at *every* social event and she'll make sure you get some good publicity for your book. But I don't have time to tell you more about it today because several of my antique ladies are waiting for me over at Buck's, where we're going to have lunch today, and I'll probably get the hot brown again because it's not too bad. Oh, darlin', they're going to be so thrilled when I tell them you're going to be hosting our next meeting. Everyone's been in a tizzy since this morning when that other man cancelled and we're so happy you stepped in!"

She paused at the oak desk by the window and picked up the pig lithograph. "Now they don't make pigs like this anymore, do they?" She laughed and returned the frame to the surface of the desk. "Darlin' I love the beautiful things you've got in this house, and I especially love this cute little piggy right here!" She walked to the door, opened it, and let herself out with a cheerful wave over the shoulder. "See you next week, darlin'!"

And with that, the whirlwind that was Frances Mengel departed.

After a deep sigh, I went to the back door and let the dogs out, and when I came back into the house the telephone under the stairs was ringing. I had a hunch who it was. "Loretty?" I said. "Is that you?"

"Yes, indeedy," she laughed. "It's old Loretty. Who was that woman who just left anyways? Someone needs to show her the difference between the street and the curb. She was parked all over the place." There was a wheezing cough from the other end and then she came back on the line. "She had on some fancy clothes, though. Had a nice car, too."

"That was Frances," I said. "I guess she's related by marriage to the Mengels who used to live down on the next block, in that huge mansion across the street from the Filson Historical Society."

"Oh, yeah, I know that place, she said. "Can't see it hardly at all from my window, but when I go down to my friend's at the end of the hall, she's got a real nice view in that direction." There was a pause and from the other end it sounded like Loretty had lit up another cigarette. I imagined her at her window, taking a long drag and languidly exhaling the smoke. "Yeah, that's the place where that guy with the temper lives, isn't it? They say he doesn't like people cutting through his property from the back alley. I heard the other day he pulled a gun on someone he found in his side lot."

I laughed. "Yes, I suppose so. I heard the same thing but he seems nice enough to me." A few weeks before, I had met the couple who had recently moved into the enormous mansion and they invited me in one day and showed me around. With its paneled and coffered library and towering fireplace mantels, it was truly one of the grandest mansions I had entered in the neighborhood.

"Well, he better not pull a gun on old Loretty, because if he does I'll give him what for," she said with a dry cackle. "So, what'd that woman want who came to see you?"

"Frances?" I said. "Oh, she informed me that she's going to bring her East End ladies group over next week for a lunch meeting. They call themselves the Antiques Club and their venue fell through so they want to use my place."

"Well, lah-tee-da," said Loretty. I heard her swirl around the ice cubes in her glass and take a drink. "I suppose they'll be expecting pheasant under glass or something fancy like that."

"I guess we'll find out because it will be catered." I walked over to the thermostat near the back stairs in the coat room. A sudden chill in the air reminded me that winter was right around the corner. I was hoping I'd be able to refrain from turning on the heat until Thanksgiving, but I realized I was going to have to break down and warm the place up.

"It's good you don't have to cook for them with Thanksgiving a few days away," said Loretty. "How you going to fit in all the stuff you got coming up?"

I was about to answer when a loud *slap* came from the foyer. It seemed to be followed by the sound of broken glass. "Loretty? I'm going to have to let you go," I said. "I think something fell and I need to go clean it up."

"Alrighty, I'll talk to you later." She hung up.

I walked back into the foyer, and there, by the oak desk, lay something on the floor. At first I wasn't sure what it was but when I went to pick it up I recognized it. It was the framed lithograph of the pig that Frances had admired several minutes before, and the glass had shattered.

Holiday House Tour

It was Saturday morning, less than two weeks later, and I stood in the front parlor and shook my head. It was hard to believe that a whole year had passed in La Casa Fabulosa. Clear lights twinkled on the Christmas tree in front of the large arched window. Outside, the frigid morning wind tossed about a smattering of puffy snowflakes before they drifted to the frozen ground. Holly branches rattled against the windowpane and in the fireplace orange flames danced, scaring off the last of the chill in the room as the grandmother clock in the foyer chimed the half hour. Soon it would be noon, and I was recounting my encounter with Frances. I had told the Tuesday night gang about the broken picture.

"So, do you think it just fell?" Skippy held a mug of hot cocoa to his lips and took a sip. "You were the only one in the house, weren't you?" He reached for a decanter of bourbon and added a generous dose.

"Yes, me and the dogs," I said. "I think Frances didn't set it down the right way after she picked it up, and that caused it to fall." I sat back in my chair and surveyed the parlor, which, like the rest of the house, had been decked out in its Christmas finery for the annual holiday house tour of the neighborhood. Six large poinsettias clustered around the base of the mahogany fireplace mantel, which had been draped with fragrant boughs of pine. Dozens of foot-tall nutcrackers, brightly painted colors gleaming in the muted light of the fire, stood sentinel in a line at the baseboard that wrapped around the room. A row of white tapers lined the shelf of the mantel, the flicker of the flames trapped in the silvered glass of the inset mirror.

Beth sat her cup down and stood up to smooth the curtains at the window. "I bet that picture didn't fall on its own," she said with a laugh. "I bet Lucy knocked it over because she was jealous of Frances."

"I don't think Lucy really has anything to worry about." Sipping my hot cocoa, I gave the tree the once-over again. One of the candy canes didn't look right so I walked over and hung it in a different location.

"She probably didn't like the competition from the East End housewives, either," said Wendy, who was sitting on the sofa with both Rocky and Bess in her lap.

"Yes, how did the lunch for the Antiques Club go anyway?" It was Ramon's sister, Silvia, who had come with Miguel, her husband, to help us clean and get the house ready for the tour. Neighborhood volunteers had arrived as well, and they were taking up positions throughout the house.

"It went fine," I said. "They all seemed to enjoy themselves and they loved hearing about the book I'm working on."

"At least it was safer than some of your most recent adventures," said Beth. "One of these days you're going to get yourself killed. Hanging out with hobos in scary basements one night and the next you're in a dangerous cemetery getting yourself caught up in a turf war between a bunch of drug addicts and a troupe of voodoo drag queens."

"All in a day's work." I finished my hot cocoa and set the cup down. From the kitchen, the aroma of baking gingerbread wafted to the front of the house, seemingly in anticipation of the several thousand visitors that would soon arrive to tour the interior.

"Well, I suppose we should all get ready," I said, looking at my watch. "Visitors will probably start arriving right at noon." With that, people got up and started moving to their different posts throughout the house. "Thanks for coming and helping out today."

At the front door, Gregory studied a piece of paper in his hand—the script he would use to welcome people as they entered—and Tad examined the anaglypta walls to make sure all the studs and faux jewels were secure. For the previous week, all our friends had worked frantically, often into the wee hours of the morning, to help us get the house ready, and the night before had been a marathon session of painting, cleaning, and adding last-minute touches to finish everything. With the coat of Venetian red paint still drying on the walls in the dining room, I surveyed the bottom floor, amazed how it all had come together at the very last moment.

There was a small commotion at the front door and, walkie-talkies squawking at their sides, several volunteers from the holiday house tour committee showed up to make sure everything was in order. After Joan Stewart, the chair of the neighborhood council, showed up and gave her okay, we were officially open for business.

Before long, groups of people began coming in from the snowy outdoors and streaming through the house. A route had been established that would first take them from the foyer and parlor up the main stairs to the third floor, where they would work their way through my office and the guest suite back down the stairs to the second floor. Then they would start with the large bedroom at the front of the house and go through the two adjacent bedrooms to the little room at the back of the house. From there they'd take the back stairs down to the coatroom before wandering through the dining room and into the butler's pantry. They'd leave the house through the kitchen, where I'd be standing by to say good-bye and offer them a taste of freshly baked gingerbread on the way out.

The stream of visitors kept up for most of the day and around five, about an hour before day one of the house tour officially ended, the traffic tapered off to a trickle of small groups and individuals. I had put the last batch of gingerbread on a tray on the table in the middle of the room and was wiping down the counters when a lone woman wandered in. When I held the tray out to her and offered a sample, she shook her head and looked around, eyes widening as she did so.

"No, thank you," she said in a whisper. "I never eat sweets." As she spoke, her eyes rose to the ceiling and she became still. "I never eat sweets, I never eat sweets, I never eat sweets."

I was struck by the visitor's singular appearance and I took a moment to study her more closely. Everything she wore seemed to be in a deep, dark purple. A heavy knit sweater hung from her shoulders and a long wool skirt brushed the tips of black pointy boots. A frizzed head of salt and pepper hair had been tied up in a fringed bandana and a large glass pentagram dangled from a chain around her neck. Oh, dear, I thought to myself. I hope she's not a gypsy or a voodoo woman or anything like that.

As if she had read my thoughts, the stranger suddenly looked at me and cocked her head. Eyes narrowed, she raised a pointed finger and inched toward me. "I can sense things that many others cannot," she said. "Don't ever doubt that, young man." Stopping in front of me so that we were practically toe to toe, the woman reached up and vigorously tweaked my nose with her thumb and forefinger.

"Hey—" I started to protest, but the visitor raised a hand to silence me and then turned to face the wall.

"Don't ever doubt, don't ever doubt, don't ever doubt." She raised her arms and flailed them at the ceiling. "I can sense the things that many others cannot."

"Good grief," I muttered under my breath so she couldn't hear me. I quickly went to the counter and pretended to occupy myself with cleaning and organizing. "Thanks for stopping by today," I said, pointing to the back door. "You can go out that way and follow the walk around the side of the house and back to the front. Merry Christmas."

When you lived in an old house, I discovered, it seemed that certain visitors invariably felt compelled to announce their psychic gifts on the spot and to declare the place haunted. Already that day I had had encounters with three other women proudly waltzing into the kitchen at the end of the tour and claiming to be "mediums" or having "the gift of sight" and I really wasn't in the mood for any more clichés or melodrama.

One of the would-be clairvoyants informed me that a young child had been buried in the walls of the basement, another said she had made contact with a young man who had lived in the house in the 1920s, and the last one had offered to come and smudge the whole house with sage and incense in a guaranteed attempt to "rid the residence of unnecessary entities"—and "all for only two hundred dollars." Although I had feigned interest and listened politely, each and every one of them struck me as a crackpot. This woman seemed no different and I longed for her speedy exit from my kitchen.

But once again, the outlandish lady seemed to have divined my thoughts. "I will go when the time is right," she said. "And not before!" Again she raised her hands to the ceiling and flailed her arms.

Cautiously, I edged toward the door leading into the butler's pantry, but the woman took a step in the same direction and blocked my way. Oh, great, I thought to myself. Trapped by another weirdo. I pretended I hadn't been trying to escape and instead walked to a shelf on the far wall, from which I pulled down an old-fashioned hand crank egg beater. When I returned to the sink I realized the lady was eyeing me suspiciously, so I pretended to inspect the beater, turning it upside down, then downside up, and finally cranking the handle with all my might to create a pleasantly rusty whirring sound.

Unconvinced, the strange woman still stared and her eyes didn't leave me when I nonchalantly walked back to the shelf and returned the old egg beater. Moseying back to the sink, I cast a furtive glance through the doorway into the butler's pantry. Where were my friends when I needed them? Maybe if one of them arrived, it would break this woman's concentration and cause her to vacate the premises. From the sound of it, however, a celebration was going on in the front of the house. Skippy had cracked open another bottle of bourbon and they had all congregated with the rest of the volunteers in the parlor, where Wendy was doling out cocktails. The last I saw Fritz, he was snuggled on Ramon's lap in front of the fire, and Rocky and Bess were curled up on their pillows in the butler's pantry, where they had slept soundly while hundreds of people passed by. I was on my own.

"You may not believe," said the woman, "but I can sense the things that the others cannot sense." She stepped away from the entryway into the butler's pantry and came in my direction. "I see the things they cannot see, I hear the things they cannot hear, I feel the things they cannot feel. And I can smell the things they cannot smell."

"Can you taste the things they cannot taste?" I said, trying to hide a smirk and figuring it couldn't hurt to ask since the oddball woman had brought up all the other senses. From the front of the house there was an enormous burst of laughter—probably someone telling a funny story about one of the people they had met on the house tour or something else comical that had happened during the course of the day. If they'd come back here, I thought to myself, they'd really have a good story to tell because I suspected this woman wasn't going to leave anytime soon and not before things got a whole lot weirder.

As if on cue, the eccentric visitor raised a finger and jabbed the air in front of her. "Blasphemer!" She hissed it in a curiously altered voice that was raspy and drew out each syllable. Then she went back to her normal voice. "Make fun of me if you wish, but I can sense the things the others cannot sense." She slowly turned around full circle and cast her glance to the ceiling. "Sense the things the others cannot sense, sense the things the others cannot sense, sense the things the others cannot sense." After completing her turn she walked over to me and for the second time I found myself toe to toe with the woman. "Did you hear what I said?" And once again she reached up and tweaked my nose with her thumb and forefinger.

"Hey," I said, gently slapping her hand away and positioning myself so that the kitchen table stood between us. "Enough with the nose already."

"Did you hear what I said?" She took a step that indicated her desire to chase me around the table.

"Yeah, I heard you," I said, taking a step in the other direction. "Sense the things others cannot sense."

"No, before that, dummy," she said, stomping a foot.

What was it with people calling me "dummy" in Old Louisville? The lady who had come to the door and told me she was friends with Big Momma Cheese had said the exact same thing. Suddenly, I narrowed my eyes and studied the woman in front of me. It couldn't be, I thought to myself, although this woman was about the same height and build. "Say, you haven't been here before, have you?"

"Me?" she said, a look of genuine confusion clouding her features. "No, never been here before. But you're avoiding my question. Did you hear what I said?" She took another step and started to come around the table.

"Yes, I heard you." I said, heading in the other direction. "But I'm not sure which part you're talking about."

She stopped short and pointed at me from across the table. "I can smell the things they cannot smell," she said, a smile of satisfaction spreading from ear to ear.

I stopped and waited for her to explain.

"I can smell the things they cannot smell," she repeated, lifting her nose and exaggeratedly sniffing three times in a row. *Sniff, sniff, sniff.* Before I had a chance to protest that I had no clue what she was talking about, she raised her eyes and pointed to the stove. "Can you smell it, too? The coffee she makes?" Then she pointed at the ceiling. "I can also smell the laundry she does. Can you?"

A creeping sensation suddenly worked down my spine and broke out in a rash of goose bumps along my forearms. Immediately I recalled the many times I had woken up to the strong smell of coffee emanating from the kitchen when nobody was there. Then I remembered all the times the distinct odors associated with ironing seemed to come from the small room at the end of the hallway on the second floor. I wondered if she could have found this out from overhearing my friends talk about the bizarre goings-on taking place in the house.

A look of puzzlement must have come over me, because the strange woman grinned, clapped her hands together, and wildly shook a finger in the air. Quickly, she darted around the table and came in my direction; I tried to keep ahead of her and moved to the other side. "Yes, you smell it, too!" she said. "You smell it, you smell it, you smell it!"

Once she was no longer pursuing me, I stopped and claimed a safe edge of the table. "Maybe I have smelled something, but I'm not sure what it is."

The woman nodded her head sagely and pointed at the ceiling. At first she didn't say anything, but then she spoke and her voice deepened and took on the odd, raspy quality it had before. "That room is the secret."

Beth emerged through the butler's pantry from the dining room and popped her head into the kitchen. Behind her stood her roommate, Lori. "What's taking you so long? The decanter's empty. We just opened another bottle of bourbon and we're all waiting for you in the parlor."

I opened my mouth and turned to point at the mysterious visitor, but she was already halfway across the room. There was a flurry of dark purple and the rustle of scurrying boots and fabric, and then the back door opened and closed with hardly a sound.

"Who was that?" said Beth. She moved to the side window and watched the figure make her way off the back porch to the walk that led to front of the house. But instead of following it to the front of the house, the woman turned and walked across the deck to the back gate. There, she opened the door, let herself out, and disappeared down the darkened alley.

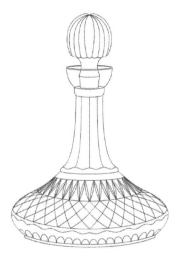

The Evil Eye

Another Christmas had come and gone at La Casa Fabulosa, and so had another New Year's Eve. After the holiday excitement subsided, the chill of winter really settled in and things slowed down a bit. January passed without too much out of the ordinary happening, although it seemed that the strange smells intensified. Most days I would wake up to the strong smell of freshly brewed coffee coming from the kitchen, always when nobody had been around to make the coffee, and whenever I happened to venture to the little second-floor room at the back of the house, a peculiar odor lingered there. Sometimes it smelled as if someone had finished ironing a batch of fresh laundry and other times I could have sworn something had caught fire and was still giving off wisps of charred wood.

During those months, if I wasn't teaching, I usually found myself before the fire in the parlor, putting the final touches on the manuscript for my Kentucky cookbook or working on the ghost story collection. Since I was cooped up and not out on the streets very much, it was hardly surprising that I didn't see Josephine at all during that winter.

Without so many distractions I soon finished the manuscript. One morning, after meeting with an editor from the publishing house, I decided to stop off at Wagner's Pharmacy for a late breakfast. A sheet of slate-gray snow clouds covered the sky as I got out of my car and walked across the street to the old brick building that housed the diner. Behind me stood Churchill Downs, the stark whiteness of the famous twin spires on the old wooden clubhouse contrasted against the dark clouds, and a long line of horse trailers was pulling into a gravel-topped parking lot. As I opened the door to go inside, an enormous stretch limo crept by and I assumed it was headed to one of the main gates, where it would deposit its passengers.

Inside, the restaurant buzzed with activity and a waitress zoomed by with steaming plates of eggs sunny side up with bacon and hash browns. Using her forearms for extra support, she held two plates in each hand as she maneuvered to a booth against the wall. I watched her set the plates down at a table with two men sitting on either side and when one of them looked up, I realized it was Godwynn Goodwynn. He had on the same get-up as when I saw him at the St. James Art Show—the wide-brimmed hat, grandfather shirt, and black vest—and his three companions were wearing the same thing. Although a faint glimmer of recognition seemed to register when he saw me, he neither said anything nor acknowledged me at first. Then his eyes lit up and he waved at me before nudging one of his friends and pointing in my direction when they all turned their heads. In perfect unison, they put their hands out in front of them and drew an invisible circle with their index fingers. The din of conversation drowned out anything they said, but it was easy enough to read Godwynn's lips when he enthusiastically mouthed the words: *Church of the Iron Hoop. Church of the Iron Hoop.* I returned the wave and made my way to an empty stool at the counter.

No sooner had I sat down when the door opened with a loud *whoosh* and a gust of cold air rushed into the restaurant. All eyes turned to see what had caused the commotion, and in walked a row of four identically—and stereotypically—clad Middle Eastern men. Each one was short and wore a white *thawb* covered by a black *bisht* trimmed in gold. On their heads were the traditional scarves known as *keffiyeh*, theirs in a pattern of red and white checks. Sauntering up to the counter and surveying the room, one of them turned and made a motion toward the door. A tall man in a tailored black suit entered, followed by another man, even taller, in traditional Middle Eastern garb. He was dressed all in white, however, and the headpiece was solid white as well, held in place by a piece of gold cord wrapped around his head.

For the span of several seconds, all conversation stopped in the restaurant as patrons took in the scene unfolding before them, but then the din resumed as they returned their attention to half-eaten breakfasts and half-empty coffee cups. At that moment, a party got up from a large round table in the center of the room and the newly arrived entourage moved in and claimed the space, the tall man in the suit keeping watch until the waitress cleared away the dirty dishes and wiped down the surface.

When she finished, the main guy sat down and settled in before being joined by the other four, two on either side. The suited man remained standing, however, presumably to better execute his duties as bodyguard, and after they all perused the menus, it appeared that he acted as translator between the men and the server as well. From the snippets of conversation, I could hear they spoke Arabic, but there was no way to tell what actual country they came from. I had heard many stories about wealthy sheiks from Saudi Arabia and other lands making trips to visit the race horses and thoroughbred farms they owned in the area but this was the first time I had seen such a sight myself. I remembered the enormous black limo out front and concluded it belonged to the new arrivals.

Before too long the waitress brought their food and the table grew silent as the five men tucked in, the tall man in the suit stealing surreptitious glances as he kept watch. I wondered if he was hungry and when he would get a chance to eat.

I had already polished off my omelet so I got up and went to pay. The cash register was located in the back part, which had an old pharmacy where trainers and other people from the track came to stock up on horse liniment and other

242

sundries, and as the server rang me up, I stood there and studied rows of yellowing photographs of early Kentucky Derby winners on the wall. I was about to turn and leave when something brushed up against me at the counter; it was followed by a hand familiarly reaching around my waist and pulling me close.

I looked down and saw that it was Cookie.

"*Gonnagimmesommadatcookie*?" He side-bumped me with this hip and flashed a lewd grin. Then he nudged me a second time for good measure and started laughing.

"No cookies here." I politely disengaged his arm from my midriff and stepped aside to put some distance between us. "There you go." I pointed to a nearby shelf of snack items. "They've got cookies right over there. Knock yourself out."

When I tried to skirt around him and get back to the dining room, he spread his arms and tried to funnel me in his direction. "*Sommadatwannadatcookie*!"

"I don't have time for this. I need to get home." I faked a dodge to the left and then went right, but Cookie spun around and caught me by the back of the waist. A waitress who had come to ring out a customer was watching from behind the counter, her eyes narrowed in disapproval as my eyes implored her for help. Instead of rendering assistance, however, she shook her head sadly, like I was a lost cause, and went back to making change for the old couple who stood there, also shaking their heads in consternation. Seriously? I thought to myself. They're looking at me like I'm the oddball?

I swatted at him, but Cookie, who hadn't stopped laughing, hung on and splayed his legs to slow me down; and before I knew it, there I was, dragging him along behind as I tried to make my getaway. "Come on," I said. "Let...go...of...me...right...now." I slowly tried to pry his hands loose.

"*Yee-haw*!" he cried in a throaty giggle. "*Gotsommadatcook-aaaay*!"

With a mighty shrug, I was finally able to dislodge Cookie from my person, and when he came at me again, I put out my arms and shoved him to a stop. I turned to leave without another word, but I almost collided with one of the four Middle Eastern men. I don't know how long the guy had been watching, but when Cookie made a move to come after me again, the man stepped in between us and shook an angry finger.

Startled, Cookie jumped back and mustered an indignant look. "*Betternotgetsommadat*," he said, in a somewhat petulant tone.

Finger still angrily shaking, the Middle Eastern man took a step closer and began shouting at Cookie in Arabic. I've only had a few lessons in the language, but the first part of his rant sounded something like "*Wald dhroot, Wald dhroot!*" and I stood by as the man continued to scold Cookie. "*Akmalakmalaklak, inta shaz akalabakbarbak hhalep charmouta!*"

243

"*Deviltricker!*" Cookie said. "*Gonnagetsommadatcook-aaay.*"

"*Nik jedak kmalakgahala malaklak, akalabakbarbak,*" said the Middle Eastern man. Or at least something similar.

"*Akmala-bak-bak, yoself!*" said Cookie. He took another step backward and raised a hand to deflect the wagging finger.

The Middle Eastern man suddenly broke off his cursing and knitted his eyebrows in confusion. Then he raised his hand higher and began casting his arm down over and over, as if in a gesture of striking Cookie with a stick or some other hand-held implement. As he did so, he resumed his angry cursing in Arabic and I got the distinct impression that he was trying to smite his opponent in both a figurative and literal sense. "*Ayeree fee wij imaak,*" he said, or something like that. "*Kanker zemmer, kanker zemmer!*"

Cookie looked like he was going to say something, but he suddenly backed away and that was when I noticed the tall bodyguard in the black suit approaching us. He gave Cookie an intimidating look and then slowly reached into his coat. Was he reaching for a gun? Was this Middle Eastern man really going to shoot someone in the middle of Wagner's Pharmacy?

Before there was a chance for the man to produce a weapon, if that's really what he was intending to do, Cookie put up his hands and headed for the door.

"*Gimmedatsommedatlater!*" he said in passing.

The bodyguard watched him leave and, after a dismissive gesture from the other man, he returned to the breakfast table, which he hadn't let out of sight.

"Pardon me," said the Middle Eastern man in heavily accented, but easily understandable, English.

"Not at all." I stepped to the side so I could continue my exit. "Thanks for your help."

But before I could leave, the man smiled and laid a hand on my forearm. "You must to take," he said. "You must to take."

"Excuse me?" Trying to pull my arm back without him noticing, I was struck by the man's singular appearance. Deeply set in a perfectly chiseled face were two eyes of a striking light blue color, and they fixed me with an intense gaze. Against the flawless olive complexion, his eyes reminded me of those of a wolf, and the more I stared, the more they seemed to draw me in.

Sensing my confusion, he reached into his robe to extract something. "I have a thing which can help," he said, withdrawing his hand from the folds of his garments.

At first I thought he was going to produce a pistol or some other type of firearm, but I quickly saw it was nothing like that. It was a colorful object, something dangling from a short string of beads.

"You need something to help you, and I will give it you." He tried to hand the item to me, but my look of confusion stopped him. "I am sorry, but I can see you do not understand," he said. "Let me to explain."

In all actuality, I wanted to leave the restaurant and get home as soon as possible, but I was transfixed by this man's eyes and the intensity of their eerie blue color. But I couldn't even come up with a verbal response, much less move my feet, so I stood there, mute, and nodded my head.

"I was born with the power of sight, you see." He raised his other hand and covered his face with it. "A caul was covering my face at the time of my birth. Do you know what is a caul?"

Nodding my head once, I told him that yes, I had heard about cauls. According to folklore, infants born with this very rare piece of thin membrane covering their faces often had psychic gifts such as clairvoyance.

"Ah, good," said the man, "then you know that people born with a caul have natural gifts lacking to many others." He paused and smiled broadly. "I can tell things by looking at people, and when I saw you, I could tell you needed something." He reached out and held up the object so I could better see it. "Please to accept."

Hanging from the string of beads in his fingers was a round piece of thick blue glass trimmed in gold. In the middle was a ring of white that surrounded a smaller circle of light blue with a black iris at the center. It was something known as a *nazar*, or the evil eye, and I had seen many of them in markets and bazaars during travels in Turkey and other countries. These talismans were supposed to ward off curses and other forms of bad luck, especially the ills inflicted by people giving you "the evil eye." As I stared at the vibrant blues of the charm and the beads from which it hung, I suddenly realized that the lighter blue matched the strange hue of this man's eyes.

At that moment his eyes narrowed, and it was as if he were privy to the discovery I had made. Once again, a broad smile spread across his face, this time exposing a set of brilliantly white teeth. "Please take," he said, pushing the talisman into my hands. "It will help you with many things, things you may not know require assistance."

The cool surface of the glass pressed tight against the palm of my left hand, I let him wrap my fingers around it before he disentangled his own fingers and returned to his companions. "Thank you," I said in a barely audible whisper as his robed form retreated. Then I opened my hand and looked down at the amulet, the concentric circles of blue and white staring up at me.

After a moment or two, I closed my fingers around the evil eye again and stowed it in the pocket of my coat. Then I walked to the door and went back outside, where the stretch limo gleamed in the dull sunlight diffused through the thinning clouds. After I got in my car and pulled out of the lot, I had to slam on the brakes to avoid hitting a careless pedestrian who stepped off the sidewalk and bolted across the street. As if I were the one at fault, she turned and gave me an evil glare, and I saw that she wore a long skirt and a colorful headscarf tied with a knot in the front. *Josephine?*

For a second, my heart caught in my throat but then I realized this woman didn't really look like Josephine. Her complexion seemed too dark and she appeared shorter. But the more I stared, the more it did look like her. Had my memory dimmed since seeing her last? Or maybe my mind was playing tricks on me.

Chuckling at my foolishness, I proceeded to the next corner and took a left back into Old Louisville. Shuffling along the sidewalk to my right was Micah, the violin case swinging happily at his side.

For the next two months I completely forgot about the evil eye, largely because when I got home that day and hung up my coat, that was the last time I wore it for a while. The frigid temperatures seemed to lift and a minor warm spell hit the neighborhood—so I didn't have much use for such a heavy winter coat. But around Easter time I woke up in the middle of the night and couldn't sleep so I decided to go for a walk and maybe find a tree to sit under. As soon as I left the bed, Fritz bounded down and followed me to the kitchen. Rocky and Bess, on the other hand, were snuggled warmly under the covers and gave no indication whatsoever that they wanted to get up. I put on my winter coat and hooked Fritz up to his lead, and off we went.

It was several hours before sunrise, so the sky still had an inky blackness about it, but already I could hear birds chirping in the trees. As I walked through the back alley to Ormsby Avenue I thought we were all alone, but as I turned and headed to Fourth Street, a lone figure coming down the sidewalk greeted us.

"Wanna wrassle?" she said with a giggle, tossing an extremely long hank of bleached blond hair back over a shoulder. At least I thought it was a she. Everyone in the neighborhood called her Tina, supposedly because crystal meth, known as Tina in some circles, was her drug of choice, but whenever I talked to anyone, they never seemed to know her real name for sure—or if she was really a man or a woman. Some swore it was a female, most insisted it was a man dressed as woman. Whatever she was, she had asked me to "wrassle" on the streets of Old Louisville and I stood there trying to figure out if this was code for something else or if she indeed really just wanted to wrestle.

Before I could answer, she started giggling again and gave my bicep a coquettish swipe of the hand. "No way," she laughed, her voice gravelly and hoarse. "You're too big to wrassle with." She looked like she wanted to say something more, but Fritz, obviously not pleased that the stranger had touched me, lunged forward and nipped her on the shin. I quickly pulled him back and Tina reached down to inspect her leg.

"Owww!" Even though there was a certain note of concern in her voice, she was still laughing when she spoke. "Bad doggy!" Quickly she determined no damage had been done and then resumed her trek down the sidewalk. "See ya later," she said. "Maybe we can wrassle then."

Shaking my head, I watched Tina's small and wiry form walk away, the ebony sheen of her face gleaming under the streetlamp as she turned and waved good-bye. Almost reaching down to her heels, her yellow-blond hair swayed back and forth as she walked to the next corner. She jaywalked to the stairs of the First Church of Christ, Scientist, went up the steps, and disappeared behind one of the huge columns.

What the heck was she doing up there? I thought to myself. She emerged from behind a large standing sconce and slowly strode from one side of the massive building to the other. The light from the sconces bounced off her as she walked and with the Grecian-inspired design of the church, she almost appeared like an early priestess keeping watch over her temple. When she reached the other side of the steps, she turned and promenaded back again, her long faux-flaxen hair pulled around her like a cloak. But what was she doing? It seemed like she was holding something out in front of her, clutched in her hands, and that she was taking rehearsed steps as she walked.

At that moment a shiver ran down my back as I was struck by an unsettling realization, the realization that just that week I had concluded my research and written a last-minute chapter about that church in my book about haunted Old Louisville. According to local legend, the spirit of a beautiful young woman who died while waiting for her fiancé on the steps of the church still haunted it today, her ghost pacing back and forth across the portico and among the massive columns in the hopes that the young man would come and release her some day.

I waited to see if Tina would make another pass across the front of the church, but she never materialized. When she didn't appear, I half-wondered if another group of swans would emerge from in front of the row of towering wooden doors, but that didn't happen either. Fritz and I looked at each other for a moment and as I studied his intelligent and understanding eyes I could have sworn he shook his head in exasperation, as if to say, "Oddballs. You got 'em at all hours of the day in Old Louisville."

I reached down and patted him on the head; then we walked over to Central Park, where we sat under a large sycamore tree for an hour, Fritz in my lap and bundled on the inside of my coat. The neighborhood had a certain enchantment about it, the magical feeling that was so typical of the early, early mornings there. Other than for some restless squirrels and a curious possum, the park seemed to be empty and we enjoyed our solitude in the pre-dawn chill.

We stayed there for an hour or so, and then we got up and walked to the northwest corner of the park. The tennis courts were brightly illuminated and I noticed that four players were hitting a ball back and forth on the nearest court. The ball made no sound as they lobbed it over the net and then returned it, and I had to wonder what had occasioned the impromptu pre-dawn doubles match at that time of year.

Walking toward Sixth Street, I looked back and studied the figures at the net. That's when I noticed that their rackets seemed to be the heavy wooden kind used back in the day. I also realized that the athletes were atypically dressed: the

248

men wore heavy V-neck sweaters and trousers, and the ladies had on long-sleeved blouses with sailor collars and pleated skirts that went down to their shins. All their clothing appeared to be solid white. Ignoring the chill that worked its way down my spine, I urged the dogs on and we made our way down to Ormsby Avenue.

Less than a half block from La Casa Fabulosa, I lifted my head and saw that a long finger of rosy red had inserted itself above the horizon, beckoning the sunrise as it were. From somebody's back yard a dog let out a long and mournful howl and a minute later several others yipped and howled as well; Fritz perked up his ears and yowled his solidarity and soon it seemed that every single dog in the neighborhood had joined in the chorus. As we entered the back alley, an eerie and enchanting canine choir sang us home.

A thin band of fog was lifting from the patch of grass along the sidewalk we were leaving behind. I looked up, and on a nearby rooftop, I saw a large owl clearly silhouetted against the backdrop of the lightening sky. A bat fluttered by and a light went on, illuminating an elaborate stained glass window from the inside. It was then, strolling over the uneven bricks and past the old carriage houses lining the alley on both sides, that I realized how much I had grown to love the neighborhood, warts and all.

Back in the kitchen, I unhooked Fritz from his leash and hung up the coat; and that's when I discovered the evil eye, in the pocket where I had stashed it after my breakfast visit to Wagner's. I hung it on a nail sticking out from the side of a cupboard and I went about the work of testing a recipe for cinnamon coffee cake with bourbon streusel. By the time the sun had fully risen, a sweet smell permeated the entire house.

As the coffee cake cooled on the counter, I opened the back door to let in some of the damp morning air. With Fritz at my feet, I stood behind the screen door for several minutes and listened as the neighborhood came to life.

"What are you baking so early in the morning?" It was Ramon, rubbing the sleep from his eyes as he poured himself a cup of coffee.

"It's a recipe for coffee cake I'm working on," I told him, walking over to the counter and cutting a slice from the still-warm cake. "Here, have a piece."

He accepted it with a grunt and started eating. "What's that?" he said, pointing to the evil eye hanging on the cupboard.

"It's a kind of good-luck charm. Someone gave it to me the last time I was at Wagner's." I poured myself a cup of coffee and blew away the wisp of rising steam. "It's supposed to ward off bad spirits and things like that."

Ramon shrugged noncommittally and finished the last of his coffee cake. "Can it make you comb your hair and put on some decent clothes?" He gave me the once-over. "You look like a hobo again."

I looked down at my pants and shoes. I didn't think my ensemble looked all that bad, but Ramon obviously thought otherwise. True, I hadn't combed my hair yet, but I wasn't planning on being seen by anyone, so it could wait. "I'll comb my hair later."

He put his dirty plate and cup in the sink. "Well, I hope you plan on combing it before you take me to the airport," he said. "I'm all packed and will be ready to go after I take a shower."

A half hour later, Ramon was back in the kitchen, suitcases in hand, and we were on the way to the airport. "Try to comb your hair every day and not to look like such a hobo when I'm gone," he said when I dropped him off. Afterward, I ran some errands and stopped to pick up lunch from Ollie's Trolley, at the corner of Third and Kentucky.

Something of a fast-food relic, Ollie's Trolley was a vestige of the days when the Ollie's Trolley chain had outlets across the country—not to mention a dozen scattered throughout Louisville, its city of inception. In addition to walk-in buildings shaped like bright red-and-yellow street cars, the extinct chain's gimmick featured a secret blend of 23 herbs and spices—more than twice as many as the Colonel used in his fried chicken—and a legendary owner, a fastidious coot by the name of Ollie, who insisted that his burgers be served rare and only with his special secret sauce. Many considered the Ollie Burger the best in the city, and that's what I got, eating it in my car on the way home.

When I walked in the back door, I found all three dogs there, waiting for me and anxiously wagging their tails. Even though I hadn't been gone very long, they bolted to the door like they had been cooped up for a whole day. But when I opened the door, instead of running off to find a patch of grass to do their business, they ran down to the deck and looked back at the house. And when I called them to come in, they stood at the bottom of the steps and looked up at me, giving no indication that they desired to return inside.

Deciding to let them have their way, I left them outside and went about getting some chores done. When I walked into the butler's pantry, I stopped dead in my tracks. There, lying on the floor, next to the sofa, was the pig lithograph from the old desk in the foyer. How it got there, I had no idea, but it was lying face down, surrounded by several large shards of glass. Shaking my head, I swept up the pieces and set the picture aside to be reframed yet again. Then I went down to the basement to check on the laundry.

When I tried to get the dogs to come back in a second time, they were sitting in the same spot I had last seen them, all three of them looking up at the house. I called out and told them to come inside, but they refused to budge. Fritz stood and sheepishly wagged his tail, but that was it. All of a sudden, I wondered if one of them had somehow managed to get the lithograph down from the desk and dragged it into the butler's pantry, but I had to admit that it didn't seem very likely. Finally, I went down and picked each of the dogs up and brought them back into the house, one by one. The rest of the day, they seemed to stay close by and they trailed me wherever I went. It was a strange feeling to have the place all to myself, and as I walked through the rooms and down the hallway, my footsteps seemed to echo more loudly than usual.

The warm weather was upon us, but nonetheless a bit of chill remained wherever I walked in Widmer House. I toyed with the idea of doing some work up on the third floor, but then I decided to get to bed at a decent hour, so I jumped under the covers and quickly drifted off to sleep. I had dozed for perhaps an hour or so when the uneasy stirring of the dogs on the bed interrupted a bad dream I was having about drag queens in a cemetery. Despite the darkness, a small patch of light from the street illuminated the bed through the window. I could see the dogs as they stood and looked toward the hallway, a low growl barely audible as Rocky and Fritz lowered their heads and stared. Pulling them toward me to calm them down, I listened.

At first I could hear nothing, but then a long, slow, wooden creak echoed outside my bedroom door. All three dogs cocked their heads and listened. I thought maybe a door had swung open by itself and I waited to hear more. A minute passed, and I heard nothing so I lay down and waited to fall back asleep. Once again, however, a long, drawn-out creak resonated slowly in the hallway and sent chills down my spine. I thought someone had surely broken into the house, and I attempted to visualize his location in relation to the bedroom.

Another moment passed, and I heard a third long groan from the floorboards in the hall, this time closer to the bedroom in front of me. All the while I could see the dogs as they cocked their heads in response to the noise, and it slowly dawned on me that I was afraid.

Almost paralyzed, I listened as something seemed to make its way up and down the hallway that ran from the large room at the front of the house to the small bedroom at the rear. After several minutes' hesitation, I finally mustered the courage to hurl myself out of bed, grab the *Louisville Slugger* propped against the wall, and switch on the light. Making as much noise as humanly possible, I rushed out of the room to confront the unseen intruder, the bat wielded overhead as I ran the length of the corridor and turned on several other lights. Finding nothing, I searched the other two floors and even looked around the attic and basement before returning to my bedroom. Somehow the house had lost the vacant and airy feeling that had caught my attention earlier in the day.

I closed the door this time and, tucked safely under the covers with the dogs, I tried to convince myself that I hadn't gone crazy and had only imagined the sounds of an intruder in the hallway. After several minutes, I relaxed, comforted by the thought that the closed door would offer some sort of protection in the unlikely event that I heard the strange noises again. Even if they did start up anew, I'd be fine, I told myself, as long as the weird noises did not bother me inside the bedroom.

Another minute or two passed, and a sharp groan on the floorboards echoed from the left side of the bed, inches from where I lay. The dogs quickly got to their feet and Fritz growled. My skin crawled at the realization that the noises had not only returned, but had also entered the room. Fighting the welling sense of panic, I forced myself to take slow breaths and reassured myself that all would be fine, as long as the noise stayed on the left side of the bed. Even though it seemed like it was immediately to the left of my bed, I told myself that it was possible the noise was really in the hallway and only sounded like it was inside the room. Several moments of silence dragged on, and I dreaded the idea that the odd creaking would eventually move around the bed to the right-hand side, where it would be harder to downplay.

Suddenly, the floor let out a long, moaning squeak that ended with a loud pop, and my eyes involuntarily squeezed themselves shut. The creepy, wooden groan had come from a spot at the foot of the bed. Despite the warm breeze that now drifted through the open window, a cold chill ran down my spine and set my heart to racing even faster. It seemed that the air was alive with thousands of little popping noises, but I told myself that it had to be the result of the wood expanding and contracting due to the warmer weather. Before Ramon left, we had hired two men to refinish some of the hardwood floors on the second floor and they had started in the big room at the front of the house the day before. I wondered if their sanding had somehow caused the strange noises I was now hearing. Whatever the reason, if the weird sounds moved all the way around to the right side, I would be leaving.

So I held my breath and waited. The dogs seemed to be holding their breaths as well. There was a loud electric pop outside, and it seemed that the street light in the alley dimmed. One minute passed, and then another, the lengthy silence compounding the tension that hung in the darkness. Another minute went by, and I slowly exhaled as quietly as possible. I listened intently and squinted to better discern any movement made in the near blackness, all the while overcome with the uncomfortable sensation that someone or something was watching me. Bess lowered her head and slowly stretched out on the bed, and I cautiously relaxed a bit, my ears still straining for the slightest noise. I turned my head to the right and struggled to make out any shapes in the dim light afforded by the windows, but I still saw nothing.

At that moment, the same long, drawn-out type of creak reverberated along the hardwood next to the right-hand side of the bed, as if an invisible visitor had taken a step or shifted her weight from one foot to the other while standing there. The loud noise faded into a soft echo, and I heard what sounded like a pluck and strum on the strings of a harp.

I flew out from under the covers, grabbed my cell phone and baseball bat, and—making sure the dogs followed behind—ran down the stairs as I pulled on a bathrobe. I picked up my keys in the kitchen, and the door slammed behind us as we ran out the back way and piled into the car.

The clock on the cell phone read 3:30 AM as I turned the key in the ignition and started to dial Skippy's number to let him know that I would be coming over to spend the night. But as I sat there and looked back at the darkened house, realizing that the windows weren't going to start glowing with an Amityville Horror orange, I reconsidered and hung up before the call went through. I was already getting a fair amount of teasing for some of the strange things that had happened in the house, so I decided to tough it out. After all, there had to be a perfectly logical explanation for the weird noises. The most likely, I concluded, was that the warmer weather was causing the timbers in the house to expand and contract, and my overactive imagination was simply getting the better of me. Nonetheless, I wasn't ready to go back inside yet. I listened to several songs on the radio, and then the dogs reluctantly followed me back into the house.

Once inside, I closed the door and listened carefully. Total silence reigned. Still trying to convince myself that I had imagined the whole affair, I sat down with the dogs in the butler's pantry and watched television until the sun came up several hours later. Stifling a yawn, I finally trudged up the back stairs to the bedroom on the second floor, content in the fact that I would be able to manage a couple of hours of sleep. As I pulled the covers up under my chin, birds chirped in the branches outside and it seemed that the house once more had an empty, airy feeling.

After I woke up, I took the dogs for a walk and when I came back the phone was ringing. I picked up and it turned out to be Loretty. "Where you been?" she said. "Called you a couple of times, but you're never around."

"Oh, I've been out and about," I said. "Probably teaching."

"Well, you've had some oddballs in back of your house, so I wanted to call and let you know." In the background I could hear a television set blaring the music for the start of a game show. "And a couple fat possums, too. Time for you to trap 'em and drop 'em off in the East End."

"Yes, I suppose it's time. It's been a couple months since my last delivery." I laughed to myself. "So what weirdoes have you seen this time?"

"Saw a couple of those bums from over on Oak Street snooping through your trash and then I saw that woman with the turban you were asking about," she said. "She was standing in the back alley staring up at your house when I saw her, but I don't know how long. Maybe she was snooping around in your garbage too. Who knows, when you're a bum."

"You saw Josephine? It's been a while since I've seen her," I said. "I thought maybe she had left the neighborhood."

"Call her whatever you want, but I don't know her name," said Loretty. "If she's standing in a back alley doing nothing but wearing a funny hat, then I call her a weirdo."

"That's fine by me. As long as she wasn't getting into any trouble."

"Like I says, who knows what that freak show was up to before I discovered her, she might have been doing a hula dance on your roof for all I know, but all I saw her doing was standing there being a nut job." Loretty coughed loudly into the receiver and cleared her throat. "I guess that's what the bums love doing best down here in Old Louisville."

"I suppose you're right," I said, waiting for one of her coughing spells to pass. "Thanks for keeping an eye out for me."

"Not a problem," she said. "I'll call you the next time I see another oddball out back. If you're home, that is. Bye."

I hung up and decided to run some errands. As I gathered my keys and wallet in the kitchen, I noticed the strong smell of freshly brewed coffee again. The two workmen had arrived and could be heard toiling away on the floors above me, so I walked up to them and inquired if either had made coffee or maybe had brought any along. When they both answered in the negative, adding that they never drank coffee, I tried my best to shake the uneasy feeling that came over me; a slight shudder crept down my spine.

Still hopeful that something logical would explain the weird noises from the night before, I also asked the two men if the sanding and the warmer weather might account for the increase in the creaks and groans that had pervaded the house in the last couple of days. One of them shrugged his shoulders and said, "It happens, I guess," but his coworker gave him a skeptical look. "I never heard it happen before," he said. Not reassured either way, I left the house.

I returned home later that afternoon, eager to check the progress that had been made on the hardwood floors. Although several days had passed since the work had started, most of the time had been spent pulling up the old carpeting and removing nails and staples embedded in the boards. Curious to see if they had managed to sand more than the front room, I walked into the house and followed the loud drone of the drum sander upstairs. The scent of fresh pine and wood shavings permeated the air, and I made a room-to-room inspection while waiting for the noise to stop.

Pleased with the progress that had been made, I walked up behind the two men and said hello when they finally turned off the sander. Both almost jumped out of their skins at the greeting.

"Lord, you scared me to death!" the older of the two said with a sigh. He looked at his companion and chuckled uneasily.

"Were you in the house, about an hour ago?" asked the other worker, casting an uneasy look over his shoulder.

I told them that I arrived home minutes earlier and asked why.

"We could have sworn someone was in here with us." Both men looked down the hall toward the small room that sat at the back of the house. "Someone kept slamming the door shut back there."

When I assured them I had not been in the house since they had last seen me and asked them if they had seen anyone, the younger one scratched his head and scowled. "No, but we sure got the feeling that someone was watching us."

"The dogs didn't get out of the front parlor when I was gone, did they?" I asked, suddenly worried that I hadn't properly shut the French doors when I left.

"No, they were downstairs the whole time," said the older man.

"Well, I'm not sure what it could have been, then." I walked to the back room and stuck my head through the door. Since it was set apart from the other rooms that needed sanding, the workers had decided to save it for last. When they finished the rooms at the front of the house they would work their way down the hallway and then start sanding the floors in this, the final room. As I stood there and studied the layout—the perfect square with a simple fireplace mantel and wider planks in the floor—a familiar odor hit my nose.

"You smell that?" It was the younger of the two men, both of which had followed me back to the room.

"Yeah, it smells like someone's been ironing back here," said the other. "Like maybe they burned something."

I nodded my head, and as we stood there the smell seemed to intensify. Despite the scent of wood and sawdust that had permeated the house when I entered it, this new odor was much more powerful. After another few seconds, I reached out for the knob to close the door, but there was movement on the mantelshelf. The large hand-painted vase I had placed there several months before was gliding along the smoothly polished surface.

As if guided by an invisible hand, it slowly slid along for half a foot, and then another foot. It continued for another foot or so and came to a stop inches from the ledge.

The three of us exchanged glances but no one said a word.

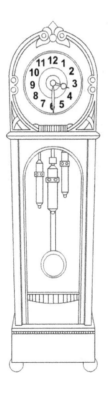

Thirteen o'clock

A couple weeks later I came home one afternoon and an unusual sight awaited me in the half-filled swimming pool in the back yard. With pink and yellow dogwoods in full bloom, Derby was a few days away and I was hoping to have the pool up and running by then. I had cleaned everything and before I left that morning, I had turned on the hose and left it to fill up the pool. When I walked through the back gate and up the steps to the wooden deck surrounding the pool, I wasn't surprised to see that it wasn't yet full.

I was surprised, however, to find my friend Kelly in the pool, floating in the shallow water on a slightly under-inflated inner tube. I was even more surprised to see that he wore only his underwear and the green and black cap of a World War II-era German Wehrmacht officer. The rest of the uniform was draped across a blue and white lawn chair. Polished black boots stood at attention under the patio table.

When Kelly saw me, he smiled and raised a hand in salute before removing the hat and waving it in the air. Overhead, the thin white stamp of a daytime full moon had left its image on a beautiful blue sky. "Mein Kapitän! Mein Kapitän! Wie geht's?" he cried out. "It's a perfect day for zee mint julep so I thought I'd stop by."

Suppressing a grin, I told him to hurry up, put on his clothes, and come inside since I didn't really want any of my neighbors to think I was having poolside cocktails with a Nazi soldier.

"Jawohl, jawohl, mein Herr!" He scrambled up the pool ladder and grabbed his uniform, then followed me through the back door to the butler's pantry, where he sat down at the small breakfast table.

While the dogs greeted him, I went to the bar and pulled out a bottle of green chartreuse, which I mixed in a shaker with mulled mint, sugar, lemon juice, and crushed ice. I poured it into two glasses and handed one to Kelly. "Here, try this instead," I said. "I saw something similar in one of my cooking magazines the other day and I thought it would taste good. It's kind of like a jazzed-up mint julep, but with chartreuse in place of bourbon." I held the glass up to the sun streaming through the window and studied the bits of mint suspended in the green liquid.

"Ah, Carthusian splendor. Carthusian splendor indeed," he said in his best W.C. Fields voice. Taking a long sip, he swallowed and smacked his lips. "Not bad, not bad at all."

I took a tentative drink and decided I liked the bright taste of citrus combined with the vegetal undertones of the chartreuse. "It's a nice change at this time of year when everyone's got mint juleps coming out of their ears."

Kelly took another swallow and put his glass down on the table. His expression became earnest. "So what's this I hear about things moving around in this house now? It sounds like it's getting serious, brother."

"Oh, you mean the vase sliding across the mantelshelf in the little room upstairs?" I pointed to the ceiling above us. "I think I may have come up with an explanation for that."

"You have an explanation for things moving on their own?" He reached down, picked up Bess, and lifted her to his lap. "Sounds like kinetic energy or invisible hands would be the explanation to me."

"Maybe," I said. "But the day that happened, I had polished all the furniture in that room, including the mantelpiece, so it was very, very slick." Outside the window, a blue jay had perched on the ledge. It jerked its head and seemed to stare at me through the wavy panes of old glass. "Not only that," I continued, "I took a level up there and checked the shelf, and it's almost a whole degree off. So it slopes slightly in one direction, and that's the direction the vase slid. That must be it."

Kelly gave me a skeptical look. "And how far did you say it moved?"

"Well, I didn't really measure or anything," I said, "but it had to be at least two feet."

"I'll freely admit that I'm no master carpenter, but I do know a little something about woodworking," said Kelly. "And I can tell you that a big vase isn't going to slide two feet because of a little furniture polish and a one-degree incline." There was a lapping noise and when we looked for the source, we discovered it was Bess. Taking advantage of her proximity to Kelly's drink, she had leaned her head over the crook of his arm and was eagerly slurping up the last of his cocktail.

"Bess!" I scolded. "What are you doing?" Laughing, I reached out to take her from Kelly's lap and return her to the ground.

But Kelly waved me off and hugged the dog closer to his chest. "In my lap the Señorita Booze Hound shall remain," he said. "Nothing wrong with a little canine cocktail every now and then, is there?" He addressed the question to Bess as he affectionately scratched the top of her head.

"Have it your way, but don't get her drunk on me," I said, getting up and returning to the bar. "It's time for another round anyway, so hang on a sec." I mixed up another batch and handed a fresh glass to Kelly.

"Thank you, thank you," he said, going back to his W.C. Fields voice. After sipping off a layer of the drink, he lowered the glass to Bess and let her lap up several tonguefuls. Patting her head, he set his drink down on the table, safely out of reach this time, and resumed the previous, serious tone. "Really, though, you need to find out what's going on in this house," he said. "It could be demonic for all you know."

I scoffed at the notion of demonic forces at work in La Casa Fabulosa and adopted a serious tone instead. "Oh, I don't know about that. If there's anything paranormal afoot, I'm sure it's not malevolent," I said. "After all, the things that happen here are perfectly harmless." I stirred my cocktail and took a drink. "And most skeptics would point out that these occurrences could be explained away."

"Believe what you will," said Kelly, "but I say there's something afoot in this house and it won't go away till you find out what it is." He raised his eyebrows and fixed me with a stare.

Instead of saying anything, I raised my glass and took another drink.

Almost two weeks had passed since Ramon had gone off to Texas, and he was set to return the next day. After Kelly left I did some yard work and tested a few more recipes for my cookbook. When I finally had a chance to take the dogs out for a walk, it was already dark. We strolled all the way down Third Street to the old Confederate War Veteran's Memorial at the University of Louisville and then returned down Second Street, where large portions of the sidewalk were framed in a canopy of flowering pear trees.

It had been a busy day, so I decided to turn in early when I got home. Tuckered out from their long walk, the dogs had curled up in the butler's pantry and gone to sleep almost immediately, so I left them downstairs. Looking forward to a long and restful sleep, I turned out all of the lights, and since it was a bit warm outside, I switched on the fan at the side of the bed before jumping under the covers. Within fifteen minutes I had started to doze, lulled by the slight breeze generated by the softly humming fan.

About an hour before midnight what sounded like three loud knocks at the back door woke me. I sat up in bed and turned on the light after rubbing the tiredness from my eyes. Not certain that I had actually heard someone knocking at the back door, I sat for several seconds and waited. Then, *rap, rap, rap!* Three long knocks echoed from down in the kitchen.

Who could it be? Was it one of the gang, stopping by, unannounced, for a night cap? It had happened before, so I grabbed my cell phone and shuffled down the stairs to the back door. Not more than fifteen or twenty seconds could have passed before I opened it.

But instead of a late-night visitor, I found no one standing in the doorway. I stepped outside and looked around. The perimeter gates at the side and back were tightly closed, and there was no indication that anyone had used them to exit the back yard. I listened intently for the sound of retreating footsteps or any signs of life and then called out to see who was there. Aside from my voice echoing off of the old bricks lining the alley, I was met with silence.

I walked back to the kitchen and closed the door. As I passed through the butler's pantry to return upstairs, I noticed the three dogs still curled up on the couch, as I had left them before I went to bed. Funny, I thought to myself, whatever had woke me up had failed to rouse them.

I wondered if I should wake the dogs to make sure they were okay but decided against it and got on the stairs instead. My left hand brushing over the smooth railing as I ascended, I paused halfway up when my ears caught a slight rustling noise somewhere off in the distance. I stopped and listened for a second, trying to ascertain the direction it was coming from. It sounded like it came from somewhere up on the third floor, but I couldn't tell for sure. Puzzled, I listened, and again, I could hear the strange noise. *Whoosh, whoosh.* I couldn't figure out what kind of sound it was, much less where it came from. I scurried to the upper floors and made my way down, from one room to the next, in the search of the sound.

After almost ten minutes I had gone into every room. Eventually, I found myself in the TV room at the front of the house on the second floor. I had decided to give up and go back to bed when the weird noise started again. *Whoosh, whoosh. Whoosh, whoosh.* I walked out in the hallway and listened. Several moments later, the same thing: *Whoosh, whoosh. Whoosh, whoosh.* I was almost positive it was coming from my office on the third floor, so I went back up and looked around.

But up on the top floor, all was quiet. I listened for several more minutes and looked around a bit, then I gave up and returned to the bedroom, thoroughly convinced that I had to be imagining things. I was about to lay myself down on the bed, when I heard the sound again. *Whoosh, whoosh. Whoosh, whoosh.* Now certain that I was really hearing something on the third floor, I rushed back up the steps and turned the light on in my office. I kept still and waited.

When the strange noise repeated itself a minute later, I felt totally foolish. I had recently installed a new screensaver on the desktop, and since I had forgotten to turn off the computer before going to bed I was hearing the sound of bubbles as they *whoosh-whooshed* to the surface of the virtual aquarium that popped up on the screen every ten minutes. Good grief. I slapped off the light and went back down to bed.

Lying in the cool darkness, I realized I was no longer tired. After tossing and turning for several minutes, I decided to pull out a my copy of *The Binghams of Louisville* and read myself back to sleep, but a minute later, my cell phone began vibrating on the nightstand.

It was Skippy. "What are you up to tonight? I'm bored."

"What are you calling so late for?"

"What are you talking about?" he said. "It's not even midnight yet."

"I know, but I was in bed already." Reaching behind me, I propped up a pillow and leaned back against the headboard.

"Why so early? You never go to bed this early," he said. "I thought we could go out and get a drink or something."

"Not anymore," I laughed. "I think I'm in for the night. Having a house has turned me into an old fuddy duddy, I guess."

"Party pooper," he said. "I don't know why you'd want to stay all alone in that big old house when you could be out somewhere else having fun anyway." From the other end I could hear him pop the top off of a bottle of beer and take a long, drawn-out gulp. "By the way, has anything else happened lately?"

"Well, it's funny you should ask, because I was asleep right before you called and something woke me up because I heard these—"

Rap! Rap! Rap! As if on cue, another series of measured knocks echoed from downstairs, presumably at the backdoor.

"Hang on a sec." I sprang from the bed, but instead of running down the stairs, I raced to the small room at the back of the house and peered through the window that overlooked the rear yard. Directly below me, I could see the steps leading up to the back door. Except for a squirrel, illuminated by the stark glare of the streetlight as it perched on the fence, the area was empty.

Quickly doing some mental tallying—it couldn't have taken me more than five seconds to reach the window—I rushed through the hallway to the large room at the other end of the house to see if I couldn intercept an interloper trying to sneak around the sides of the house. I threw open one pair of shutters, lifted the window and looked outside. Other than some spooky shadows thrown by the neighbor's shrubbery, nothing showed itself in the front yard. Across the street loomed the dark form of the Hillebrandt House, buttery light shining through a handful of square windows. I looked up to the top floor, but Loretty's window was dark.

I waited a bit to see if the light would flash on and off, but nothing came, and I closed the window and shutters before returning to my cell phone, which I had thrown on the bed in my haste to discover the source of the knocking.

"Sorry," I said, picking up the phone. "You still there?"

"Yeah. What was that all about?" In the background I could hear the soft strains of jazz music lilting from his Bose player.

"That's what I was going to tell you about." I walked out into the hall and flipped on the light, suddenly overcome with thirst. "Someone keeps knocking at the back door, but when I get there, they're gone. Maybe I'm hearing things." I nodded my head and headed down the hallway for the stairs.

"You mean those loud knocks I heard through the phone a minute ago?" He sounded alarmed. "I guess I must be hearing things, too, because I definitely heard knocking."

"So, I'm not going crazy then?" I approached the back stairs and reached out for the railing.

"Well, I'm not saying that you're not crazy, but I did hear knocking." Skippy laughed.

I was about to take my first step down the steps when someone knocked at the back door a third time.

"Here we go again," said Skippy, his voice trailing off as I dropped the hand holding the phone down at my side and sprinted to the window overlooking the back step. *Rap! Rap! Rap!* The knocks echoed once more, and a few seconds later I stood at the rear window, looking down over the back yard.

As before, the back yard was empty, and it didn't appear possible that someone could have knocked and disappeared altogether in a split second. Wondering if someone was playing a prank, I put the phone back up to my ear and ran down the stairs to the foyer. Giving Skippy a breathy progress report, I yanked open the front door and walked outside. I walked around the house and eventually I found myself in the back yard.

"Did you find anyone?" he asked.

"No." Taking one last look around the back yard, I scratched my head. "If there was someone here, they must be awfully fast," I added. Then I walked around the other side of the house and returned to the front door. The door locked behind me, I walked into the kitchen and poured myself a glass of orange juice.

"What are you going to do?"

"About what?"

"About the oddities in your house."

"I'm sure it's not that bad," I said. There's got to be a logical explanation."

"Uh huh." He didn't sound very convinced.

I finished my orange juice, rinsed out the glass and set it in the sink before turning out the light in the kitchen. "It was probably some kid playing a prank on me or something."

Rocky, Bess, and Fritz snored softly on the sofa in the butler's pantry. I walked past them and went to the foyer to turn out the light. "Or you," I said. "Are you sure you're not out there doing this to me?

"I'm at home listening to Diana Krall, and I haven't been out all day," he said. "That's why I was calling you. I was getting stir crazy."

"Well, then somebody else must be pranking me."

"Call me if your head starts spinning around and you start throwing up pea soup all over the place."

"Sure thing." A laugh escaped as I mounted the servant's stairs but then I cut myself short and stopped mid step. Two large windows covered with lace curtains flanked the exterior wall to my right, and I was startled to see that the bottom frill of the curtain nearest me appeared to be jumping about and skipping over the sash. It seemed that invisible hands had reached up under the hem of the curtain and were fluffing the material. Taking a step backward, I waited for the jumping curtain to settle down, but instead of ceasing, the activity increased and the frilly bottom part of the curtain started jumping even higher off the sash. "Um–"

"Um what?" Skippy stopped laughing. "What's going on now?"

I reached my hand out tentatively to see if a breeze could be felt, but there was no sign of wind or any other force that might be causing the curtain to flutter.

"What's going on?"

I began to stutter a narrative of what I was seeing, but the lacy piece of fabric suddenly stopped fluttering and settled down against the windowpane. Then, as suddenly as it had stopped, the lower edge of the curtain flew up and started to flap in front of me. "You're not going to believe this," I said, "but I'm in the back stairwell and one of the lace curtains on those big windows is going crazy on me."

"Curtain going *crazy*?" he said with a laugh. "What are you talking about?"

"I don't know." I took another step back. "It's fluttering around like there's a strong wind blowing through the window."

"Well, is the window *open*? There's probably a draft or something."

I considered the possibility and reached out my hand to double check the window. Then, I recalled something that made me withdraw my fingers. "No, there's no draft coming from these windows at all." I thought back to a day two weeks before when I had spent most of the afternoon painting the wainscoting and wooden trim in the back stairwell. "The previous owners had these windows nailed shut, and I caulked and painted over them myself a couple of weeks ago." With that, the curtain stopped fluttering and fell back against the pane.

"There is something odd going on in that house. You want to come over here and spend the night?"

Cautiously, I put my hand up to the window to make sure a crack large enough to let air through hadn't appeared around the glass somewhere. Not so much as the faintest breeze could be felt. "No, I'm fine. It's probably nothing at all. It must be a weird draft coming down from the third floor or something." Then I backed down the stairs and entered the foyer, where I studied the face of the grandmother clock tick-tocking away. It was already after one.

"Alright, suit yourself," he said. "I'm going out for a drink. If you need anything, call me."

I hung up the phone and went to the bedroom, making sure to use the stairs at the front of the house. Two minutes later, I was back in bed with the pillows propping me up so I could finish reading the chapter I had started earlier. By the time the grandmother clock chimed the half hour, sleep had started to reclaim me. I put the book on the night table, turned out the light, and rolled over under the blanket. Within several minutes, I drifted off, the faint chirp of crickets coming through the open window next to my bed.

Sometime later, the same insistent knocking roused me. Grumbling to myself, I opened my eyes and listened. It came again: *Rap! Rap! Rap!* "Good grief!" I said out loud to no one in particular. "You must be kidding." I hugged the pillow closer and refused to get out of the bed. "I'm ignoring you, whatever you are, so go away."

Downstairs, the clock in the foyer struck two, the melodious clang of its somber chimes filling the house. I squeezed my eyes shut and easily willed myself back to sleep, stirring only slightly when a lone chime off in the distance marked the next half hour.

Rap! Rap! Rap! I instinctively grabbed the cell phone when the next set of knocks woke me up shortly before three. Eyelids drooping heavily, I confirmed the time and mumbled into the pillow. "Pound all you want, but I'm not getting out of bed." I covered my head with the pillow.

Once again the rapping noises came, this time seeming to come in response to my complaint. It sounded like it originated in the small room at the back of the house, however, so I raised my head and listened. Several uneventful minutes passed, and I cautiously lowered my head. After several more minutes I closed my eyes and tried to sleep. But the noise came again: *Rap! Rap! Rap!*

I groaned and hopped out of the bed. Fighting back the sleep that tugged at my eyelids, I trundled down the hallway to the room at the rear. Flipping on the light, I walked through the door and looked around and saw nothing. I stooped and peered out the window to see if anyone was in the back yard, but there was nothing there, either.

I turned to leave the room, but stopped when a faint whiff of smoke met my nostrils. Slightly acrid, yet pleasant, it smelled like someone had started a wood fire. I waited another half minute and became alarmed when the smell of smoke began to intensify.

Convinced that a fire had broken out in the kitchen, I ran down the back stairs, past the dogs still sleeping on the couch, and turned on the light over the stove. Sniffing loudly as I moved along, I examined the outlet behind the stove and then moved to the one behind the refrigerator. Once I convinced myself that neither of them appeared ready to burst into flames, I checked the other plug-ins on the wall. All was well in the kitchen, where there wasn't the slightest trace of smoke or odor.

Then I opened the door to the basement and went down for an inspection, but everything was fine there as well. I went back upstairs and quickly ran from room to room, relieved to discover that the smell of smoke had dissipated.

Ten minutes later I stood in the second-floor hallway outside the little room, anxious to return to bed and salvage at least a portion of the night's sleep. The light still burned in the small room, so I walked down the hall to turn it off. But as I entered the doorway, I was quickly overcome by the pungent smell of charred wood. I looked around the room and was amazed to find no sign of a fire. I yanked the chain on the ceiling fan and opened the window on the other side of the room, but after five minutes, the strong smell of smoldering wood still lingered.

I got down on my hands and knees and examined each of the outlets in the room. None of them felt warm. None appeared to give off the odor, so I pulled a chair out from a nearby dressing table and stood on it to inspect the light fixture that dangled from the ceiling. That didn't seem to be the cause, either. I put the chair back and stood in front of the fireplace, where the odor was most intense. Maybe I smelled residue from a long-ago fire, I thought to myself.

Dong. Downstairs, the grandmother clock in the foyer marked the half hour with its usual single chime. Leaving the room, I looked at my cell phone and saw that it was half past three. *Dong.* I scratched my head and debated calling the fire department. *Dong.* I suddenly became aware that something was not right. *Dong.* I waited for a couple of seconds, and then I realized the clock was still chiming. I raced out of the room and ran to the front stairs. *Dong.* I paused on the landing before going down, the measured tick tock of the pendulum becoming more audible. I grabbed the railing and tried to ascend the steps slowly and silently as the chimes continued. As my foot hit the very last step, another *Dong* rang out from the grandmother clock, and then I saw the swaying pendulum come to a stop as the clock went silent. It had chimed thirteen times again. One by one, I could feel the hairs on the back of my neck bristle and stand up.

The cell phone began to vibrate in the pocket of my bathrobe. Skippy was calling again so I flipped it open and cast one last suspicious glance in the direction of the now-quiet clock before walking up the stairs.

"What's going on? Why are you calling so late?" I asked.

"What are you still up for?" he answered. "I just drove by your place on the way back from the bar and saw lights on in every room of your house. I almost stopped and came to the front door, but I decided to call instead."

"Oh, I thought I smelled smoke so I was looking for a fire." I turned out the lights on the bottom floor and returned to the second floor, where I made my way down the long hallway to the little room at the back of the house.

"Fire? Did you find anything?"

"No, but it smelled like it was coming from the back bedroom on the second floor." I entered the room in question and inhaled deeply before I extinguished the light switch. All the odor had vanished. "I'm going crazy." I walked up to the third floor and made sure the lights were off.

"Figures," he said. "A lot of the weird stuff seems to happen back there."

I returned to my bedroom, crawled back into bed and turned off the light. "Well, there was some weird stuff going on in the foyer as well," I said. "The clock starting chiming and wouldn't stop. When I went down to check on it, the clock stopped. And I swear it just chimed thirteen times."

"I told you something odd is going on in that house. I'm not that far away. You want me to turn around and come over?"

Chuckling, I lay back on the pillow, letting my eyes adjust to the darkness. "No, don't worry about it. I'm getting worked up and psyching myself out," I said. "And besides, if there's really anything here and it wants me to know, I'm sure it will let me know."

At that very instant, there was a sharp click in the hallway outside the bedroom, and bright light flooded through the open door and into the bedroom.

Someone had turned on a light.

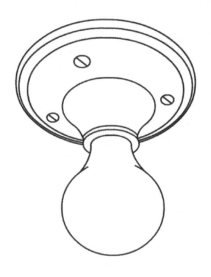

Candle

Beth helped herself to chicken and dumplings. "So, what did you do?" It was the week after Derby weekend and we all sat around the table in the dining room. I had been feeling spooky all day, and the TV soundtrack from *Twin Peaks* was still playing in the parlor, the haunting strains of the music wafting across the foyer and into the dining room.

"I almost had a heart attack, that's what I did." I passed around a basket of hot rolls. "I held my breath for a bit and then I finally got out of bed to see what it was. Skippy came over five minutes later and nothing else happened."

"So? What was it?" Wendy poured herself some wine and raised her eyebrows.

"The light in the linen closet," I said. "It came on all by itself."

"You actually stayed in the house after the light came on all by itself?" Laura sounded incredulous.

"Yes." I wavered a bit at the realization that everyone was staring at me as if I had lost my mind. "But we've had problems with that light before," I explained. "I think there's a short in the wiring or something."

"You ever have any problems before with it coming on right at the instant you say if there's anything spooky going on in the house something will give you a sign?" Skippy sat back in his chair and waited for an answer.

I tried to think of something smart to say, but instead I shrugged my shoulders. "It guess it was a coincidence," I said.

"You know what Kurt Vonnegut said about coincidence, don't you?" Laura looked at me and waited for an answer. All she got was a blank look from me, so she continued. "He said coincidence is God's way of remaining anonymous."

"Huh, is that so?" I took a bite of food. I was going to take the opportunity to express my own thoughts on coincidence, but the loud buzz of the doorbell interrupted our conversation and the dogs started barking. "We expecting anyone else?" I asked, looking around the table. "Did crazy Kelly say he was stopping by?"

"Not that I know of," said Ramon, returning from the kitchen with a fresh bowl of salad.

"Guess I'll see who it is." I reluctantly scooted out my chair and went to the door. On the front step, a grizzled old gentleman in a gray suit stood and looked out at the street. I muttered softly, feeling around in my pocket for some spare change in case he was a beggar. I opened the door. "Can I help you?"

The old man turned to face me and smiled, his face lighting up with kindness.

"Hello, sir." He took off his hat and rumpled it between his hands. "You have a magic house. You know that, don't you?"

Outside, a beat-up gray Chevy Impala—a 1960, I thought—puttered up to the curb and pulled over. A chubby woman with a beehive hairdo leaned over to the opened passenger-side window and peered up at the house, a pair of cat-eye glasses scrunched up at the end of her nose. Her steering wheel was covered in pink fur and a pair of furry dice hung from the rearview mirror. The scene looked like something straight from a David Lynch movie and I wondered if the *Twin Peaks* music had anything to do with it.

Unaware of the quirky scene playing out behind him, the man smiled broadly and nodded his head. "Oh, yes," he said. "She has the magic in abundance, your house."

I gave an inward groan. "Is that so?"

He reached out a hand, and I noticed he had his fingers crossed. Using his crossed fingers, he made the sign of the cross before me.

"Thank you. Does that mean I have to do anything special or can I go on living here like I have been?" The visitor didn't take note of my sarcasm so I continued. "Hey, since she's a magic house, maybe she can start to pay some of her own bills." I thought about the depressingly large stack of bills on the library table in the foyer. The mortgage payment was considerable and the chickens of all our restoration projects were coming home to roost.

"With a magic house come much responsibility." He slowly cast a glance over his shoulder and I followed his gaze to the wimpy hedge. Although almost a year had passed since the bushes had been planted, it didn't appear that they had grown an inch. "You take care of the front yard, you take care of the back yard. You take care of the gardens inside the house," he said.

Gardens inside the house? What was that supposed to mean? Other than a couple of Boston ferns, we didn't have much plant life in La Casa Fabulosa, something that had always been a bone of contention between me and Ramon. Ramon wanted plants in every single room; I didn't, citing the fact that they were messy and that, despite his best intentions, he was always killing them.

The old man pointed past me and laughed. "Magic. Every house have a magic garden."

"Alrighty then—" I stepped back inside the house and got ready to shut the door.

But then the man's dark eyes widened and the smile vanished. A finger rose and pointed at me. "You have seen," he said. "You know this house have the magic." I was struck again by the man's unusual accent and I wondered if he wasn't the same old Cajun guy that my friend Jill had told me about. He did sound the same and he fit the description, but I couldn't be sure. Before I could interrogate him about his origins, he leaned in and whispered. "The candle on the second floor, she come on all by herself." Then he turned around and shuffled down the walkway. At the sidewalk, he turned left and headed toward Oak Street. I went inside and closed the door.

In the dining room a swell of laughter rose from the table. "Was that another panhandler?" asked Skippy as I sat back down at the table. As usual, the dogs were hanging around in anticipation of stray crumbs and under-the-table treats, so I picked up Bess and put her in my lap.

"I don't think so. He didn't ask for anything at all. He stopped by to tell me this is a magic house."

"Oh, that's nice." Beth sliced into an apricot tart and started to pass pieces around. "Another weirdo on the front porch."

"Was that all or did he say anything else?" Laura accepted dessert and spooned a dollop of whipped cream over it.

"Not much, but it got a bit spooky, actually. He talked about 'gardens inside the house' and said I knew what he was talking about. Candles coming on all by themselves on the second floor and stuff like that."

"Candles?" Skippy grabbed a decanter of port and started filling glasses. "How about lights in the linen closet coming on all by themselves? Does that count?"

I moaned. "I hadn't even thought about that." As the port made its way around the table, we considered the possibilities and discussed the most recent spate of eerie coincidences. Before long, we were reminiscing about the many oddballs and oddities that had made themselves known during our relatively short time in La Casa Fabulosa.

When I wasn't paying attention, Bess lapped up the last of my port. She didn't even look sorry when I scolded her.

269

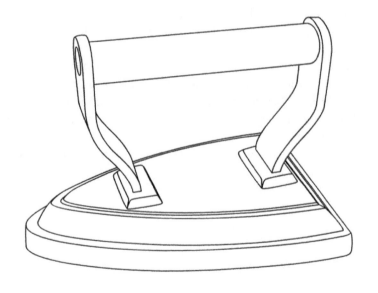

Discovery

"Whew! That smell sure is strong today!" said one of the workers as they walked through the back door into the kitchen a few days later. He wrinkled his nose and looked around the room. "Did you ever figure out where the burning smell is coming from?" When I responded that it must be coming from the neighbor's house, he looked like he wanted to say something else, but he didn't.

"We'll start on the last room today and should be done in another day or two," said the older of the two men. They headed upstairs to do their work, and I left to run some errands. Outside, a hawk was circling in a brilliant, cloudless sky. When I went to get in my car, an enormous black snake shot out from underneath it and slithered across the alley, where it skirted the side of the neighbor's carriage house and disappeared in a tall fringe of grass and wildflowers.

When I returned later that afternoon, the strong coffee smell in the kitchen had faded, only to be replaced by the familiar smell of a hot iron and fresh laundry. I scratched my head and looked around, then walked into the next room. Upstairs, I could hear a loud scraping noise, the irritating sound of wood against wood. It appeared to come from the linen closet on the second floor, and from the loud footsteps running back and forth, it sounded like the workers had decided to concentrate on that room instead of the small room at the back of the house. I couldn't figure out exactly what they were doing, however. It sounded like they were pulling out the huge wooden drawers for sheets and pillows, and then pushing them back in again. In, out, in, out...

I was about to run up the stairs and get an explanation when the back door opened, and in walked the two workers. For a second I stared at them with stupefaction, but then I remembered the time I thought Ramon was up in the linen closet, but he wasn't.

I bolted upstairs to the wooden closet, already knowing what I would find. Although the cupboard doors remained open, and the large storage bins and drawers were pulled all the way out, no sound could be heard, except the two workmen as they trudged up the steps behind me.

"Let me guess," said the older gentleman as he reached the top of the back stairs, "you heard all kinds of racket in this linen closet here, like someone was running around and pulling out those big wooden bins there."

Before I had a chance to continue, the younger man cut me off. "Man, this place is haunted! That's all there is to it. We kept hearing strange noises the whole time we were here, and it felt like someone was watching us, too." He looked at the other man.

"Yep. We took our lunch break an hour ago because we couldn't stand it anymore and didn't want to be here alone. This here door kept slamming shut, too." He pointed at a door outside the linen closet that divided the long hallway on the second floor into two sections of equal length when it was closed. Even though I had heard it slam shut many times, I always assumed it had been the result of the breeze from an opened window.

"And come take a look at this," he said, motioning for me to follow him to the small room at the back of the house. "Remember that iron smell you were always complaining about? The burnt wood and all that?" He opened the door and pointed inside. The room had been stripped of its outdated carpeting, exposing the beautiful century-old heart-of-pine flooring underneath. He stopped in front of the mantel and indicated a spot on the floor. "See that? We've sanded and sanded, but we can't get rid of it. Too deep in the wood, and it's there to stay."

While the wood had lost much of its original luster due to years of neglect and build up, I could still easily make out the dark shape he pointed to. It was about five inches long, and triangular, but the two longest sides were slightly rounded. With a slight shudder, I realized I was staring at a burn mark on the floor, one left behind by an old-fashioned flat iron. A long time ago, someone in that room had been heating the old iron in the fireplace and the ironer must have inadvertently set it on the floor, where it charred a permanent mark in the wood.

The wheels started turning in my head. I ran back to the dividing door in the middle of the hallway, and as I stood and stared, things slowly started to make sense. I closed the door, and realized it divided the front half of the house from the back half. The front half included the original lady's day room we now used as a study, the former nursery, and another bedroom, all of which had interconnecting doors and doors that opened onto the front part of the hall. From the hall, one could mount the carved oak stairs to the rooms on the third floor, or take them down to the public rooms of the house—the parlor, foyer, dining room, and small bathroom under the stairs. I finally realized what the small room at the end of the hallway on the second floor had been used for.

I explained this all when friends arrived for our weekly dinner a couple of days later. Opening the door in the second floor hallway, I ushered them through to the back half of the house and then closed the door again. We stood in the dark rear corridor and studied the layout in silence. Doors granted entry to the large linen closet, several smaller closets, a bathroom and water closet, and the small bedroom at the very back of the house. The plain back stairs led down one flight to a small coatroom and the cellar stairs, and then into the butler's pantry and the kitchen at the back of the residence. For the most part, all the odd activities in La Casa Fabulosa had centered around the back part of the home. The little room on the second floor, the linen closet, the kitchen, butler's pantry, coatroom.

"Oh, I see!" said Laura. "The back part would have been where the servants worked and had access. That's where they cooked and cleaned and did laundry."

"And that room?" said Tad, pointing to the little room at the end of the hall. Our heads slowly turned to the small room where at one time a hot flat iron had charred its mark on the floor. "That must have been the maid's room."

"That would make sense," said Beth. "So do you really think Lucy could have been a former servant here?" We all crowded into the small room and gathered in front of the hearth. The workers had completed their project the day before and now the floors gleamed with wood stain and a coat of polyurethane. Without a word, we all stared at the burn mark and mentally debated the possibilities.

We continued the conversation over drinks downstairs. Laura had volunteered for cooking detail, and the stories and discussion continued as we passed around rolls fresh from the oven and a large tray of grilled fennel with a shallot and bourbon vinaigrette. After that, we sat for hours and enjoyed pot roast, corn pudding and scalloped potatoes. Before dessert, I set out a tray of fresh fruit and cheese.

Dessert that night consisted of homemade paw-paw ice cream and freshly baked butter cookies, two of the last recipes I had been developing for my Kentucky-themed cookbook. By the time the dishes had been cleared away, we all knew what had to be done.

Carrying lighted candles and walking from room to room in the servants' area of the house, we all followed Wendy as she reassured Lucy that she was free to enjoy the house as she wanted. No one wanted to bother her, Wendy explained, and we understood that, ever the diligent servant, she was keeping watch over her part of the house. After the impromptu blessing we returned to the front parlor, where we drank coffee, passed around the bourbon, and talked till the wee hours of the morning. From that night forward, there were never anymore unexplained noises or would-be paranormal events at La Casa Fabulosa.

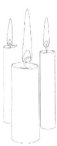

Voodoo Finale

Silvery dark storm clouds had swept in over the neighborhood and the rumble of distant thunder hinted at a spring shower. I zipped my windbreaker all the way up and left through the front door. As I went down the front walk, a blue and black sparrow zoomed by, its wing tilted perpendicular to the ground. The gang was coming over that night and we were making Cuban food for Victor, who had moved out a couple of months before but came back for frequent visits. Since empanadas, yucca, black beans and rice, and roast pork were on the menu, I decided to make mojitos to drink. Although I had plenty of mint, I didn't have any limes so I decided to walk to the Kroghetto. I hoped it would be a Cookie-free day.

I grabbed a bag of limes from the produce section and tried to think if I needed anything else. I was out of honey, so I got a jar, and then I remembered that we had used up all the candles the other night during Wendy's spur-of-the-moment consecration of the house.

I found a dozen white candles and then walked to the checkout line with the fewest shoppers. As I pulled out my wallet to get my bankcard ready, I froze.

There, right in front of me, stood Josephine.

She wore a flouncy green skirt with a white peasant-girl blouse, and a metallic-looking turban had been wound around her head so that not a single strand of hair could be seen. Holding my breath, I kept still and took a step back so she wouldn't see me. When it came time to move my cart forward in the line, I tried to do it as quietly as possible so as not to arouse her ire, but a squeaky wheel gave me away. She turned to look at me, but I averted my gaze, trying to look invisible as my fingers danced over the assortment of candy bars. When I looked back, she gave me a brief, unrecognizing, once-over and then returned her attention to the front.

Josephine dangled a shopping basket at her side while an old man in front of her argued with the cashier about whether or not a coupon was still valid. After a minute or two I still hadn't advanced, and I tried to make myself relax a bit—until my eyes beheld the contents of Josephine's shopping basket. Inside were only three items: a bag of limes, a jar of honey and several tapered candles—white.

My eyes widened to twice their normal size. Quickly, I grabbed a Baby Ruth and added it to my purchases, thinking that if I disturbed the balance of items in our shopping baskets I might be able to halt the emergence of another voodoo day.

But Josephine stopped swaying and shifted her weight. She pivoted a bit to the left and stared at the candy selection in front of her. Don't do it, I thought to myself. But, slowly, she reached down, grabbed a Baby Ruth bar, and tossed it into the basket.

"No way!" I said it loud enough that she turned around for a second to see who I was talking to. Realizing that the fates had presented me with a very rare opportunity, I decided then and there to introduce myself. If Josephine was a real voodoo lady, I definitely wanted her on my good side. Maybe she'd like to come over and meet the Tuesday Night Dinner Club.

Cautiously, I inched the cart forward. "Psst. Josephine," I said, leaning over the rail of my cart. But she didn't hear me and looked straight ahead. "Hey, Josephine," I tried again.

Seeing how nobody was responding to my greeting, the woman behind me cast a quick, puzzled glance around and then cautiously moved her cart ahead. The man with the coupon had finally started to gather up his groceries and was leaving.

"Hey, Josephine," I repeated in a louder tone. I even stretched an arm out to the side and waved to get her attention.

The head under the turban spun around and the woman looked at me, a confused expression on her face. "Huh?"

I put on my best smile. "I only wanted to say hi, Josephine," I said, extending my hand and prepared to make introductions.

The woman narrowed her eyes and looked around suspiciously. "You talking to me?"

"I wanted to introduce myself," I said. "My name's David and I live over on Third Street."

"Who you callin' *Josephine?*" She jammed the hand not carrying the basket down onto her hip. "My name's Marsha!" Her head swiveled to the right and she pursed her lips while fixing me with a skeptical look.

My heart was pounding in my throat. "Oh, sorry. You're not. . . Josephine?"

"Nah-uh." She swiveled her head in the other direction and mustered another disdainful look.

"No voodoo?" I said in a faint-hearted voice.

"Voodoo?" she crowed, vigorously shaking her head. "Crazy weirdo!" As she proceeded to lay her purchases on the conveyor belt, she continued to grumble. "I don't know why I even come to this store. Nothin' but a bunch a freaks and crack whores on up in here."

"Sorry." I felt myself shrink by inches as the others in line looked at me like I was an oddball. "I had you mixed up with someone else."

Throwing her money down at the cashier, Josephine quickly gathered up her bag and prepared to leave. At the last minute, however, she turned to give me one last chewing-out, but she stopped dead in her tracks when she spied the contents of my cart.

Her mouth snapped shut and her eyes widened as she studied the bag of limes, the jar of honey, the candles, and the Baby Ruth bar. Then she took several slow steps backward while giving me a worried look. As she stared at me, it seemed that the faintest glimmer of recognition registered in her eyes, but then she shook her head, as if trying to rid herself of an unpleasant thought, and she bolted out the door. The cashier rang up my order as if nothing had happened.

Outside in the parking lot, I opened the Baby Ruth and looked up. Storm clouds roiled the sky, but it hadn't started raining yet. Chuckling at my goofiness, I set out for home and ate the candy bar as I walked the first block. Had I really spent more than a year pursuing a non-existent voodoo woman? Or had I simply confused this Marsha lady with someone else and was Josephine really out there yet? All of a sudden, I realized that it didn't matter, and I picked up my pace in hopes of beating the rain.

As I crossed Oak Street, I looked down to the corner of Fourth and Crazy, and I noticed a woman pushing a shopping cart piled high with what appeared to be sticks and other things. She had reddish brown hair and wore a long black coat, but I refused to entertain the notion that she might be the Stick Witch, or any other elusive neighborhood character.

Approaching 1228 South Third Street, I looked up and saw the three bats darting to and fro over my front yard. It seemed that they were playing an aerial version of tag and I could almost hear them calling back and forth to each other. They fluttered out over the street and then flew up to the gable and disappeared.

As I turned and made my way up the walkway to the front door of La Casa Fabulosa, the skies opened up and a downpour washed over the colorful façade. A deafening thunderclap rumbled high overhead and my enchanted neighborhood prepared for a soaking.

Epilogue

The buzz of the cicadas was deafening. The neighborhood was wilting in the stranglehold of the sweltering heat of the last day of August in 2007—fall was still three weeks away—as I worked my way from the top floor of La Casa Fabulosa down to the front door. All the furniture had been moved out several days before, and my footsteps echoed in hollow thuds as I passed from one empty room to the next. Void of furniture, rugs and drapery, the three-story building had resumed the imposing mien that had greeted us almost eight years before.

Unobstructed by the clutter of everyday life, I was free to confront the memories that had sought refuge in each of the vacant spaces. Images of get-togethers and dinner parties, friends and family who had come to visit, countless hours of renovation and work, unnerving nights plagued by unseen footfall during the first year. It was time to leave Widmer House, but it wasn't Lucy who had caused me to flee.

No, it was something much more frightening: a sub-prime mortgage.

After more than a year of struggling, we had finally realized that the time had come to let the old place go. Worried that it might fall into the hands of someone who wouldn't give her the attention she deserved, I was happy to discover that someone who had read about the house in my book *Ghosts of Old Louisville* was in the market for a haunted house. He was especially intrigued by Lucy's story and promised to carry on the good work.

When I talked to the new owner several months after he moved in, he mentioned strange noises and odd footsteps around 3:30 a.m. had been keeping him awake, and that his cats were acting strange.

I kept in touch with the new owner for the first few years and we'd email every several months; then I started to hear less and less from him. The front yard became overgrown and tendrils of ivy began creeping across the façade of La Casa Fabulosa. The gold leaf and gilding on the façade started to fade, and chips of paint flaked away here and there. In addition, several major windstorm wreaked havoc on the city, and one day not too long ago as I drove by La Casa Fabulosa, I noticed one of the chateau finials was missing from the roofline.

Very recently, a former neighbor informed me that the new owner had vanished and that nobody in the neighborhood knew what had become of him. As far as they could tell, the house was abandoned and empty. Little by little, La Casa Fabulosa is starting to look more and more like a haunted house.

One day, right before moving out, I received an unexpected visit from an elderly lady who said her grandmother had been one of the first owners of the house. The woman asked to come in and see the place, and I was more than happy to oblige her. As I showed her from room to room and listened to comments about what changes had taken place and how she approved of the decorating, I grew anxious to hear her comments when we reached Lucy's room at the back of the house. Sure enough, she confirmed that the maid had indeed lived in that room, but other than that, she couldn't recall anything in particular about this individual. Her grandmother, she said, complained that bats always seemed to be flying around the house, day or night.

When I asked if she remembered the maid's name, the old woman shook her head and said she couldn't recall it for sure, but she said it might have been Lizzie.

Lucy? Lizzie? They are very similar, so I wondered if the stories about Lucy were true after all. Standing there in the foyer, near the wall where pictures had kept falling for no apparent reason, I pressed the old lady for more information. One thing she did remember, she informed me, was that her grandmother's maid had come to her as a young girl, and that even though the woman was very fond of the servant, she always complained about her mischievousness. With a chuckle, the old woman told how her grandmother was constantly chiding the girl for eavesdropping when visitors came. Instead of staying out of sight in the back part of the house as servants always did, the young girl liked to sneak to the small landing on the front staircase and listen to conversation in the parlor, making sure she stayed just out of sight in case someone exited the parlor and discovered her perched there.

I thought about the times I had heard footsteps on those stairs and wondered if the mischievous young housekeeper had wanted to eavesdrop and nothing more. Each time I had the distinct impression that someone was trying very hard to stay out of sight.

Was La Casa Fabulosa haunted by the ghost of a former servant named Lucy or Lizzie, or was it all merely a series of strange coincidences? Personally, I've chalked a lot of it up to an overactive imagination and a good deal of happenstance, but you never know.

Although I don't have nearly as many voodoo days as during that first year in Widmer House, every once in a while a spate of coincidences will pop up and make me think. One morning not too long ago, for example, I woke up chuckling after having a dream about possums. I went downstairs, made my coffee, and turned on the TV. The channel that was on was running a documentary about possums. A few minutes later, as I stood at the back window, looking into the stand of trees that separates our yard from the neighbors, I noticed a small possum hanging upside down from its tail. After a minute or two, it swung up and grabbed the next branch before scampering away into the leafy canopy.

Later that afternoon, as I returned home from a round of errands, I found myself in a minor traffic jam because something had blocked the traffic a block from my house. After craning my head out the window, I discovered that cars in both lanes of traffic had stopped to let something cross the road. At first I thought it was a cat or a dog, but once the traffic started moving again and I was able to see the creature creeping over the sidewalk and into a well-manicured lawn, I discovered that it was a possum. Not only that, she had six babies riding on her back and before rounding the corner of a house and disappearing from sight, she turned and looked at me.

At that very moment, the second when our eyes met, all of her offspring lifted their heads and did the same, and it caught my breath and I had to smile to see her face sweetly framed by those of her children. I was left pondering how many times in their busy daily routines most people are fortunate enough to find out that their traffic jam is due to the crossing of a mother possum with young ones on her back—and I came to the conclusion that it was probably a very rare occasion and I considered myself very lucky.

Speaking of possums, I finally captured the last family of fat possums in the basement and set them free out in the East End when the weather warmed up. And none too soon, either. Bess had discovered a gap in the heating grate from the basement to the kitchen and learned that she could drop her doggie treats through it to her possum friends below. Our little black cat, unfortunately, never did return to her little closet under the stairs. I'm sure someone in the neighborhood took her in. That's how people are in Old Louisville.

Sadly, the dogs are no longer with us, either. In 2004 Fritz developed problems with his throat and after half a year of visits to specialists and unsuccessful operations we had to have him put to sleep. When my first book of ghost stories came out the following year, I made sure to dedicate it to him, in memory of the many nights he sat next to me as I worked on the manuscript in the front parlor. In 2010 we lost Rocky and Bess, both at the age of fourteen. Rocky developed kidney issues and Bess had a stroke. I dedicated the next two ghost books to them. The same year we also had to have Edwin put to sleep. He was another little rescue schnauzer we had adopted in the meantime and he had congestive heart failure. Losing three dogs in one year was hard and we haven't gotten around to adopting new ones since then. I have missed having furry companions, though, and it's about time to see about getting another batch of schnauzers.

For some reason, Ramon has it in his head that we should get a golden doodle, but I've been stubborn and told him I only want schnauzers. He's persistent, though, and keeps saying he wants a golden doodle. He insists that if people see me walking down the streets with a golden doodle I will look like less of a hobo.

Now we live in a different part of town, not far from Old Louisville, but I miss living among the big old mansions and the eccentrics and oddballs in that enchanted neighborhood. Around the corner from my current house, a cozy stone cottage from the 1940s, is a large park where I go for daily walks. Sometimes, when I can't sleep or have things on my mind, I get up very early and take my stroll while it's still dark outside.

Or, if the urge strikes me, I'll jump out of bed in the wee hours of the morning—often at three or four—and I'll head over to the park and follow the path to the top of the hill, which is crowned with an imposing brick structure built as a mansion in 1944, after the 154-year-old original burnt to the ground. Nearby, I find a tree, usually one looking down the hill and across the bottom half of the park, and sit under it. It's not quite the same as Central Park at night, but it's an inspiring experience nonetheless. That's when deer steal forth from the adjacent forest and play on the meadow, and owls in the tree tops hoot back and forth to each other. And if I wait long enough, raccoons venture down from the branches and continue their nighttime quests for food.

I see a fox every now and then, and many possums. Very rarely will I spy another human creature of the night, and if I do, I always remain quiet and hidden in the shadows so I don't startle anyone. And even if I do see someone on a very late-night stroll, they are never pushing creaky shopping carts, although—strangely enough—I did spy one the other day at the bottom of the creek that cuts through the park.

In Old Louisville shopping carts aren't much of a problem anymore. Not too long after my first book came out, the Winn Dixie at the corner of Fourth and Crazy closed its doors and went out of business, so there went half of the rogue shopping carts in the neighborhood. Then, finally giving in to complaints and neighborhood demands, the Kroger on Second Street implemented a wheel-locking system to prevent shopping cart theft from their store, and now, thankfully, abandoned shopping carts on the streets of Old Louisville are something of a novelty. Just recently, however, the Second Street Kroger went on the market with an asking price of $1.6 million, so who knows how much longer it will be around. The rumor is that Old Louisville will be losing its only grocery store very soon. Whatever goes in there, everybody will still call it the Kroghetto.

Sometimes, a wave of nostalgia will overcome me and I'll wake up in the middle of the night and drive ten minutes to Old Louisville and find a tree in Central Park and sit under it. Invariably, there are people who wander by at all hours of the night, but as I push my spine against the trunk of the tree in an attempt to stay hidden from them in the shadows, my ears will strain to hear the rattling wheels of a rusty shopping cart bumping along the sidewalk. The real sound never materializes, though, and I'm left reminiscing about the good old days in La Casa Fabulosa.

Although we don't have our get-togethers every week like we used to, that tradition carried on till after we moved out of La Casa Fabulosa and I still see most of the old friends on a regular basis. We still love to sit around and tell stories whenever we're together.

As far as I can tell, the new place doesn't have any ghosts or weird things associated with it, but I did have a strange experience right after we moved in. We had only been there a couple of weeks and it was the Thursday before Derby weekend. I came home in the evening after teaching most of the day, and when I pulled into our street there were cars parked all over the place because a neighbor was throwing a party. We now live on a very narrow, hilly street and I was amazed to see so many cars lined up on our side of the street when I came home that night. After I went to bed about midnight and saw that cars still lined the street, I wondered how long the party would last.

Several hours later, at half past three to be precise, I awoke because a knocking was coming from downstairs. At first, I lay there in bed, asking myself if I had really heard a knocking or if it was something else; but then the knocking came again and it became clear that somebody was at the front door, which was immediately below the room I was in. Seeing that it was still dark outside, I checked the time on the cell phone on the nightstand, and my first reaction was to assume that a partygoer had backed into one of our cars as he was trying to get out of our street. Before I went downstairs, however, I walked around the foot of the bed to the only window in my bedroom, which happened to look down over the front door and the front steps, just to make sure that someone was really there.

I saw a man in a yellow oxford shirt and beige trousers, his arm raised as if he had rapped on the door. He had graying hair, which seemed to be in a crew cut, and his overall appearance was that of a man from the 1950s. I had the distinct impression he had been at the neighbor's party, but when I looked at the street, it seemed that all the other cars were gone. Puzzled, I took the stairs down and went to the front door to see what the man needed. In all, it really couldn't have taken me more than ten seconds to get down there because the bedroom sits at the very top of the stairs, and the stairs end in the foyer, steps from the front door. But when I got downstairs and opened the front door, there was nobody. When I turned on the porch lights, there still was nobody to be seen. And our front yard is big enough that I should have been able to see the man walking away if he was still anywhere in the vicinity. But as it was, he was gone, apparently vanished into thin air.

Immediately I tried to rationalize the situation, telling myself that I still must have been half asleep and that because I had taken so long coming down the stairs, the man at the front door must have given up and left, but I was left with an uneasy feeling nonetheless. I looked at the grandmother clock ticking away in its new location nearby and my mind went back to all those nights during the first year at La Casa Fabulosa when I found myself awake in the early morning hours, trying to figure out what was going on.

The place we live in today is an airy limestone house built in 1946. It's not as large or opulent as La Casa Fabulosa but it's big enough and more than comfortable. There are great picture windows in the main spaces and one of my favorite things about the house is that there's a library tucked away behind a door hidden in the north wall of the living room. I've got most of my books in there and lots of my favorite things and it's where I do most of my writing nowadays, although I do like to spend my free mornings at Day's, a local coffee house. There are window boxes full of red geraniums at the new house and although it's in the city it sits on a lot with large trees that provide shade and make it feel like we're in the country at times. The yard is much bigger than the one on Third Street, but it's not really that nice.

While most of the lawns in the neighborhood are tidy and manicured, ours is sort of a mess. In some parts, there are too many tree roots and shade for grass to grow and in the parts where there is grass, there are mole tracks and burrows all over the place. Ramon wants to get poison to get rid of the moles, but I haven't had the heart to do that yet and keep managing to put it off. I don't think some of the neighbors appreciate this, though, because the other day a guy walking by with his dog gave me the stink eye when he looked into the yard and saw all the ruts. I'm sure he wouldn't approve of the fact that I'm always throwing scraps of food out into the back yard instead of into the trash either. I figure why throw out anything edible when there are creatures who will eat it? At night, the possums and fat raccoons come out and scamper through the back yard to root through the piles of scraps I leave for them and I feel like I've done something useful in feeding somebody.

I still love cooking today and it seems that I'm always testing and developing new recipes to try out on my friends and family. Eventually, I went on to write three cookbooks and a restaurant guide for Kentucky, but in the meantime I've given the food writing a break because every time I wrote a cookbook it seemed I'd gain at least 20 pounds from all the sampling and recipe testing and with every new book it kept getting harder and harder to lose the weight afterward.

I cook all the time and love having people over, and whenever I can, I still frequent my favorite restaurants in Old Louisville. Several years ago, someone purchased Juanita's Burger Boy and really cleaned it up. The ambience is definitely less seedy now, but the food hasn't really changed and it's still open 24 hours a day so it's a great hangout if I ever find myself wide awake at three in the morning and in need of a cup of coffee or a place to write. They also cleaned up the Tavern and really spruced up the menu to boot, but they're not open 22 hours a day anymore. As a result, it's hard to find the same mix of night owls, drag queens and salty locals that used to be the norm. Nonetheless, it's still a great place to pop in for a drink or a knockerburger and it seems that interesting characters can still be found at the bar every now and then. The other day I was in there for a meeting and I saw a figure hulked over the bar. Although the person wasn't in drag, much less wearing a black leather leotard like that Halloween night in Eastern Cemetery, I could have sworn it was one of Mama Wawa's acolytes.

Eastern Cemetery has undergone some changes as well, and for the better. In 2013 a local man by the name of Tony Harpole started the Friends of Eastern Cemetery, a volunteer group that generally meets there on Sundays to keep the place from falling into ruin. They've cleaned up and reset headstones, trimmed and maintained the rough expanse of tangled weeds and overgrowth that dominated most of the green space, and they've done a great job of raising awareness in the city. I keep meaning to go and help out, but Sunday afternoons are usually pretty busy for me, so I haven't been able to yet. My friend Sean Stafford is a regular volunteer, though, and he keeps me apprised of the progress they're making.

I first met Tony Harpole one day at the courthouse, where he showed up to sit in on one of the first days of a murder trial I was writing about. We got to talking and he mentioned his plans to start a group dedicated to the preservation of the cemetery, and he also told me about the Stigmatorium, a pet project of his. The Stigmatorium, as it turns out, is a kind a makeshift museum of the macabre set up in his boat restoration business in an old warehouse in Louisville's West End. Stop by and you'll find old caskets turned into coffee tables, skulls, funeral art and any numbers of pleasantly gruesome artifacts. It's a shame he can't move the whole place to Old Louisville.

Not to worry, though, because an acquaintance of mine recently opened a similar kind of establishment near the corner of Sixth and Oak, not even two blocks away from the Witches' Tree. Her name is Cathe Crabb and she named her shop "Unorthodox" for obvious reasons. In addition to authentic Victorian witch hunting kits you can find all kinds of things for the very discerning shopper: hundred-year-old moose antlers, lockets filled with dirt from infamous serial killer Ed Gein's grave, a Civil War era bone saw, brothel tokens, embalming fluid bottles, antique baby caskets, nun puppets, a taxidermy rat dressed as the Pope—things that every respectable household needs. I love it that we have a shop like that in Old Louisville and I love it even more that Cathe chose Oak Street for the location of her business.

Although I've moved out of the neighborhood, it seems that I'm in Old Louisville now more than ever. If it's not a committee meeting or a board meeting for some annual neighborhood event that calls me down to Old Louisville, then it's a tour group or school group wanting to know more about the neighborhood. The word has really gotten out about Old Louisville and more and more people are showing interest in it. Some are coming to visit; others are moving here from other parts of the country, like Carrie Sweet, who moved here from California. She bought a big place over on First Street and I got to meet her during a photo shoot at her house, which she graciously opened to me and photographers Franklin and Esther Schmidt while we were working on our coffee table book *Old Louisville: Exuberant, Elegant, and Alive*. I found out that Carrie had read my ghost books and was a paranormal buff, so she's a regular hangout of mine and has even become a research assistant for one of my most current projects.

One day I received a somewhat mysterious request to give someone a private day tour of the city, and when I showed up at the Seelbach Hotel to meet the guest, it turned out to be none other than famous filmmaker Baz Luhrmann, who had come to town to scout out potential locations for the new Great Gatsby movie he was directing. In the novel, F. Scott Fitzgerald's Daisy Buchanan character comes from Louisville and Luhrmann wanted to explore the parts of town Daisy would have frequented. After touring the lovely Highlands neighborhood where she lived, we headed into Old Louisville and the director's eyes immediately lit up when he saw the array of old homes and mansions. He had an assistant with him and they immediately started the camera rolling as we strolled down Millionaires Row and through Belgravia Court into St. James Court. After stopping in front of the Pink Palace, we continued down the sidewalk past the antique houses and we came to stop in front of the splashing Venus fountain at the center. After a lengthy silence and a long look around, Luhrmann nodded his head slowly and said, "This neighborhood is simply enchanting."

As we drove back into the downtown area along Fourth Street, there was a commotion on the sidewalk as we stopped for the light at the intersection with Oak. I looked over to where a shopkeeper had dozens and dozens of tropical birds, mostly macaws and parrots, on display in a variety of wooden cages and on large perches that seemed to take up half the block. Flapping brightly colored wings, the creatures were squawking and screeching to high heaven at a scuffle on the ground in front of them, where two people appeared to be wrestling. One of the figures stood up and broke away from the other and that's when I saw it was Beau, smiling and in his heavy trench coat despite the July heat, and Tina, her ankle-length bleach bond hair tousled and in severe disarray as she squealed and tried to convince him to go another round. In the crowd of onlookers cheering them on stood Candy the transvestite I had met the night in Fort George. She had on flouncy pink summer dress, and next to her stood a rotund man with a bald head and a handlebar mustache, wearing a red and white striped unitard just like an old-fashioned strong man at the circus. I didn't see any cast-iron barbells, but I'm sure he had to have a set nearby.

After years and years of studies and neighborhood meetings, it seems that the corner of Fourth and Crazy might finally be getting a much-needed makeover, and very recently the city invested a good deal of money to improve and beautify the streetscape in that area. There's also been an incredible push to bring in more restaurants and business establishments, and you can already see things starting to turn around. Whether or not this will have any effect on the amount of questionable characters and colorful oddballs who tend to mill about at the corner of Fourth and Crazy has yet to be seen, however. The other day I noticed what appeared to be a drug deal going down in broad daylight as I drove by.

Two blocks later, after I turned and was passing my old house, I happened to see a figure with a violin case shuffling along the sidewalk. Sure enough, it was none other than Micah Chandler, who, since I first spotted him all those years before, has become a regular fixture in Old Louisville, downtown, and along Bardstown Road. He is seen frequently in various parts of the city, and his volunteerism and impromptu street performances have made him something of a local icon. People call out as he passes and he often stops so people can have their pictures taken with him. It is always a hit when one of my tour groups runs into him along the streets of Old Louisville. Micah was recently in the news when an unkind soul stole his violin, but by the next day, it was replaced by a good samaritan and Micah was back to his sidewalk concerts as if nothing had happened.

I run into Cookie every now and then, usually near the corner of Fourth and

Crazy, but he has mellowed out over the years and, fortunately, I don't have to worry about him appearing out of nowhere and grabbing me anymore, although for a number of years he insisted on talking about cookies whenever we came across each other. I eventually consulted a dictionary of urban slang, and just as I had feared, the cookies he was referencing weren't the kind you bake in an oven. It seems that he still gives me a lewd grin any time we see each other, but we usually don't talk other than to exchange brief greetings.

Frances Mengel and I kept in touch and for several years I was a regular speaking guest at various events for her clubs and organizations. She's still out in the East End and will be pushing one hundred in not too long and we talk once or twice a year. Last month she was sitting at home alone when one of my books apparently flew from a shelf and landed at her feet, so she called me to tell me about it.

For a couple of years, I would get a weekly call from Loretty, perched high up at her window in the Hillebrand House, and she would tell me about the sundry oddballs and weirdoes that she tracked through the neighborhood with her father's World War II-era field glasses. Anytime she saw a possum in the back yard she would call and inform me as well. Then, one day, I realized I hadn't heard from her in almost a month. Anytime the phone rang for the next several months, I would rush to it, hoping to hear Loretty's gravelly voice and the tinkle of ice cubes in bourbon on the other end, but I never heard from her again. Although she had never told me her last name, I probably could have found out and tracked down some information about what happened to her, but I was afraid at what I might discover. Every time I pass the Hillebrand House I always look up and imagine her sitting at the window, keeping watch over the neighborhood.

Throughout most of the year we offer guided walking tours of the neighborhood. Not too long ago, *The New York Times* named my tours as one of the things not to miss during a visitor's "36 Hours in Louisville." Daily at 11AM and 1PM there's a history and architecture tour and then at 7:30PM there's a tour of "America's Most Haunted Neighborhood." This tour is based on my eleventh book, *True Ghost Stories and Eerie Legends from America's Most Haunted Neighborhood*, which is a compilation of the most popular stories and legends from my previous ghost books, which have been edited and updated.

One of the stops on this tour is a large house at 1435 South Fourth Street, two blocks away from La Casa Fabulosa, and which has become the subject of a recent writing project. Carrie Sweet has been invaluable as a confidante and research assistant on this book. The house in question was built around 1899 for the family of Richard Robinson and for many years it sat, largely ignored by the residents of Old Louisville.

That all changed on the evening of June 17, 2010, however. That night around

9:30 a call was made from the house to 911. The caller was Jeffery Mundt, a local man who had recently moved back to the Louisville area and who had purchased the large mansion with the intent of turning it into a bed and breakfast. Shortly after moving into the house, he had met Joseph Banis through an online hookup site and the two became a couple. The night of the 911 call, however, things were a bit rocky for them and Jeffery told the 911 operator that he was locked in a bedroom on the second floor and that Joseph was outside with a hammer, trying to break down the door so he could kill him. When police arrived a short time later and arrested Joseph Banis, everybody thought that would be the end of the matter.

But Joseph Banis began talking and the claim he made was a startling one. A man, he said, had been murdered the year before, sometime in early December, and was buried in the basement. Although they didn't believe him at first, detectives started to take Banis seriously when they discovered that Jamie Carroll—the alleged victim—had been missing for the last half year or so. When officers returned later that night with a search warrant, they found a large plastic storage container under several feet of dirt in the basement. In it was the body of James Carroll, who had been shot and stabbed. A sledgehammer had been used to fit his body into the container. Known as *Jamie* to many of his friends, Carroll was a hairdresser from eastern Kentucky who also performed as a drag queen by the name of Ronicka Reed.

Banis and Mundt were both charged with the murder of James Carroll, but both insisted that the other was responsible. Three years later, in 2013, Joseph Banis and Jeffery Mundt had their days in court, each in separate trials. In March, a jury convicted Banis for the murder of Jamie Carroll, and several other charges; in May, a jury acquitted Jeffery Mundt of the most serious charges. For his part in the crime, Mundt received an eight-year sentence; Banis was sentenced to 25 years to life.

But there's much more to the story. As more details emerged, it was revealed that drugs, kinky sex and counterfeit money were also involved. In addition, the large house where the murder occurred has a slightly spooky past and, for a time in the early 1900s, doubled as a sanatorium. Not only that, the negative publicity threw Old Louisville into the spotlight and many were left with an unpleasant taste in their mouths after the soft underbelly of the neighborhood was exposed.

Of course, I saw the potential for another book in this old house and the working title is *The House in Old Louisville*. After two years of research I've finally gotten down to the actual writing, but it's been slow going and I don't foresee the book nearing completion for another two years. In the meantime, I will keep writing about the neighborhood and telling anyone who will listen why I think it's such a special place. An enchanted neighborhood, despite its imperfections.

On nights when people sign up for our ghost walk of the neighborhood I regale visitors with stories from my most favorite houses in Old Louisville. They hear about the Conrad-Caldwell House, the Pink Palace, and the somewhat hidden areas like Fountain Court. One of the stops is the old house where Jamie Carroll met his tragic end, and which was recently purchased and lovingly restored. When the tour goers hear the details of the murder and subsequent trials, their eyes grow wide with disbelief and this disbelief generally turns into fascination when they discover the house's strange history. Perhaps it's because the details are so fresh in the local memory or maybe it's because they're so bizarre, but whatever the reason, *The House in Old Louisville* has generated a lot of buzz and people are looking forward to the book. I kind of envision it as the Louisville version of John Berendt's wonderful book *Midnight in the Garden of Good and Evil* with a touch of Truman Capote's *In Cold Blood* thrown in for good measure.

Like I said, it's going to be a while before the book is finished anyway, and in the meantime I have to figure out how to come up with a story that tells the truth while not coming off as overly gruesome and sensational.

Toward the end of the evening tour, we always stroll down Third Street before heading back to Central Park and one of the last stops is La Casa Fabulosa. Standing in front of the old house, I give the tour-goers a brief rundown on the history of the building and point out some of its architectural features.

Then I tell them it's where I used to live and that for the first year in the house, would-be paranormal events seemed to be a regular occurrence. Footsteps in the middle of the night, the grandmother clock chiming thirteen o'clock, strange smells, and things moving of their own accord. When it comes to the oddballs in the neighborhood, I usually avoid those details. Nor do I tell them that there was a time when witches and gypsies could be found in the neighborhood and that for a while I thought a voodoo woman was stalking me.

I figure they can find out those things on their own, so I tell them Old Louisville is a place that holds lots of secrets. All it takes is a little curiosity and the desire to scratch the thin veneer between the past and present before an enchanted neighborhood starts to reveal itself. It's an enchanted place full of old houses and history, one with its fair share of oddballs and oddities as well. I encourage them to come back and explore on their own, and then the group makes its way back. As we leave, I always turn and smile at the fading façade of La Casa Fabulosa. All these years later, and the hedge around the small front yard has finally grown and filled out so that now it towers over me.

I make sure to reach out and brush it with my hand as I walk away.

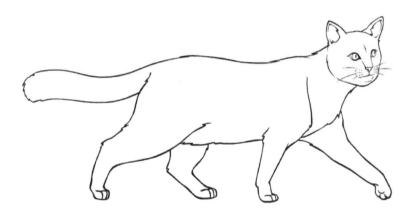

Acknowledgments

Thanks to the people who read my manuscript, or portions thereof, and provided valuable feedback and edits along the way. They include Jeanine Pickett, Julia Blake, Kelly Morris, Jerry Rodgers, Alice Monet, Mark Werner, David Williams, and Mary Popham, who is always so generous in the detailed and wonderful feedback she provides.

For the illustrations, I would like to thank Prasanta Biswas; thanks as well to Victoria Davies, who did the wonderful cover design.

In addition, many others have supported me and encouraged me in other ways—people like Sena Jeter Naslund, Leslie Daniels, Sean Stafford, David Seaman, Rick Brown, Omar Figueras, Tim Pardue, Kim and John Crum, Jason Hill, Cindy Brady, Jacob Bennet, Nicholas Siegel, Ron and Jane Harris, Bob and Eva Wessels, Caroline Kaufmann, Holly Rudolph, Terry Meiners, Rachel Platt and the others at WHAS11, Michael and Rhonda Williams, Kära Donathan, Herb and Gayle Warren, Hank and Anne Triplett, Nancy Gall-Clayton, Gabriele Bosley, Mari Lively, Nancy Wentzell Walker, Nancy Cogan, Carrie Sweet, Charles Patrick, David Green, Erinn Lee, Christy Camille Roy, Dawn Anderson, Catherine Kiely, John Paul, Darlene Metts, Kelly Creagh, Debbie Creagh, Jenn Leipold, Sandi Knapp, Mitzi Fields Root, Heather Funk Gotlib, Lisa Wilder Elble, Bill Goodan, Angelique Stacy, Susan Shearer, Laura Wallace, Don and Chris Lowe, James Oslin, Kevin Kouba and Rick Tabb, Carol Galbreath, Suzanne Hurst, Joe Impellizzeri, Bobbi Wiechert Parrish, Lillie Arundel, Sonya Lewis Stone, Suzy Johnson, Suzanna Starr Williams, Vito Gobbo, Barbara Lechner, Grace Gorman, Edna Holz aka Momma Skippy, Laura Handler, Jon Huffman and Barb Cullen, Marianne Zickuhr, Carlos Manuel, Andrew Hudson, Bonnie Omer Johnson, John and Tracy Fischer, Jamie Pearce, Abigail Smith, Holly Elaine and Edward Goodyear, Susan Sams Priest, Susan Dallas, Nicole Twigg, Larry and Judy Franklin, Debbie Robie, Chelo Garcia, Margie Cook, Odina Lienenluecke, Aunt Jane and Uncle Charlie, Silvia, Isabel, Olivia, and Miguel Zañartú, and Ramon Garcia.

And to the many others who aren't named here but who did make appearances in this book – thank you!

As with other of my projects, some passages or iterations thereof in *Voodoo Days at La Casa Fabulosa* appeared first in books about the haunted history of Old Louisville that were published by McClanahan Publishing House. University Press of Kentucky has acquired the rights to these books and will reissue them under their label.

Learn more about author David Dominé at
http://daviddomine.com/

If you want to learn more about Old Louisville and see some of the places described in this book, come and take a guided walk with *Louisville Historic Tours*. Walking tours depart daily at 11AM, 1PM, and 7:30PM (March 15-November 15) from 1212 South Fourth Street (near the corner of Fourth and Crazy!) and by appointment in the off-season.

Call 502-718-2764 for details and to make reservations.

Get more information at http://louisvillehistorictours.com/